I0592449

Knowledge and Opinion

Essays and Literary Criticism of John G. Neihardt

John G. Neihardt
Edited by Lori Holm Utecht

University of Nebraska Press
Lincoln and London

Publication of this volume was assisted by
The Virginia Faulkner Fund, established in
memory of Virginia Faulkner,
editor-in-chief of the University
of Nebraska Press.
Acknowledgments for the use of copyrighted
material appear on page x, which constitutes
an extension of the copyright page.

♾

Library of Congress Cataloging-in-Publication Data
Neihardt, John Gneisenau, 1881–1973.
Knowledge and opinion : essays and literary criticism of
John G. Neihardt / John G. Neihardt ; edited by Lori Holm Utecht.
p. cm.
Includes bibliographical references and index.
ISBN 0-8032-8381-4 (pbk. : alk. paper)
I. Utecht, Lori.   II. Title.
PS3527.E35 K58 2002
814'.52—dc21   2001052236

Contents

Preface

John G. Neihardt's critical writing comprises over twenty-five hundred reviews and essays written between 1910 and 1942. This massive body of work contains a feast of absorbing reading—my challenge has been in narrowing selections. This is not a sampling of the "best" of Neihardt, although many fine pieces of his writing can be found here. My goal is to provide a representative, rather than a comprehensive, collection, providing the reader with a sense of the scope of his critical writing. I have followed Neihardt's lead in choices for presentation; he was less interested in reviewing the popular titles of the day than in exploring with his readers books from a wide range of disciplines offering fresh and thoughtful examinations of the human condition.

I have silently corrected obvious typographical errors found in the newspaper copy. Original punctuation and archaic or unusual spellings of words or names have been left intact, even when inconsistent, for example, in the appearance of multiple spellings of "Shakespeare." A particular challenge involved the readability of microfilm copies of newspaper columns. Empty brackets indicate missing or unreadable text; when possible the brackets enclose the most likely reading or, at times, my conjecture.

I wish to express my appreciation to Florence Boring Lueninghoener for generously turning over all materials gathered with John Neihardt in the initial stages of compiling his critical work and for her reminiscences and advice. I am grateful to Dr. Susan Rosowski for her support and insightful critique as my dissertation director and to readers Dr. Paul Olson and Dr. Frances Kaye. Thanks also to Hilda Neihardt, Coralie Hughes, and the John G. Neihardt Trust and John G. Neihardt Foundation Board of Directors for their unfailing support of the project. I am grateful to the Nebraska Humanities Council for a grant that helped support initial research and to the staff of Western Historical Manuscripts Collection who were invaluable in gathering pertinent material from the Neihardt collection. Carol Vogt's meticulous help in researching correspondence was invaluable. Thanks to Elodi Emig for the Greek language assistance. To Linda, Alyssa, Sam, Mardell, Lynn, and Julie, my appreciation for help locating, typing, proofreading, and listening.

"The White Radiance" and "Literature as Environment" were reprinted from *The Giving Earth* by John G. Neihardt by permission of the University of Nebraska Press, copyright ©1991 by the University of Nebraska Press. Essays originally appearing in the *Post-Dispatch* are reprinted by the permission of the *St. Louis Post-Dispatch,* ©1926–36. My thanks to those institutions for their assistance.

Introduction

When John G. Neihardt accepted a request from Joseph B. Gilder to review *As Old as the Moon* for the 1 January 1910 edition of the *New York Times Saturday Review of Books*, he launched a critical writing career that lasted more than three decades and produced nearly three thousand reviews and essays.[1] He also began a public conversation in which he responded to thousands of books produced in the first third of the twentieth century, assessed the criticism of his contemporaries, and guided a general reading public in a thoughtful consideration of its time and the importance of art in interpreting and enhancing human existence. This John Neihardt—critic, essayist, journalist—is not particularly well known to readers familiar with his writings about the American West. Without a consideration of the full scope of Neihardt's writing, however, it is difficult for those readers to form an accurate picture of his legacy.

Central to Neihardt's critical philosophy is the responsibility of the artist to the rest of humanity. He charged the artist, gifted with deep insight and powers of synthesis, to interpret a rich world lying just beyond the range of ordinary consciousness. The artist does this by evoking a sympathetic response to sculpture, painting, music, or poetry. However, this world that the artist has insight into is so unfamiliar to everyday experience and so highly charged with meaning that it is a struggle to find a method of translating the vision. Language, developed for direct communication, is a particularly limited means of expressing vision, so the artist must draw on symbolism, metaphor, and new rhythms and patterns to suggest the vision that cannot be told.

The same powers that allow the artist to interpret vision can be used to heighten awareness in the practical realm by pointing out the individual's connectedness to all creation and all time. Neihardt believed that his location in a particularly troubled century placed on him additional demands. Like many of his contemporaries, he saw life for twentieth-century inhabitants of the Western world as fraught with unsettling change: a technological explosion and corresponding industrialization, population shifts from rural to urban settings, the crumbling of old values. His writing life encompassed two world wars and the economic depression of the 1930s. He believed that his geographical location outside the power centers of urban America gave him a unique perspective from which to comment on the contemporary scene and that his calling as poet demanded he respond to what he saw. His first response came in the form of his writings of the western American landscape. A second response came in the way he carried out his responsibilities as a son, father, friend, and fellow inhabitant of this troubled planet. A third response can be found in his work as a literary and social critic.

An exploration of Neihardt's critical writing helps enhance our understanding of Neihardt the artist, giving insight through our readings of his discussions of his contemporaries into what he attempted to do in works such as *Black Elk Speaks* and *A Cycle of the West*.[2] What also emerges is a picture of an intelligent, compassionate human being, one often out of step with his contemporaries, who composed and articulated a thoughtful, cohesive philosophy regarding the artist's relationship to the world and the ability of that artist to guide others into a broadened awareness of the mysteries that envelop us all.

Neihardt's motivation for embarking on a career as literary critic was financial, taken up as a way to subsidize the writing he considered primary, though ultimately it delayed as well as accommodated that writing. In 1912 living in Bancroft, Nebraska, Neihardt prepared to begin the project that would dominate most of his working life—his epic of the American West. He envisioned a five-part celebration of the heroic spirit that drove the exploration of the trans-Missouri River country. His wife, Mona, encouraged him to begin at once. Dedicating the time necessary to such an undertaking, however, would mean a severe strain on his family's already limited resources. He had been writing occasional reviews for Joseph Gilder at the *Times*, and that arrangement suggested an answer to his financial concerns. Neihardt wrote to editor H. V. Jones of the *Minneapolis Journal*, offering his services in raising the standards of the newspaper's literary page.[3] Jones was sufficiently interested to invite Neihardt to Minneapolis (with the Neihardt bank account emptied to purchase a new nine-dollar suit and round-trip train fare) and sufficiently impressed to offer him a job, with a starting salary of fifty dollars a week.

Whatever the practical reasons behind Neihardt's career as a literary journalist, he found the forum of newspaper reviews congenial to his idealism. He had strong opinions about the state of contemporary literature, about the purpose of literature in a culture marked by constant, wrenching change, about the role of the artist as an interpreter for culture. Through a vehicle such as the *Journal,* he could guide a reading public through the flood of books produced annually by commercial publishing houses.

John, Mona, and baby Enid moved to Minneapolis in the spring of 1912. Neihardt's first writing for the *Journal* appeared 15 September 1912 under the heading "Review of New Books" on page 7 of the Women's section. For this opening page Neihardt reviewed two books of political essays by John Jay Chapman and included an essay on "The Renascence of Poetry."[4]

Neihardt enjoyed life in Minneapolis. He browsed the shelves of second-hand bookstores, enjoyed lively debates with his colleagues, and kept busy reading books and writing his column. However, in spite of its charms, city life was not as conducive to the writing of his epic as the quiet, rural village, and after a year the family moved back to Bancroft, where Neihardt received books and returned columns by mail.

In Bancroft, Neihardt rented a small building that stood behind his house to use as a study. The first three days of the week he read books and wrote his columns. The rest of the time was spent working on *A Cycle of the West.* The mail was Neihardt's principal source of contact with the outside world, and Enid and brother Sigurd shared the ritual of the daily walk to the local post office. Holidays without mail service were a "distressing delay in the progress of life."[5]

Though the new arrangement made it possible for Neihardt to give attention to the writing of the *Cycle,* his schedule was a demanding one. In a pattern that was repeated throughout his writing life, Neihardt alternated among periods of frustration when he was obliged to put aside the epic to go pile up cash, times when he watched funds disappear as he took leaves of absence to work on the *Cycle,* and times when he drove himself to nervous exhaustion trying to answer the demands of multiple writing commitments. In a letter to George Sterling, Neihardt told of one such episode: "I've been reading too much along with my other work, and day before yesterday I went to pieces. . . . I read 12 books in 7 days besides writing reviews and working on *The Indian Wars.*"[6]

Neihardt's writing for the *Journal* had its own frustrations, including occasional conflicts with his editor. Jones was conservative, a champion of business. He worried about Neihardt's liberal politics and once warned Neihardt, who occasionally handed out leaflets for the Socialist party, not to "fool around with those damned Socialists—they'll never get you nowhere!"[7] Neihardt wrote Sterling: "My *Journal* boss loves Jesus to distraction and he has the heart of a rat."[8] Neihardt often presented ideas that were at odds with his editor's conservative notions. He described one such occasion in a letter to David Starr Jordan:

> I may have told you that I do reviews for the *Minneapolis Journal.* During the summer, the editor began to groom me for the Sunday editorial page; that is, he planned to have me do the Big Talking for the paper. Well, I began to talk for him—there was an explosion in the editor's office. I was informed that not only was I unpractical but that I did not understand Jesus Christ. (All of which may be quite true!) In reply, I pointed out the fact that if the *Journal* were to employ in succession all the forward-looking thinkers in all the nations, it would have the same trouble with each of them that it was having with me. I also stated that there were values somewhat greater than any editorial salary he could pay me. He didn't discharge me from the staff; but I am not making the Big Talk for the paper, and when I slip a bit of liberalism into my reviews, the blue pencil generally finds it, though now and then I do get some things across, for it appears that the editor is not infallible in the matter of detecting liberalism![9]

Though Neihardt's ideas were of a different cast from those of Jones, Jones respected Neihardt and gave him a good deal of freedom in selecting books to review, even those books that attacked the existing social system. Neihardt's interests are reflected in the wide range of subjects covered, including science, politics, economics, philosophy, criticism, poetry, and literary trends. He reviewed some of the bestsellers, but more often selections ran to books that gave him a chance to lead readers on an exploration of ideas being put forward by some of the best thinkers of the day.

The appearance, location, and regularity of Neihardt's column for the *Journal* underwent frequent changes between 1912 and 1922, the year Neihardt ended his affiliation with the newspaper. The Sunday "Review of New Books" became, by October 1912, "Some of the New Books." In January 1913 the headline changed again, to "New Books—Book News." This full page had several articles, apparently by multiple authors, all of them unsigned.

A weekly column, "The Book Nook by John G. Neihardt," the first work bearing his name, first appeared 4 November 1913, a Tuesday. During this time, a literary column written by Sinclair Lewis, "The Book of the Week," could sometimes be found on the same page. Though the two writers had different ideas about literature—Lewis in the realists' camp, Neihardt with the traditionalists—no rivalry is apparent.

"The Book Nook" continued until 16 June 1914, at which time a four-month gap occurs. Additionally, the column was interrupted for occasional short periods during the rest of the decade. Lucile Aly notes that during the war cutbacks in advertising by publishers were so severe that suspension of the column was necessary.[10] When Neihardt's column resumed after the four-month hiatus, in October 1914, it had been retitled "The Journal's Book Review" and appeared with no byline or signature.

Even without a byline, reviews or essays of substantial length usually have some sort of Neihardt marker—for example, prose stamped with his wry humor or the inclusion of recurring themes, such as the importance of the classics—that identify the writing as his. Note the similarity between an excerpt from a review in the *Journal*—"desire grows by that upon which it feeds, and . . . he who desires more and more of the world's goods is seeking a goal that flees from him with a speed always equal to his own speed in pursuit"—and a passage from *The Song of Jed Smith*:

> It seemed the goal was learning that a goal
> Is just the fleeing shadow that you cast,
> Until pursuing teaches you at last
> What mattered was the light upon your back.[11]

Sometimes a signed review can provide evidence to substantiate attribution of an unsigned review. For example, Neihardt discussed H. L. Mencken in two reviews for his signed column in the *Post-Dispatch*; these reviews have several points of similarity to reviews of Mencken books in the *Journal*. Neihardt notes a Mencken façade of not taking himself seriously: "Mencken can be wrong, and doubtless often is; but he can't be dull; and if he ever takes himself overseriously he has the good taste never to let his readers know" and "[Nathan and Mencken] are brilliant young fellows who take nothing seriously but themselves, and feign to laugh even at themselves."[12]

Some recurring Neihardt themes appear in the unsigned essays: the elitist assumption of New York as the heart of American identity, the tendency to mistake the symptoms of cultural maladies for the disease, the writing of Mencken and the other moderns as a natural "compensating tendency toward disintegration" in response to "rigidity in the social or cosmic order of things."[13] These textual evidences, coupled with Neihardt's own record of his affiliation with the papers, usually provide ample credence for attribution.

The Neihardts left Bancroft for the more temperate climate of Branson,

Missouri, in December 1920. Neihardt continued the arrangement of receiving books and sending columns by mail until November 1922, when his writing for the *Journal* ended. He resigned when Jones insisted that he return to Minneapolis to spend more time editing his column. Neihardt later learned that Jones had not intended an ultimatum and was sorry to lose his talented editor. The last column, under the heading "The Readin' and Writin' of Books: News, Views, and Byplay, with Reviews by John G. Neihardt and Others" appeared 5 November 1922 and included a review of *The Revolt Against Civilization* by Lothrop Stoddard.[14]

From November 1922 until March 1926 Neihardt did not have the vehicle of a regularly published column for his criticism, but he was certainly not out of the stream of contemporary literature, nor was he silent. His letters to friends are full of ideas about literature; he wove his literary opinions into regular public readings and lectures; he contributed occasional essays to literary publications. In the mid-twenties as part of consideration for a position in the English department of the University of Nebraska, Neihardt was asked to present a series of lectures discussing his theory of art. What became two lectures on "The Creative Dream" and "Common Sense" were presented in October 1925 and published that same year as *Poetic Values: Their Reality and Our Need of Them*.[15] A third lecture, developed later, was on "The Cultural Mood of Our Times."

In February 1926 Neihardt was offered the literary editorship of the *Kansas City Journal-Post*, a position he held for only six months. Neihardt welcomed the opportunity to reengage the public on contemporary issues. Trends that he had noted in his writing for the *Journal* had accelerated rather than abated, and he was eager to lend his voice to the public discussion.

Neihardt's first column for the *Journal-Post*, "Book World Comment and Reviews" appeared 7 March 1926. The newspaper announced his column in the same edition: "John Neihardt to Write Book Surveys for *Journal-Post*." One of the two pieces on that first page, "The New Reading Public," challenged the contention that nothing worthwhile in literature is being produced, heralding Neihardt's position with the subhead, "This Is an Important Age in Literature Despite Flood of Seemingly Worthless Books Which Seem to Bury Masterpieces and Works Worthy of Serious Attention."

Just a month after his first column appeared in the *Journal-Post*, Neihardt was approached by Leigh Leslie of Omaha about the possible syndication of his column in several papers throughout the Midwest, including the *St. Louis Post-Dispatch*. *Post-Dispatch* Editor George Johns was so interested in Neihardt's work that he offered him a position as literary editor of that newspaper with a starting salary of one hundred dollars a week and the freedom to shape the page with little interference. Not only would the income provide financial security for his family, but Neihardt also felt that he couldn't turn down an opportunity to speak in such a respected, widely read newspaper, the flagship of the Pulitzer publishing empire. The position also brought him under the managing editorship of Oliver K. Bovard: "'OKB' in Journalism was like 'FDR' in politics. He was regarded as the greatest managing editor of his day."[16] In 1928 Bovard was rated "first among American newspapers executives."[17]

The family moved to St. Louis, and Neihardt went to work setting up the literary page. He wrote some of the reviews and edited additional contributions to fill the Saturday page, working with associates such as George Johns, Marquis Childs, Irving Dilliard, Joseph Meek, and Bart Howard. His arrangement with Johns gave him mornings at home to work on the *Cycle* and afternoons at the newspaper office writing and editing the feature. His first writing appeared 30 October 1926 under the heading "Literary Views and Book News," with his initials after his contributions. In his first appearance he reviewed books by John Erskine and John Dos Passos, Sir Oliver Lodge's book explaining Einstein's theory of relativity, and Willa Cather's *My Mortal Enemy*.[18] In "The White Radiance," Neihardt wrote of the need for a wider vision and the importance of conceiving of all literature as organic.

On Tuesday, 7 December 1926, the page became a column, appearing Monday through Saturday. Neihardt invited guest columnists to share their views on contemporary literature, usually featured in the Wednesday column. He included contributions from such literary figures as Robinson Jeffers, Albert Bigelow Paine, and William Rose Benet.[19] The new title for the column, "Of Making Many Books," included Neihardt's byline and, according to daughter Hilda Neihardt, was suggested and designed by Mona and comes from Ecclesiastes 12:12: "And further, by these, my son, be admonished; of making many books there is no end." The biblical allusion reflects Neihardt's recurring theme of the importance of the critic in guiding the reading public as it picks its way through the flood of books produced by a business-minded publishing world.

Neihardt earned considerable respect from Joseph Pulitzer and Bovard and enjoyed camaraderie with his peers, who affectionately referred to him as the "brain department."[20] This respect provided stability during the inevitable disagreements over content of the columns. Neihardt recorded a mild dispute with Pulitzer, based on a misunderstanding of a brief note in one of his columns, a speculation on what might be the response to a return of Jesus: "It must have been noted by those who keep in touch with the stream of books that one Jesus of Nazareth has become quite popular of late. . . . It used to be said commonly that if Jesus should return He would be crucified again, and that by His own professed devotees. One wonders. Is it not more likely, in view of His present popularity, that a fat movie contract would be offered to Him? Ours is a progressive age."[21]

The rival St. Louis newspaper, the *Star*, published a letter in "Everybody's Column" signed "Offended," which reprinted the paragraph along with a pointed comment about sacrilege, and someone drew Pulitzer's attention to the piece.[22] Pulitzer sent the article to Neihardt with a note, "Please see me at your leisure." Neihardt described the incident to Florence Lueninghoener: "My convenience was the first elevator. . . . He said, 'Now, Mr. Neihardt, you have often said you were surprised you haven't been criticized for what you wrote.' I said, 'Will you let me speak first?' Then I said, 'I made a mistake. I used a rapier when I should have used an axe.' " After Neihardt's explanation that he was, indeed, on the side of Jesus, Pulitzer responded by saying, "This isn't the first time I made a fool of myself."[23]

Neihardt continued to struggle both to meet his duties as critic and to make progress on the work he considered vital—the writing of the *Cycle*. He received permission to move back to Branson and mail his columns beginning in July 1930, and he took occasional leaves of absence, to write *Black Elk Speaks*, for example, in the summer of 1931. Hints of this other side of Neihardt's writing life sometimes surface in his columns. In reviewing a book by Dhan Ghopal Mukerji, Neihardt reminisced about a visit by the mystic to the poet's home in Bancroft, a visit also recorded (though the visitor is not identified) in *Poetic Values*.[24] Occasionally, in writing about books by western writers, he included research, anecdotes, or first-hand information, as when he noted some inaccuracies in Charles Eastman's *Indian Heroes and Great Chieftains*. He corrected the placement of Reno's men in a gully, since Neihardt could "say with certainty that Reno intrenched himself upon a high and ragged hill to the east of the river valley." He also challenged Eastman's location of Sitting Bull's graveyard as outside Fort Yates: "The writer of these paragraphs has himself sat in the moonlight upon the grave of Sitting Bull, burning good tobacco to the memory of that great chieftain."[25] In June 1931 Neihardt revealed his excitement over his three-week conversations with Black Elk, where he was "sitting at the feet of a poet fit to dine with the finest spirits that have sung in his discordant world and are now among the tallest of the dead."[26]

Neihardt planned to return to the *Post-Dispatch* in January 1932, after completing *Black Elk Speaks*, but that return was postponed due to the economic depression. Pulitzer proposed a reinstatement of a regular Sunday column in July 1932, and Neihardt resumed the column from Branson; the weekly, rather than daily, column provided some financial security while allowing adequate time for work on *The Song of the Messiah*.

The atmosphere was changing at the *Post-Dispatch*; in fact, Neihardt's work was being more closely scrutinized than in the past. In a 1930 letter to long-time friend Julius House, Neihardt had wondered that he was allowed to continue writing as he did, "for I say things with death in them for the whole present world-scheme." He did not think it possible that his editor misunderstood his meaning, for "Clark McAdams is an intelligent radical."[27] However, by 1932 McAdams was rejecting some of Neihardt's choices, one of them Steffan Zweig's *Marie Antoinette*. Neihardt conceded McAdams's right to hold back publication of a review but defended his position:

> According to the *Publisher's Weekly*, the book is a national best-seller in the non-fiction list, and has sold especially well in St. Louis. That is why I spent 14 hours in reading its more than 700 rather closely printed octavo pages, although 50 pages would have been sufficient for me had I been reading for my own benefit. . . .
>
> I wonder if my article would have seemed offensive to many. Surely those who had been enthusiastic about the book would find my necessary references to sex extremely mild by comparison and the others might well have inferred that I was rather "on the side of the angels"—or, what is better, on the side of historical accuracy![28]

A letter from Neihardt to Pulitzer at the end of 1933 indicates this increased watchfulness and the additional pressure for the column to reflect popular trends: "I promised to write you each week, for awhile, regarding the books reviewed in my columns. This week I am featuring [Mark] Sullivan's *Over Here*, giving a shorter article to Dorothy Parker's *After Such Pleasures*. . . . both of these, as you will note, are leaders at the moment. Soon plans for having outstanding books within a week of their publication will be working."[29] In the letter Neihardt refers to a recent meeting: "[T]echnically speaking, I suppose I was 'on the carpet,' but I had no such feeling," and he mentions the inclusion of some letters of appreciation received from readers, "fairly typical of the considerable number" received in a year.

Neihardt's responsibilities and salary at the *Post-Dispatch* increased in 1936 at the request of Pulitzer, who wanted to restore a full Sunday literary page. While the rest of the family stayed in Branson, Neihardt moved back to St. Louis with daughter Enid, who was to serve as his secretary, and set up the page, usually reviewing two books himself and assigning the rest to staff. Contributors such as F. A. Behmyer, Ferd Gottlieb, Marie Bliss, and H. M. Williams, whose initials had appeared occasionally in the weekly column were now joined by Dorothy Jean Coleman, Frances Dawson, Irving Dilliard, and O. F. Fink in a list that eventually swelled to fifteen. Incidentally, Ollie Fink's connection to Neihardt soon became more than professional; in January 1937 he and Enid married in a quiet ceremony with Enid's brother, Sigurd, and his wife, Maxine, as witnesses.

Neihardt's writing for the *St. Louis Post-Dispatch* came to an abrupt end in July 1938. Neihardt became the victim of an internal struggle for control of the newspaper that had been going on for some time. Neihardt, in a note to Aly, told what happened:

> When the young Pulitzer (the 3rd) came back from college to become a power in *P-D* affairs, the reactionary trend began to be noticeable . . . At first, his influence was vague, but it grew and occasioned talk in the staff. Then the *P-D,* the great, free, progressive paper, edited by the great OKB (a radical in the progressive sense) actually endorsed Landon for the Presidency!! There was kidding with a lot of concealed scornful laughter, all over the *P-D.* It was pure farce comedy, as the intelligent members of the staff (that's most of them) saw the matter. Now this, of course, was accomplished over the opposition of OKB. There were other reactionary moves, generally concerned with financial retrenchments, which were strenuously opposed by OKB, who represented the morale of the old *P-D* under the first and great, Pulitzer. . . .
>
> Finally, in 1938, when OKB was on vacation . . . the literary page of the *P-D* was abruptly "discontinued," in keeping with an efficiency engineer's report to the effect that the page cost "17,000 a year and did not bring in anything like that much revenue!" . . .
>
> OKB returned from vacation and shortly afterward resigned. . . . Before he left the *P-D* he made a speech behind closed doors to his entire staff. One reason that he gave for his resignation was the termination of my service. He said in the typed copy I saw: "When Neihardt left the *Post-Dispatch,* much of the spiritual power of the paper left with him!"[30]

Neihardt completed the circle begun thirty years earlier in once again writing for the *New York Times.* It seems fitting that one of Neihardt's last pieces of critical work concerns a book about a hero of the American West written by a respected colleague: Mari Sandoz's *Crazy Horse: Strange Man of the Oglalas*. In the review he paid tribute to Sandoz's portrayal: "Here is a glorious hero tale told with beauty and power."[31]

In looking at Neihardt's thirty years of critical writing, one can see subtle shifts in position, responses to cultural changes, a maturing of voice, and a softening of some earlier harshness, and yet the underlying critical principles remain the same. Neihardt as a thirty-year-old artist standing poised to claim his place in the literary landscape and the mature man of sixty demonstrate a remarkable symmetry of outlook. Neihardt may have been a young man when he took on the challenge of publicly staking out the territory of his critical principles, but he had arrived at those principles carefully through his education, his personal readings of the ancients and the moderns, and exchanges with his peers. He had thoughtfully examined the world of ideas around him and had developed strong opinions in response to his "time-mood," a phrase he used to describe the cultural atmosphere of a particular time and place.

Like many of his contemporaries, Neihardt saw a culture where old values were crumbling and a social climate marked by upheaval and human suffering. He identified the time around 1911 or 1912 as the beginning of a period of cultural anarchy in the United States. In a May 1916 column he noted that four years previously he had linked the "democratic idea and modern art tendencies, especially those which may be characterized as impressionistic," pointing out that democracy, in its excess, can lead to ignorance and unrestraint.[32]

Neihardt traced the cause of the dominant time-mood, beginning with the invention of the steam engine and following through the French Revolution and the triumph of laissez faire. The steam engine was a key marker in the movement toward an industrial society, and a laissez-faire system reflected a shift in the politics of power in the economic realm. He cited the French Revolution as a reversal of the previous dominant world trend. Until that point, Western society had been moving toward concentration, arriving, finally, at absolute monarchy not only in the realm of politics but also in all human activity. This final stage of concentration reached a point of rigidity that had to break. "It did so in the great upheaval at the end of the eighteenth century, and there began a panic rush in the opposite direction; for when men flee from any hell, Heaven will seem to be as far from that place as it is possible to go."[33] The natural reaction was a tendency toward absolute individualism that had engulfed his time, with the higher values—ethics, religion, literature, and art—just beginning to be affected.

Neihardt saw a culturewide reliance on scientific materialism as a reinforcement of anarchic trends in the artistic realm. The amazing results of a dedication of energy to technological advances had enshrined objective ways of seeing and knowing and led to a corresponding rejection of subjective experience. In reality, Neihardt believed, science and mysticism were part of a continuum. Responding to a letter discussing Rabindranath Tagore's *Gitanjali*, Neihardt recalled the cultural mood at the time of the book's appearance:

> It was in 1912, the year of *Gitanjali*, that the great world-wave of impressionism struck the realm of our higher values over here like a hurricane. (I use the term, impressionism, to signify the tendency to repudiate all standards that are the result of the race's accumulated experience, and to set up individual caprice as a guide.) The world war that began two years later was a major symptom of what was happening to our world. We are still living in a cultural chaos. This is not to be deplored, only understood, if possible. . . .
>
> Surely, it is not surprising that Tagore's fame should have waned along with so much that was good—and *is* forever. Time moods sweep across the world like cloud shadows across the landscape. As they pass, they seem everlasting, and they determine the dominant persuasions of men. But the sun goes on shining.[34]

Neihardt believed that this cultural chaos was also expressed in contemporary criticism, and he found little of value when he surveyed the critical scene. Although his criticism was itself a part of the popular press, his reading went beyond that forum; his library shelves contained scores of books of criticism by writers such as Walter Pater, Henry James, Leo Tolstoy, J. E. Spingarn, Paul Elmer More, Irving Babbitt, H. L. Mencken, George Jean Nathan, George E. Woodberry, Sir Arthur Quiller-Couch, and Lewis Mumford.[35] For his literary criticism, he also drew on the writing of thinkers in disciplines outside literature, such as Upton Sinclair's and John Jay Chapman's social criticism, John Elof Boodin's philosophy, Oswald Spengler's view of history, F. W. H. Meyers's research on human personality (as well as Meyers's literary criticism), and Ananda Coomaraswamy's writings on the Vedanta. Including the more than four hundred volumes of social commentary, theology, philosophy, and criticism reviewed in his column, the titles with which Neihardt was familiar make up a respectable list.

Neihardt positioned himself in opposition to most of the currents of critical thinking of his day, sometimes overtly, engaging in dialogue as he challenged another's response to a work or literary principle, and sometimes subtly, but always with an underlying awareness of other voices in the conversation. On the one hand were the academic critics who dismissed much of contemporary literature as worthless. They are, he said, "offended by the character of much of our successful literature, [and] leap to the conclusion that contemporary writing is pretty much a false alarm and that genuine literature is 'the surviving product of dead authors—the longer dead the better.' "[36] On the other hand were the "hoarse screamers" who were themselves the product of the same time-mood sweeping through the cultural realm, and who "trim their sails to catch the veering wind."[37] It was this group that Neihardt saw as being most vulnerable to the trends of contemporary thought, a condition that makes valid criticism difficult, if not impossible.

Headlining the list of the latter group were critics such as Ford Madox Ford, who, according to Neihardt, praised everything so uniformly and with such shouting that he had no voice left to announce a truly remarkable book when it came along;[38] Dr. John B. Watson, the father of behaviorism and eminent critic of the shouting variety; and Frank Harris, "than whom, perhaps, there is none whomer." Neihardt's selection of quotations suggest that he is hard-pressed to take these critics seriously, quotations such as "Great work, Major, this literature, the greatest a man can do; and you do it greatly" (Harris), the assertion that "It will be little less than a scandal if this book is not read enormously widely!" (Ford), and even the claim by an unnamed critic that anyone who didn't read *All Quiet on the Western Front* would be a traitor to the human race. Neihardt had a little fun at the critics' expense: "Doubtless during the course of the war-book craze we'll be guilty of all sorts of misdemeanors if we don't fall for every outburst of war-book ballyhoo. . . . Note the possibilities: mayhem, arson, simony, sodomy, murder in the first degree, also in the second and third degrees, burglary, body odor, driving while intoxicated, spitting on the sidewalk, adultery, jay-walking, assault and battery, etc. etc.!"[39]

Neihardt took more seriously the criticism of the moderns, the "New Republic Group" or "American smart set," as he sometimes referred to them, critics such as Louis Untermeyer, H. L. Mencken, George Nathan, and Edmund Wilson. Neihardt argued that the writing of the moderns is actually anarchic and "represents no more than a belated reflex of the old individualism." He accused Untermeyer of "mistaking the end of his nose for a mountain" and for falling into error when he assigned the tag of "democratic" to the writing of Amy Lowell and Carl Sandburg.[40] He considered Mencken and Nathan brilliant young men, but their smug sense of urban superiority exposed them as true provincials in the intellectual realm, and their attitudes were representative "not of independent philosophical thinking, but of the general anarchic atmosphere of their time."[41]

Neihardt ridiculed the extreme of the modernist movement, which he termed "impressionism," exemplified by the writing of Gertrude Stein, Ezra Pound, and James Joyce. His use of the term "impressionism" can be confusing, especially when directed against writers and critics who also positioned themselves against impressionism. Neihardt agreed with modernist objections to the grasping materialism of American culture, the emphasis on that which served commerce, and a lack of a national consciousness in American letters, and he agreed with the search for a "usable past."[42] He didn't agree with what the moderns chose to fill the void and believed that those choices actually propelled the disintegration that was at the root of these mutually acknowledged problems.

He expressed his scorn for supporters of the movement, as in this discussion of the Parisian magazine *Transition,* devoted primarily to American expatriates: "Monsieur Jolas is very positive on one point. 'We are no longer interested,' he says, 'in the bourgeois forms of literature... Language, which heretofore has been chained in traditional regimentation, must be dissolved and re-created with new elements.' We must, it appears, have free self-determination for words, which too long have been subject to the bourgeois tyranny of lexicographers and grammarians. By and by even the most patient little word gets sick of having its meaning and even its relation to other words dictated to it. 'Make the dictionaries and grammars safe for democracy' is our slogan."[43] The attacks against modernist writers are cleverly written but are often dismissive to the point that it's hard to tell if Neihardt made a sincere effort to understand what they were trying to do.

Although Neihardt found much in his readings that was disappointing, he continued the search for genuine criticism, a creative art that draws on the "universal interest in the best that men have thought and felt and done throughout the ages" to avoid the extremes of either a violent radicalism or a wooden conservatism.[44] Neihardt respected critics who upheld a criticism grounded on literary tradition—Woodberry, More, Babbitt, the early Sherman. Sometimes referred to as "Puritans" or "of the genteel tradition," these writers came under attack by a younger generation of critics, including Mencken, Nathan, Walter Lippmann, and Van Wyck Brooks, who challenged what they considered to be a dry, academic literary tradition, a lack of an American identity in American letters, and a rigid, stifling insistence on archaic forms and standards.

Neihardt disagreed with this assessment, admiring much of the work of the critics of the genteel tradition. George Woodberry was an early and ongoing influence; Neihardt had several volumes of Woodberry's essays in his personal library and initiated a correspondence with the essayist in which he approaches hero worship. He expressed his thrill at receiving an answer: "At most, I did not expect more than a line or two from you; and here I have a delightful letter to cherish," and closes, "This is a young man's letter to a master. My loquacity will be forgiven."[45] Woodberry's influence on Neihardt can be seen particularly in Neihardt's conception of the American landscape as epic material, which Woodberry examined at length in *America in Literature*.[46] Woodberry, like Neihardt, was opposed to most contemporary realistic fiction and saw literature as the selection and combination of the raw material of experience into an organic whole. He argued that the "scale of experience with which literature deals . . . begins with the narrow circle of the writer's own life and widens out through his city, people, nation, his age, until it includes humanity as such" and that "the end of poetry is to illuminate life from within the consciousness of the reader."[47]

Neihardt also claimed Irving Babbitt as an influence, citing Babbitt's discussions of the wave of impressionism that struck America about 1912 as instrumental to his own interpretation. He pointed to Babbitt's *Masters of Modern French Criticism* as one of the earliest books to draw attention to the "anarchic effect of the democratic idea as misinterpreted and misapplied in the realm of the higher values."[48] Babbitt's discussion "explained and clarified [Neihardt's] thinking about what was happening to our culture in 1912 and after," and he built on those ideas in his application of theory to specific books, "illustrating the effects of the anarchic principle in all fields of thought and theory."[49]

Neihardt agreed with Quiller-Couch that it is natural but dangerous to turn one's back on the favored literature of previous generations, that arbitrary terms like "romantic" and "classical" serve to muddy critical discussion, and that Matthew Arnold improved the means by which to assess literature by introducing an authority based on standards, or "touchstones," of right taste.[50]

Neihardt admired Stuart Sherman's early writing and expressed ideas similar to Sherman's call for an authentic American identity to end the imposition of a New England slant on the American consciousness. Sherman, like Neihardt, was opposed to a dictatorial eastern elite: "The grimmer members of the modern school say, in effect: 'We are going to exclude from the audience of significant modern art the following classes: children, nice young girls and boys, old maids, old fogies, the entire ruck of the bourgeoisie, and all people who insanely insist that they are happy and contented. We shall address only stern, unblinking adults, such as are at least theoretically pessimists and we intend to give them their first full realizing sense of the abyss.' "[51] Both Sherman and Neihardt called for a new type of realist, one bringing a more synthetic view, although they came to widely divergent conclusions regarding who in contemporary literature fit that description. Sherman pointed to such writers as Sherwood Anderson, D. H. Lawrence, and Willa Cather as the embodiment of his brand of the new realist; in Neihardt's eyes, each of these writers expressed the fragmentary nature of the modern condition.[52]

Neihardt considered the writing of Paul Elmer More to be an expression of genuine criticism. He agreed with More's call for a restoration of humanistic values and a natural aristocracy in letters, a "stable class, based upon intellectual and spiritual superiority."[53] Neihardt took exception to a "highbrow" contention that the "lower orders" are incapable of reading, much less appreciating, literature. His vision was also built on an elitist leadership but called, rather, for a "vertical cleavage" based on "gradations of intelligence and essential humanness," rather than a horizontal social stratification.[54] He considered Irving Babbitt's contribution on the humanistic outlook to a collection of philosophic essays "a very fine example of what competent thinking may be" and expressed appreciation for George Santayana's fine distinction of a historical humanism as "essentially a revolt against absolute sanctions for human conduct, based upon supernatural conceptions," which, Neihardt noted, "reads superficially like a description of the prevailing modern mood, against which the humanism of Babbitt and his followers is a protest."[55] He disagreed with Charles Potter's assertion that humanism is a new religion, countering that it "is an admirable system, and it is ably presented by Mr. Potter, but it is very old."[56]

Neihardt's definition of humanism varies slightly from both historical and modern definitions and is tied to his conception of a continuum of human experience encompassing the practical as well as the artistic realms. Neihardt's conception of humanism links social with literary criticism:

> The values of art are . . . fundamental ethical values in the broadest practical sense . . . and any society, however complex, will be civilized in proportion as it admits these values as real and integral in its scheme of practical things. To regard the arts as merely entertaining, or as a means of escape from reality, is to miss the point utterly and to lose the values. These values are called humanistic, and for a good

reason, as we see; but if we should give the name animalistic to the values of materialistic science, we might make our meaning clearer for those who must have all their ideas neatly boxed off from each other; but all values must be interdependent, as the parts of any whole are interdependent. To ignore the higher is to have no human justification for the lower; and to deny the lower is to have nothing upon which the higher may act.[57]

Genuine criticism, in Neihardt's use of the term, must take into account this larger view of the continuum of human experience in its look at contemporary literature.

When reviewing a book for his column, Neihardt held himself to the precepts he admonished others to follow. He began with respect for the effort put into a book, especially by an inexperienced writer, believing that one who had labored long deserved careful consideration of the finished product. In a review of a book by Humbert Wolfe, Neihardt wrote, "Those mysteriously gifted critics who can review a book by looking at the outside of it or, at the most, by glancing at the first few pages, are not likely to be lucky with this item. . . . But long before half of the thousand lines are read, the reader has run the gamut from wit to beauty, from satire to sublimity."[58]

In the reviews, Neihardt often referred to some small nugget buried deep in a book or described spending several nights trying to get the full flavor of the author's message. He often noted some contribution made by a book that did not necessarily qualify as enduring literature—for example, Earl Van Zandt's *Yank the Crusader.* "[T]here is some value in any record of human experience, even though the gifts of the recorder may be slight, and a book such as this before us should not be judged by the higher literary standards, but rather by the good intention of the author."[59]

Authors wrote to express their gratitude for the thoughtful attention Neihardt gave their work. What stands out in the letters is an appreciation for the fact that Neihardt dug deeply enough to make a fair assessment.[60] He showed as much consideration to aspiring authors who sent their manuscripts to him for his opinion. In a letter to Pemberton Parker, Neihardt noted that he wrote "extraordinarily well" but that he would write better if he didn't try so hard and advised him to write as though he "were obliged to buy [words] at a dollar apiece" to guard against overwriting. He gave detailed suggestions, citing examples by page, but he also offered recommendations regarding the larger structure of the writing and ended with words of encouragement and an offer to take a look at a subsequent draft.[61]

Even books that Neihardt didn't find particularly commendable he considered important as indicators of the prevailing social climate. In a metaphor repeated several times in the column, Neihardt likened these books to straws in the wind, books that reflect rather than shape world thought. These books are necessary for an understanding of one's particular moment in time. The literature of the day is "news of how the human spirit is reacting to the social environment, to the prevalent hopes and fears, the characteristic enthusiasms, prejudices and whimsies of its moment."[62]

Neihardt saw much that was of value in contemporary literature. The problem for the ordinary reader was finding it. Publishing companies, like the rest of a society enamored with technology, had turned to mass production and marketing to drive sales. What had been a "gentlemen's business,"—select publishing houses that brought out a few carefully chosen titles each year—had become major commercial concerns that produced a deluge of printed material marketed with the same savvy as soap flakes. While this situation made books more readily available, it did make it difficult to be a selective reader.

Neihardt felt himself particularly fitted to serve as a guide for a reading public looking for good literature. He had spent his life in the company of "the great ones" of classical antiquity as well as immersed in the books of his day. Even before he took on the role of reviewer he was an avid reader and book collector; during his stints with the newspapers the volumes that passed through his hands numbered in the thousands. In 1917 he wrote of reading one thousand new books and scanning as many more in the previous six years; in a 1930 review he told of reading fifteen hundred books and scanning many more in the years since 1922—almost a book a day, half of those read, half scanned.[63] Neihardt's personal library at the time of his death contained over five thousand volumes. He was certainly aware of the trends of literature, both past and present.

Neihardt's geographical and philosophical position on the fringes of contemporary culture gave him what he felt to be a vantage point from which to observe more clearly the dominating trends. He pointed to Stuart Sherman, professor of literature at the University of Illinois, as an example of a critic who had operated under similar favorable conditions. Sherman had developed an autonomous criticism primarily because he had developed it in isolation, far from the Eastern literary power circles, and when he moved to New York, he was no longer able to resist the mood of the dominant group. Neihardt noted this event with disappointment but understanding, remarking that it is difficult for the artist to maintain perspective in the midst of the contemporary whirl.[64]

According to Neihardt, the poet is both gifted with an insight not available to most people and charged with responsibility to interpret that vision. Neihardt acted on this responsibility in his writing of the *Cycle*, but he also considered his literary and social criticism to be a way of interpreting vision. He saw himself in a particular role with a particular audience—a general, yet thinking, reading public. He believed that most people are unaware of the subtle influences that buffet them and shape their perceptions, unaware, indeed, that these forces exist. His task, in his columns, was to provide some means by which they might consider their society and respond thoughtfully.

In writing to this audience, Neihardt attempted to point the way to the good idea or to reveal the larger relationships among those ideas. Neihardt maintained that the world's wisdom has not changed since the time of the ancients; it is merely the store of facts that has shifted. Art reveals the relationships among the facts: "Art in its largest sense is applied philosophy working in the concrete stuff of our experience. Its business is to reveal, by various strategic means, the larger relations between the facts of human experience. In its highest forms, the relations revealed are those that endure, so far as we are able to know; and that is far enough in our finite purposes. At least the relations revealed are unchanging in our little world of ever changing facts that seem to boil like quicksand. Our store of facts has increased enormously since the Greeks of fifth century Athens; but their human truths remain true."[65]

Although our world is constantly stumbling upon new facts, the truth of the relationships remains the same, which is why there is still a place for Socrates and Shakespeare. It is the role of the artist to reveal these relationships to the uninitiated.

In carrying out this charge, Neihardt invited his readers to join him in a grand adventure of exploration and conversation. In one of his introductory columns to the *Post-Dispatch* readers he wrote, "[I]t will not be assumed that anyone can have a corner on the truth, and accordingly those among our readers who may have well-considered literary opinions to express, may do so here. Such communications will be welcomed. However we may disagree, we shall be as comrades who look upon discussion as adventure."[66]

He worked to develop camaraderie with his readers, creating a style that is inviting rather than didactic. He sometimes paused in the middle of a complex interpretation to make sure his reader was keeping up. He was playful in his use of language, with a sense of humor that could produce a delightful sting. He freely expressed his passion for literature and helped his readers imagine the rich relationship between author and reader. He so effectively created the mood of being caught up in a book that his reader is with him as he reads far into the night, fully aware that the lights should have been put out hours earlier. He reminds his reader of the presence of the author in the text, as when he writes, "Now and then . . . the author seems quite unconscious of the fact that he has run away and hidden from his anxious lay reader, who must wait helplessly until the Professor returns, looking exactly as though he had never been away at all."[67]

At the suggestion of a reader, Neihardt issued a challenge to use the coming autumn as the impetus to start on the "effort to live a bigger and better life" by returning borrowed books. He paints a picture of himself looking mournfully at the empty spot where some cherished volume once stood and reminds the borrower, "We lent you those books because we loved you, wished to share our enlightenment with you—and thus it is you thank us! Can you wonder that we are sorry for ourselves?"[68] Neihardt communicated his passion for books, describing his ventures into dusty secondhand bookstores and the thrill of finding a first edition or special inscription on some longed-for title. In short, Neihardt worked to make criticism what he charged others to make it—living, vital, creative, itself a work of art.

Neihardt did not direct his efforts toward an academic or intellectual audience, nor was he writing for the crowd admirer who wanted to remain a part of the crowd. He wrote with an eye on that ordinary reader who loved literature and wanted to examine what that relationship meant in expanding the horizons of his or her world. Letters from his readers testify to Neihardt's success in meeting his goals for the column. He often received personal letters of appreciation; others took the more public forum of the "Letters from the People," as the writer of this note: "What other paper, here or abroad, publishes every day a column on books more imbued with perfect understanding and appreciation than John G. Neihardt's? There is true culture, not only of the mind but of the heart, in his criticisms that brings to his readers a wider vision of life—and what is the real purpose of literature if not that?"[69]

Accepting the role of critic gave Neihardt the opportunity to explore and fine-tune, over a period of thirty years, his own critical principles. His columns provided him with a forum in which to speak freely, a chance to play with and reshape his ideas in the context of a public exchange. He accepted the freedom along with the responsibility and did not hesitate to go against the mainstream, make mistakes, or change his mind. His voice grew stronger and surer over the years, mellowing in some respects, growing more insistent in others. In the main, however, the principles that formed the foundation of his critical stance in 1911 were the same principles of his mature work.

Shortly after its inception, the weekly column in the *Post-Dispatch* became a daily one, and with the inauguration of the new format, Neihardt articulated for his readers the critical perspective from which he would view the new books. He wrote of the importance of taking the long view of literature and considering current publications in the context of that view. Literature is a reflection of the ever-shifting life stream, and while experimentation with new forms is a necessary process in staving off rigidity and death, pushed to extreme it can result in the perverse and grotesque. He noted that a mob spirit, blown by an Eastern urban mentality that was itself subject to the same winds, characterized contemporary literature. In later columns, he pointed out the dangers of relying solely on the evidence that an objective world provides, and he connected prevailing cultural trends to the realm of higher values, pointing out their manifestation in philosophy, religion, ethics, and the arts.

Central to Neihardt's conception of the function of art and the responsibility of the artist was a belief that art is enduring and that an evaluation must look at a work of art in the context of its place among the works of the ages. Neihardt turned often to the classics in his assessment of contemporary literature, believing that literature is a living thing, at once connected to the past and reaching out beyond its own time to the future. The artist is the inheritor of a tradition and builds on that inheritance with individual experience. By ignoring tradition, the artist is cut off from the source of poetic power: "For it is mainly by appealing to memory that poetry works its magic: and the individual memory is too brief, too fragmentary. The racial memory, rich with the distilled experience of countless men and women, is necessary; and racial memory is literary tradition."[70]

The critic needs this sense of all time in making any kind of valid assessment of contemporary literature. Drawing on a metaphor from Shelley, Neihardt likened this perspective to a "white radiance," a pure stream of light encompassing the spectrum of color. It is easy to become convinced that the reds or the yellows of a single generation are the colors of eternity, but it is the responsibility of the critic to point out that they are but single fragments. These fragments are important but cannot constitute the entire focus of one's gaze: "To scorn the red is to have no sympathetic understanding of one's own time—and that is a pitiful disaster. To seek the larger human values in that one necessarily transient key, is to miss the larger values."[71]

The epic poet is most fitted to paint this vision of the larger human scene, and Neihardt's sense of himself as epic poet infuses his critical writing. In the essays written for the *Times*, Neihardt surveys the literary landscape and calls for a poet to write the epic that the story of America demanded, a job, of course, that he soon took up himself. In a review of Charles A. Hanna's *The Wilderness Trail*, Neihardt speaks with authority about the available histories of the West and identifies the subject as epic material. He talks of the opening up of the Midwest to trade as "the start on the last lap of civilization's age-long westward journey about the globe," and ponders why no one has taken up the subject: "In reading of the romantic lives of such men as these and their prototypes in the fur trade of the northwest, one wonders that America has not produced a full-sized National epic."[72] In a review of Edwin Arlington Robinson's work in 1912, he speaks once again of the stories of the West as "the material our not impossible epic poet might use."[73]

Neihardt moved quickly from tentative explorations to a claim of authority to speak out for the western landscape as epic poet. By 1920 Neihardt had published three of the "Songs" of his *Cycle of the West*, and his epic consciousness carried over into his critical writing. In his preface to *The Song of Three Friends* (1919), he wrote of contemporary literature, "We lack the sense of racial continuity. For us it is almost as though the world began yesterday morning; and too much of our contemporary literature is based upon that view. . . . But what we call the slow lapse of ages is really only the blinking of an eye."[74]

It is not surprising that Neihardt's poetry answers the call of his critical writing, but this doesn't presuppose a criticism written as apologia for his poetry. He demonstrated a strong commitment to his vision of the American West, spending nearly thirty years on a project not likely to garner a large share of popular acclaim or much financial reward. The same principles driving the writing of the *Cycle* appear in his columns.

This very commitment to a personal vision, however, makes him subject to his own particular biases, no matter how fitted he believed the epic poet to see beyond the immediate moment, and some of his pronouncements have not worn well with time. Neihardt could recognize the biases coming out of urban power centers but failed to note the biases that might come from one who enjoyed a position of privilege in a patriarchal culture. He acknowledged that it was a "driving, predatory breed" that pushed from Europe into America with a conqueror's disregard for the people already occupying the land.[75] While he respected much of what he found in indigenous culture, he was a proponent of assimilation into "our" culture:

[That time] may never come; for we may never become a homogeneous people, cherishing in common all our great traditions. Perhaps
our country is too large; perhaps too many unassimilable people have
swarmed already upon our shores.

Nevertheless, it is something worth hoping for."[76]

In insisting on continuity as a reference point, Neihardt neglected to
consider that some long-standing traditions might deserve dismantling and
that a common inheritance based solely on a Western male definition is a
limited perspective, indeed.

While considering the past an essential link to who we are today, Neihardt
didn't stand with his back to the twentieth century. He was very much an
eager participant in his time. He also welcomed new forms of literature;
he had, in fact, written some of his early poetry in free verse and at one
point explored with a fellow poet, Louis Ledoux, the idea of publishing
their correspondence in which he defends the new form against Ledoux's
attacks.[77]

Insofar as experimentation gives fresh form to the creative impulse, Neihardt applauded the energy directed to new movements. He was, however,
opposed to experimentation for its own sake—the kind of experimentation
that had its expression in an undisciplined art that substituted individual
caprice for standards. Walt Whitman's influence on modern literature was a
glaring example of such a trend, Neihardt believed, for would-be poets, not
able to imitate Whitman's genius, followed only his style, which resulted
in sloppy, undisciplined verse created by versifiers who were not willing
to learn their craft and, in their scramble to be noticed, turned to ever-
more grotesque posturing. Although Neihardt recognized that these views
were apt to bring him the label of "traditionalist" or the scornful epithet
"Victorian," he insisted on reminding readers of connections to a rich past.
Nevertheless, the labels chafed. In a note commenting on the manuscript of
Aly's biography he wrote, "Let's not say 'traditionalist.' My opponents would
love that bald word. I was the poetic rebel against tradition in 1907 (Bundle
of Myrrh period.) My insistence in my criticism was not upon tradition but
upon essential organization, cosmos as opposed to the prevailing cultural
chaos."[78]

Freedom is realized only by obedience to unyielding law, Neihardt says:
"I suspect that these 'vers librists' confuse the meaning of 'freedom' and
'license.'"[79] The movement did have its benefits according to Neihardt,
however: "Perhaps it will be seen later that the 'free form,' so greatly

emphasized, was the least important feature of the moment. It is clear, at least, that most of the unquestionably sound accomplishments in the poetry of the last fourteen years [since 1912] has been through the adaptation of old forms to the liberated spirit of the times. The whole question has been argued with much heat among the cliques, and all the while it has remained true that should a great poet appear he will write greatly in any form he may choose."[80]

Neihardt saw in contemporary fiction a movement away from the essential organization he demanded of literature. Realistic fiction could provide a brilliant copy of life, but it did not provide the wider view implicit in art, focusing instead on the fact, which is essentially transient. Neihardt connected the rise in the popularity of realistic fiction with a feminization of literature, a preoccupation with the personal and fragmentary. He believed that to be great, poetry must "reveal demiurgic power," that the great poetry of the world was "distinctly a masculine product," masculine because characterized by a "creative integrating vision." Too much of contemporary realistic fiction, written by both men and women, was characterized, rather, by a "painstaking accumulation of details—a sort of emotionally heightened gossip on a large scale."[81]

Art works on the individual, according to Neihardt, by pointing out the relations among the facts of human existence and by enabling the individual to participate in the grand scheme of life. Art's purpose is not moral, but it must be ethical, must have at its core an essential truth:

> At this point there may be some who still suspect that I am confusing literary with moral values; that I am persuaded to regard literature as a means of telling man how to be "good"; that I think a book is good if it deals with good characters and acts; bad if it deals with bad characters and acts. The idea is abroad but I know no such distinctions. I still sometimes read my Rabelais and, as anyone knows, much of him, in our time, is unquotable. Much oftener I read the *Agamemnon* and Aeschylus, in which the husband is slain by the wife who boasts of her deed. It would be easy to name a great many such books, ranging from remote antiquity to recent times that are to many of us like stars that do not set. There are also many happy books that glow throughout with human kindness and are dear. On the other hand, I find it hard to fight my way through those "sunshine" books in which the half starved, crippled little hero, always smiling and talking like a Sunday School, is inevitably rewarded by the good rich lady. Fairy stories, moving in the rainbowed land of Never, Never, may be very precious.

A rude and grotesque wit, instinct with vision, may, by audacious misrepresentation reveal the true with laughter. But a lie won't do.[82]

Neihardt was not immune to the pessimism that he noted in much of the writing of his contemporaries. While usually the determined optimist regarding the human race, especially when taking the long view, he was at times discouraged by the foibles of individuals and the grasping policies of world leaders. One place he let down his guard was with Julius House: "Silence is perhaps the answer that a god would give to all this turmoil and folly; but we are not gods, and the best our writing can do is to act as a cry to forlorn individuals here and there in the growing darkness—'Here too am I—sad and puzzled and still believing desperately that there are real human values to be cherished even in utter loneliness.' "[83]

More often, and nearly always in his columns, he guarded against pessimism and admonished others who used their gifts in a destructive pattern:

> Strange beauty is to be found in the book, as in all of Cabell's work; and ever from behind the beauty, as a satyr leering out of gorgeous foliage in some haunted wood, peers a salacious, mocking spirit. "Breed and die!" it jeers. "All your notions about beauty and sanctity and wisdom, all your conceptions of super-brutal values, all your religions and your moralities and your ethics and your gods and your music and your poetry—what are they but the fig leaves of romance hung over the brutal fact that men merely breed and die?"
>
> If Mr. Cabell believes this, one wonders that he should consider it worth the effort to say so. And the very genius which he employs in saying it would seem to render his thesis absurd.[84]

While admitting that this world can be an unhappy place, Neihardt chose to direct his gaze toward the nobility of the human spirit. His belief that this world is an illusion created out of the human consciousness led him to the conviction that the better "world-craftsman" is not Cabell and his ilk but the outmoded, beleaguered idealist. It is here that we find the seeds of Neihardt's conception of the purpose of art and the role of the artist.

Neihardt stressed the power of poetry to expand consciousness. Most inhabitants of the West limit their interpretation of their world by using only evidence gathered by the senses. Neihardt argued that all humans have the capacity to enlarge ordinary, sense-bound consciousness, "for we live in mystery and some glimmering of awe must at times break through upon the darkest mind." The poet can be the catalyst: "An artist, we may say, is one whose habit it is to view the world from the vantage point of states more or less removed from the standardized state of ordinary living, and who has a special technique for representing the wider experience by fusion with the narrower, to the end that his vision may be shared."[85] When someone experiences the momentary flash of art's power at its height, that person undergoes a sense of exaltation in a loss of self. Neihardt likened this experience to the merging of the raindrop with the sea, the raindrop losing its individual identity but taking on the larger identity of the vast sea.[86]

Neihardt explains this expanded consciousness with a parable of a valley surrounded by high mountains. The people who live in the valley are convinced that they cannot climb the slopes to view what is beyond, and they define their world only by what they see around them. However, a few of the valley dwellers are sleepwalkers, and while others sleep, they ascend the slopes and return to tell what they have seen. As the sleepwalkers report their view, the people of the valley reshape their interpretation of their valley. Their perception of the valley has not been wrong, merely limited, and the sleepwalkers' stories enrich their understanding.

It is not easy, though, for the sleepwalkers to tell what they have seen,

for language has been developed to meet the need of those who have never left the valley, and there are no words for aspects of the valley from the height. Accordingly, through the ages, these sleepwalkers have developed new languages, new techniques, whereby it may be possible to re-create in the minds of valley men some semblance of the vision of the height. . . . Some strive with color, some with visual form, and some strive to present the mood of the vision by weaving sounds into enchanting patterns. And some use words in ways unknown to common valley parlance, creating a rhythmic flow of pictures in the mind of him who hears; and this way is more suggestion than telling, more singing than speech; and were it all a telling, less would be told.[87]

Poetry can bridge the gap between an ordinary, limited state of consciousness and the outer boundaries of awareness: "[T]he act of creating a poem—or any work of art—is an act of translating; and if pure poetry could be created, it would not be literature; it would be music; just as pure music could be conceived only as enchanted silence."[88] The greater the artistry of the tellers, the better able they are to translate mystery.

Another metaphor Neihardt uses to explain how the poet interprets his vision compares a sudden flash of insight to brief illuminations produced by lightning. The description of a landscape obscured by darkness is not wrong, merely incomplete, and new details, new relationships, and expanded boundaries revealed flash by flash are thrilling additions to understanding. The real challenge to the recipient of this flash of awareness is not in understanding but in communicating that understanding to another, especially what is revealed at the boundaries of consciousness. Boundaries, for Neihardt, are places of power where the commonsense world blends into a landscape of mystery. Creative vision is born in this borderland at the edge of ordinary states of consciousness, and high art is defined in terms of its success in translating those outer limits of awareness:

> [M]inor poetry is produced . . . so near to the standard spot that the sense of time and space is still strong, tending to limit expression to the moment and the place. . . . On the other hand, major poetry is produced in the further reaches of the outer field, so distant from the standard spot that the sense of space and time is weakened, or even lost by fits; the moment and the place grow vague, as remembered in a dream, or vanish as memories of the day in the strangely conscious profundity of sleep. The symbols of expression become generic, the fundamentally human is emphasized, the sense of individuality weakens or dies out, the universal is substituted for the particular; for here the poetic process is taking place in human depths "That yield no foam to any squall of change."[89]

No matter how important a world force Neihardt believed poetry to be, however, he knew that his culture did not place a high premium on poetic values. Rather, the prevailing doctrine of the twentieth century, at least for the Western world, was scientific materialism, the culmination of a century of reliance on a sense-based view of the world.

Neihardt considered materialism to be a dominant factor in the conduct of life, a force of which the public, however, was unaware. As scientific materialism, it was the theory that the universe could be explained in terms of matter and motion, the former conceived as the substance of our commonsense world, the latter as an infinite varying of relationships between the ultimate particles of matter. According to this theory, these multiple relationships result in all forms and all phenomena, even consciousness, and anything not physically measurable cannot be real.

Though this cultural reliance on physical authority is so entrenched in the Western mindset as to appear universal, other cultures have developed different patterns. Neihardt explored Eastern mysticism in particular as a possible alternative, an approach that rejects a view of the world interpreted by the senses as illusory and gives primacy to subjective ways of knowing. While conceding that an Eastern view could add a sorely needed spiritual component to Western perspective, Neihardt believed that it was too alien a concept for westerners and too limited in itself to be embraced wholeheartedly.

Neihardt conceded the many benefits of science but cautioned against relying on one perspective to meet all human needs. Scientific advancements, as impressive as they may be, still answer only the needs of humanity at the brute level. Neihardt questioned the value of our ability to travel faster, communicate more rapidly, and produce more if that which is produced does not make us more humane: "It is altogether possible to live the ethical life of swine while enjoying all of the vaunted blessings of materialistic science. We know this to be true, because it is being done on a vast scale with conspicuous success. . . . Why do we save labor—to the end that laborers and their families may go hungry? Why fight tuberculosis in the slums— that the number of those who live the lives of rats may not dwindle? For what are they to live?"[90]

Neihardt argued that a strictly sense-based, scientific view does not leave room for poetic values, and the prevailing mood of early-twentieth-century culture was scientific. "Science is matter-of-fact, whereas poetry is of the imagination. Men with the scientific outlook cannot be poets or even love poetry." Neihardt noted, however, that science, though ostensibly in opposition, actually partakes in the poetic: "[W]ithout imagination, modern science would have been impossible. So obvious is this that in its higher reaches it approximates the poetical."[91] He observed a growing tendency among some scientists to look beyond the discipline's reliance on sensory data only and believed that, in an unusual twist, science and literature had exchanged roles. Particularly because of work done by physicists Niels Bohr, Max Planck, and others, many scientists had come to a realization that their theories were inadequate and that "there are values that do not admit of measurement and 'scientific' proof."[92] A similar metamorphosis had taken place in mathematics where, "in their farther reaches the mathematical mind and the poetic mind become all but indistinguishable."[93] Literature, on the other hand, had become more "scientific," as writers turned to a literal, sense-based portrayal of the world referred to, erroneously, Neihardt contended, as "realism."

Neihardt's writings against dominant trends are part of a concerted attack on a prevailing cultural view, a warning that a model based on sense-bound science is not only inadequate but also destructive. He proposed a new way of looking at life that is neither a sense-based nor an idealistic perspective but a synthesis of the largest view possible, given our circumstances and our limitations as human beings.

Neihardt did not insist that we reject the scientific world, only that we recognize its limitations, that life itself is the goal, and art and science are both merely means by which to live more fully. Neihardt called us to follow the artist's lead in peering into the borderlands of consciousness, convinced that we can reshape our vision of the valley in which we live. He argued that the world has not always fixed its faith on materialistic science and will one day turn its gaze toward another object, that it is, in fact, already moving in that direction. He asked,

Can it be that the poet and the physicist are merged in Bohr and Planck, the poet and the mathematician in Einstein? Is this not inevitable, since they are men? And if the modern theories are not science, but poetry, should we devotees of the poetic values be scornful? Should we not rather rejoice to believe that the old notion of antagonism is an illusion, and that both the scientific and the poetic belong to one flowing circle of human reality? And if this be poetry, what is its theme but the ancient longing to know? And the symbols of its expression are the circle in space and time—symbols of human limitation—pictures of the human dream, always essaying an infinite journey and always returning upon itself.[94]

John Neihardt's critical writing adds a layer of complexity to the sketch that has been formed of him thus far. Much has been written about the joining of his voice with Black Elk's and about his epic, *A Cycle of the West*. But he also speaks to us in important ways in his critical writing, and we can benefit from his guidance, as did the readers of his newspaper columns, in finding the best that literature has to offer. We might not agree with all, or even any, of Neihardt's assessments—opinions are subjective; new interpretations lend additional perspective to the literary and social outlook, and we look at the world's literature through the lens of our own particular time-mood. But Neihardt's critical principles can enlarge our view, and we can use them as a starting place for new conversations or a reshaping of old conversations as we consider this particular sleepwalker's vision from beyond the valley.

Neihardt believed that poetry lifts us out of the mundane circumstances of brute existence and offers a stunning vision of a world previously wrapped in darkness. Perhaps the vision is illusion, but, as he told his readers during the early years of the twentieth century, the illusion is ours to choose. Poetry reminds us that by responding to the highest call of our humanity we can peer with the poet as he stands "upon a swimming peak and [beholds] the valley as a tiny pool of shadow in a vast of starlight, as though he had peered a moment upon an outer world."[95]

I
TRADITION

ONE

As from a Height of Time

John Neihardt was an enthusiastic participant in his particular time and place. He considered his life rich in family, friends, work, and contact with the land. He also enjoyed the contemporary intellectual scene and welcomed new books, new thought, new discoveries. As much as he enjoyed the cultural atmosphere of early-twentieth-century American life—his "time-mood," in his term—he recognized that his moment in time was only a small fragment of the whole of human experience.

One of Neihardt's oft-repeated themes in his critical writing is the difficulty of distancing oneself from one's particular time-mood. When looking at literature or life, the view from inside the moment is, of necessity, fragmentary and clouded by the whims of fashion. One way to step outside a particular time-mood is to view contemporary literature in the context of the accumulated wisdom of the ages. Neihardt did not suggest that we ignore the present, for not only is this moment rich in and of itself, but it is also the link between what has been and what is yet to come. He recommended, rather, that we step back to take the longest view possible and add to our impression of the moment the perspective of centuries of the best of human thought.

Neihardt pointed to the dangers of taking the position of either of these two extremes—one of limiting perspective to the present moment, the other of excluding that moment: "We are witnessing a struggle between two conceptions of poetry, that of tradition and that of impressionism. No doubt, as in all similar struggles, neither party is entirely right. The impressionist forgets that no time can be independent of the past out of which it has grown; and the stickler for tradition, on the other hand, forgets that imitation is a form of suicide, and that real art is the result of a creative continuation of tradition, not of a slavish obedience to it."[1]

The long view—the view implicit in art—can temper a "slavish obedience" to the past. It can also lead those moderns who consider current society the pinnacle of achievement to recognition of the transience of the moment and the fallibility of the moment's discernment.

THE WHITE RADIANCE (1926)

It is a well-known fact, and one that has furnished vast comfort to many a misguided literary aspirant, that contemporaneous literary criticism has very often proven ridiculously inadequate. Recently there has been published a volume entitled *Famous Literary Attacks*, in which are gathered together a few choice vials of critical wrath poured upon the heads of those whom now we view as masters.[2] It is a rather portly book; yet it is only one of many such that could be compiled. Also, if the compiler's appetite for grossly mistaken literary judgments were not appeased after so great a feast of futile ire, he might prepare an equally imposing collection of ill-fated eulogies.

Many an alleged immortal has succumbed to the inclement social weather of our world; and many an apparently puny infant has survived the croups of cultural autumns and the colics of new fruitage in the green.

Such a library of misconceived opinion as has been suggested here would make jocose reading for those of us who share the curious and fairly prevalent delusion that we, the first moderns, stand triumphantly unbunkable upon our height of time. But there are reasons for suspecting that we are now living in a time peculiarly liable to gross errors in literary judgment.

Literature is merely one of many social phenomena, and the literary activities of any age are to be considered first of all with reference to the prevailing social background. Growth in society proceeds, like any other growth, by alternate periods of increasing strain—which may seem almost static in their peacefulness—and periods of sudden release and unfoldment. Slow-moving pictures of a developing plant have been seen by almost everyone, no doubt, and will be remembered in this connection. The period of release and violent unfoldment which we are now experiencing may be viewed as having begun with the French Revolution which was, broadly speaking, the triumph of the individualistic idea over the monarchic idea. The extreme of concentration had been reached in the reign of Louis XIV and the centrifugal, so called democratic, movement began. Its influence was apparent in the fundamental realm of economics long before it began to affect what we call the higher values—those of literature, the arts, philosophy, religion, ethics. It was not until about 15 years ago that individualism, long triumphant in industry, struck our realm of higher values like a whirlwind. Whether or not the storm has attained or is about to attain its maximum violence, who can say? We know that many very respectable old signboards are flying all over the place and that many a private window, once turned serenely upon a world of what seemed eternal certainties has been broken in by the chilling blasts of doubt.

To realize the change that has taken place in literary attitudes, as a result of individualism worked out to its logical conclusions, one has only to consider the rigid rules that were laid down by absolute critical authority for the writers of pre-Revolutionary France. The monarchic idea, long established in the lower realms of human activity, had penetrated to the realm of art. Then tradition was everything; now it is practically nothing. Taste was then a fixed thing imposed upon the individual by unquestionable authority; but what taste now? The past was then the standard for the present; but now, to most, there seems only the loud moment, enormously prolific of contending whim—a bewildering spectacle!

It is the latter point that brings us to the matter of importance in attempting to judge the literature of our own time. We are witnessing the anarchic effect of extreme individualism in literature as in life. It is only the social body that lives on and on. The individual life is but a moment in the life of the race. During an age when the social body is conceived as a unit, to which individual interests must be sacrificed, the past has a tremendous meaning. For a generation dominated by the individualistic attitude, it is not unnatural that the living moment should loom larger than all time.

The result is that, being cut off from the long process that has given us all our human values, we now tend to become provincials in time. Just as the provincial in the usual geographical and social sense judges all things by the prevailing conceptions of his province, scorning the larger world, so do we now tend more and more to appraise our own literary products solely in the light that is peculiar to our agitated moment. The attempt to render absolute judgments with only the data of a limited reference scheme has always been the supreme tragedy (or is it comedy?) of human thought. But in an age like ours, it is very likely to become the rule.

The long and dearly bought experience of men, in the matter of ascertaining dependable human values, is momentarily ignored in our overwhelming passion for novel experiment. We lack the synthetic sense in literature as in

life. We do not now commonly conceive of literature as organic. Its past for
most readers seems to lie dead somewhere on the far side of an impassable
gap. The literature that really concerns us greatly as a people is largely a
sporadic phenomenon growing out of the peculiar mood of the time.

Being a revolting generation, impatient of all restraints, we are certain to
overestimate the essential value of those works that most violently express
the antisocial mood; and yet all of our genuine values are in their very
nature social.

Doubtless Shelley had no thought of literary criticism when he wrote the
strangely luminous lines: "Life like a dome of many-colored glass, / Stains
the white radiance of eternity," but he expressed a truth that is applicable
here.[3] The light of understanding and persuasion by which men live is
constantly changing. New generations develop new social moods within
which, as in a colored atmosphere, all views are colored. When the light
of the time is red, as we may say, most men will think the truth is of that
color; and the blues and yellows of other generations may seem absurd or
pathetic or merely curious.

Yet what is any color but a fragment of some single white radiance? And
what is the white radiance in our special application of the figure, but a
vision of the larger truth about men and the human adventure in general,
as opposed to the merely fragmentary view in keeping with the bias of the
moment?

Eternity is a long, long stretch, and we can not follow our poet so far.
Human literary history is much briefer, and here and there, throughout
the whole length of it, flashes of the white radiance may be noted by those
who have the eyes to see. Even in our own confused time of stormy red the
white ray breaks in many a single line or passage; and now and then a whole
book may glow with it. But it is the red that wakes the loudest clamor.

To scorn the red is to have no sympathetic understanding of one's own
time—and that is a pitiful disaster. To seek the larger human values in that
one necessarily transient key, is to miss the larger values.

More than once has the restless general consciousness of men passed
through all the shades and colors of the social spectrum from the naïve
germinating violet on through the slowly maturing blues, the flowering
greens, the mellowly fruiting yellows and the tempestuous revolting reds.

But the truth about the light was never to be perceived by the split ray.

LITERATURE AND THE UNLETTERED (1926)

For a book reviewer who was in the game before the days when the Many
in America seemed suddenly to discover the pen, and who, since early

childhood, has been somewhat aware of the great human spirits that have
passed through our world, enriching it with their readings of the wonder
and the beauty and the hurt and heroism of it all, there are certain to come
moments when the literary turmoil of the day seems a pitiful futility. There
is not a season now that does not bring forth several "masterpieces," hailed
raucously by our most highly accredited critical hucksters, and the average
life of these masterpieces is a matter of a few best-selling months.

So greatly do we seem to be embarrassed with literary riches, that great
works of literature must die each spring and fall to make room for the
inevitable new crop of prodigies and portents. It is no wonder that a slight
falsetto note is to be detected in the voice of our contemporary enthusiasms.
Read among the advertisements of any publishing season what the most
"authoritative" critics have said about the latest wheezes. What a din of
superlatives! It is strangely like the screaming of hysterics. Yet, season after
season the crowd believes again, and reads what it is told to read. It does
so for the same reason that it uses Cleanso and will have no substitute, or
eats Vitoshavings for its breakfast, or wears the latest thing in hats or coats
or collars.

The loudest shouting wins where there is nothing but an empty ear.

Are we, then, justified in assuming that our authoritative critics, who
specialize in singing hosannas for each new literary vogue as it develops,
are the conscious agents of a shrewd selling scheme? Some may be; but it is
probable that most are not. When the mob-spirit is abroad and mighty, it
is extremely difficult for any individual to retain the power of independent
judgment. If you have ever been caught in a multitude intent upon lynching
a fellow man, you will know just what is meant. Or if you have ever found
yourself in the midst of a vast revival meeting crowd when the frenzy of
salvation was at its height, you will know how hard it is to keep your balance
where the mob-mind rules. Whatever else we may become through the
cultivation of our higher human powers, fundamentally we are gregarious
animals; and to be unlike is always to assume a fearful burden. Is it not
said that one might as well be dead as out of fashion? And this most men
believe.

It was along about 1911 that the mob spirit began to operate conspicuously in the realm of American literature. Hundreds upon hundreds
suddenly qualified as poets, for the difficulties of that ancient and noble art
were obligingly removed. Vulgarity became the vogue, and uncouth hoboes
could become outstanding literary figures over night.

The literary center of gravity shifted rapidly southward across the human
equator, and there it sticks today; for are there not two primal urges to which

the least literate of men can readily respond? And perhaps hunger is the less compelling of the two.

The revolt that we are witnessing in letters is essentially a sansculotte revolt. The crowd is making pigstyes of the temples and the palaces and guillotining the mighty of the old regime. The democratic principle, in its literal sense, has been defeated almost everywhere as a political concept. It is in the realm of the higher human values that the principle has won a temporary triumph; and this, perhaps, for the simple reason that the masters of the modern world do not take those values seriously. If the mob were to attempt to do in the realm of material values what it is now doing with howling temporary success in the realm of literature and the arts, would there not be armored cars patrolling all our cities and machine guns stationed at strategic points along our streets?

Just as the momentarily victorious masses of the French Revolution sought to obliterate the long human past by creating a brand-new calendar, beginning with the year of their emergence, so now it becomes the fashion to deny our literary heritage, as though literature had begun some fine day last week, say shortly after breakfast.

The insurgent mass has never been able to hold an advantage it has won. It is essentially an amorphous thing, lacking the integrating power of a long past commonly remembered. Its characteristic values are not of time. It is capable of destructive violence, but the mob spirit never can create. Now and then come periods when apparently nothing but general violence can clear the way for the ancient life-stream of the world that has been checked by the slowly growing clutter of obsolete custom. No doubt we are in such a period now; but while attempting to understand our period we need not mistake the odor of garlic and onions and neglected alleys for the breath of inspiration, nor destructive violence for creative power.

TWO

Ancient Seers

In taking the long view, Neihardt turned first and foremost to the classics of Greece and Rome, the heritage of Western culture. He admired the heroic spirit of Homer, the wisdom of Socrates, the power of "that shaggy old god of them all—Aeschylus."[4] To Neihardt, the cultural achievements of the Greeks have seldom been paralleled; their wisdom and spiritual development unmatched.

There is evidence in the following essays of Neihardt's extensive grounding in the classics, including his familiarity with the standard English translations as well as the works in their original language. Having read the classics of Rome both in Latin and in English, Neihardt knew that poetry loses something of its beauty in translation, no matter how gifted the translator. Wanting that intimate experience with the texts of ancient Greece, he set about teaching himself Greek and even began a translation of the *Agamemnon*.

These essays also display John Neihardt's playful humor and his feeling of kinship with his readers as they venture together into a world in which he obviously delights. We see several of Neihardt's recurring themes: the idea of synthesis as a creative principle, the value of myth as evidence of humanity's noble reach exceeding its grasp, the idea of greatness being a loss of the individual in something larger than self. This loss of self is something that the individual human ego must often be tricked into. What has historically inspired greatness has been the belief, by the individual, that a particular act will bring glory or power or immortality. In reality, the greatness comes from the sacrifice of that individual to the greater social good.

GALVANIC SHOCKS IN ESSAY FORM

REVIEW OF *LEARNING AND OTHER ESSAYS*, BY JOHN JAY CHAPMAN
(NEW YORK: MOFFAT, 1910)

We hear so much discussion of the literary poverty of the times that, if we are not forewarned, we are apt to regard a new book much as we regard a piece of toast at breakfast, listlessly, and with a vague mental observation: "Come, here is some more toast; let us dispose of it and be at more serious operations!" Now this state of mind is not to be defended, only explained. It is the attitude of an age in which more is devoured than is digested.

When we wish to be quite unoriginal we can do no better than to remark that the printed output of to-day is chiefly twaddle. Having made this remark, all our friends will promptly agree with us, which fact in itself ought to inspire us with some suspicion. But it doesn't; and so, when next we feel in the mood for reading, we purchase a book which our bookseller tells us is going to "have a big run," and emerge from our latest mental debauch well prepared to repeat our former unoriginal remark. For, with the vast majority of us, reading is not an intellectual delight, but (to coin a doubtful phrase) a mere optical automatism made possible by a lazy fondness for vicarious excitement. We forget in making our unoriginal remark that a symphony concert may be in progress while most of us are just around the corner absorbed in the strains of a hurdy-gurdy!

These oblique remarks are inspired by the thought of a number of recent books, but Mr. John Jay Chapman's latest collection of essays is immediately responsible.

There are books, logically thought out, excellently written, that, when you have gone through them, leave with you an impression of knowledge rather than of wisdom. You respect them, but they do not leave an awe about you. They do not give you that vague but persistent feeling that a universe presses in all about them, that if you open them lightnings will leap out and show you a whole world lifted momentarily out of darkness. *Learning and Other Essays* somehow leaves an impression not to be adequately explained when the book is thought of in detail. It cannot be said of it in a comfortable, final way: "This much it has taught me." The secret of its influence seems to lie in what might be called its electric quality. It does not think for you so much as it makes you think. It is a rapid series of faint galvanic shocks that leaves you more active than it found you, and you will find the real book growing within you after the printed one is closed. All of this is, perhaps, only another way of saying that the author has written with a margin.

It is proverbial that America has gone mad over utilitarianism. Nothing seems to be too sacred for appraisal in dollars and cents. Classical education has little prestige with many of us because it does not "fit us for the struggle," as we say, with an air of worldly wisdom.

In spite of our remarkable power along so-called "practical" lines, there is something of the "bounder" about us as a nation. Even in our rural communities a man, possessing none of the intellectual inheritance of the race, elevates himself and family above his neighbors by purchasing an automobile. Since these things are unfortunately true of us generally, Mr. Chapman's opening essay on "Learning" contains a most important message for our time. He does not attack us for our deplorable plunge into materialism; being a philosopher, he explains it, points out the remedy: "There are, then, in the modern world these two influences which are hostile to education—the influence of business and the influence of uninspired science. In Europe these influences are qualified by the vigor of the old learning. In America, they dominate remorselessly."

The following passage should be blazoned on all billboards and cried up and down our streets:

> To-day science knows that the silkworm must be fed on the leaves of the mulberry tree, but does not know that the soul of man must be fed on the Bible and the Greek classics. Science knows that a queen bee can be produced by care and feeding, but does not as yet know that every man who has had a little Greek and Latin in his youth belongs to a different species from the ignorant man. No matter how little it may have been, it reclassifies him; he breathes from a different part of his anatomy. . . . Drop the classics from education? Ask rather, Why not drop education? For the classics are education. We can not draw a line and say, "Here we start." . . . We started long ago, and our very life depends upon keeping alive all that we have thought and felt during our history.

In other words, classic literature is the continuous consciousness of humanity.

Mr. Chapman wisely lays stress upon the importance of nursery training as a means to a higher education. "The focus of all cultivation is the fireside," he says. "The whole future of civilization depends upon what is read to children before they can read to themselves."

Just at present, the misnamed "funny paper" and cheaply written "juveniles" are devoured in great masses by the youngsters, many of whom, if properly started, could find wonderful playmates in the Odyssey. By way of proving that Mr. Chapman is not one of those idealists who see everything but the evident, let us quote one more passage from "Learning": "Now the truth is that the higher education does not advance a man's personal interests except under special circumstances. What it gives a man is the power of expression; but the ability to express himself has kept many a man poor. Let no one imagine that society is likely to reward him for self-expression in any walk of life."

As indicated by the above quotation, what we need is a love of intellectual development for its own sake, less love of appearance, more love of being something worthy, whether our neighbors know it or not, regardless of how much money it will bring us.

Excellent Aeschylus Translation

REVIEW OF *AESCHYLUS WITH AN ENGLISH TRANSLATION*, BY HERBERT WEIR SMYTH (LONDON: HEINEMANN, 1926)

There has been published very recently a new and excellent prose translation of the seven dramas of Aeschylus, the great Greek tragic poet. This is news, but naturally there have been no extras announcing the event. Neither have the literary auctioneers in our leading journals shouted themselves hoarse over the fact. They were already hoarse from telling the world about the best selling masterpiece of the day. And that is quite as it should be, for when is a masterpiece of the moment to receive hoarse acclaim if not during its moment? And after all, Aeschylus has been dead about 2,400 years. Also, he had his day—a long a brilliant day, as days of mortals go—and there was no lack of shouting. Some few are shouting yet in a still, small way; but there are and should be louder noises. The murmur of a gnat in the ear must seem louder than even the music of the spheres.

Since there are sure to be among our leaders some who are not acquainted with Aeschylus—and why should anyone hesitate to admit such a fact in a world "so full of a number of things" worth knowing?—it may be well to state that he was, for our Western world, the inventor of what we know as drama.[5] Strange as it may seem to some movie fans, drama grew out of a religious rite.

Before Aeschylus, this rite consisted in the dancing and singing of a chorus about the altar of the god Dionysos or Bacchus, who was invented to symbolize the spirit of life that came in the spring and went away in the fall. The poet Thespis had been bold enough to introduce an interlocutor, whose function it was to question the chorus, thereby leading the singers into new lyric outbursts. Thus it was possible to tell the story of the god in greater and more interesting detail.

Aeschylus added the second character, thus greatly extending the scope of the rite and making dramatic action possible. The goat was sacred to the god, and the singers of the chorus wore goat skins. Their song was therefore called a goat-song, and goat-song in their language is "tragodos." The English form of the word is tragedy.

Really Quite a Fellow

But perhaps this is not enough to convince an American, not acquainted with Aeschylus, that the father of drama was really quite a fellow. "How much did he get out of it?" is a question that might be asked. Happily we may say that Aeschylus came to be one of the best-sellers of his time. There were, of course, no printing presses in those days. The dramas of Aeschylus were published in the theaters of the Greek world, and they had a "great run" for many, many years. The house was always packed and the poet seems to have been almost as great a drawing card as Rudolf Valentino ever was. Also, he won the Pulitzer Prize twelve times after losing it for fifteen years straight, and he got to thinking it was a part of his salary. He counted on it for the rent. In a manner of speaking only; for the prize seems not to have been paid in cash. Perhaps the Athenians were too primitive to know that everything has a cash value. A "tragic victory" seems to have been much like an "A" mark received in school for good conduct. That wouldn't buy the poet's tobacco, even though he "rolled his own." There is nothing very impressive in that direction. Fortunately we can do much better, as the following story will show.

Book Borrowers Then, Too

It is said that when Ptolemy Evergetes, who ruled over Egypt during the third century, B.C., came to realize that his great Alexandrian library contained no copy of Aeschylus, he decided that he would have a complete copy regardless of expense. Athens, so the story runs, had the only complete copy in the world, containing perhaps as many as ninety plays. (The names of eighty are known and fragments of over seventy are in existence.) Ptolemy proposed to Athens that the manuscript be loaned to him for copying. But Athens had probably loaned books before, like the rest of us, and knew that sometimes even the nicest people forget to return borrowed books. Athens demanded security and Ptolemy gladly put up fifteen talents. That was a lot of money in those days—so much that even a movie star would not regard it as small change. And having put up the money, Ptolemy kept the book. After that, whenever he saw Athens coming down the street, he dodged up an alley. Athens is said to have contemplated a declaration of war, but thought better of it, for Ptolemy was a husky chap.

And that was the beginning of one of the greatest catastrophes in the history of literature. For in the seventh century A.D. Omar, the second of the Mohammedan caliphs, burned the Alexandrian library. He figured it this way: "If," he is said to have stated substantially to a reporter of an evening newspaper of the time, "If all those books contain material that is in the Koran they are clearly unnecessary. If, on the other hand, they contain material contradictory to the Koran, they are pernicious. In either case, they will make a fine bonfire."

Omar Logical Enough

Omar was logical enough; but we lost all but seven of the plays of Aeschylus; and if, as we have good reason to believe, the lost plays were equal to those we have then what a man that was! Even the seven extant plays, though marred with occasional corrupt passages, place Aeschylus among the few supreme poets of all time and his influence has been tremendous in our world.

"From whose pocket was Shakespeare seen to draw his hand? The pocket of Aeschylus," says Victor Hugo.

Seven plays out of possibly ninety by one of the greatest spirits that have passed through this world, and our oldest copy of these is an imperfect manuscript in Florence, Italy, that was copied by some unknown scribe from some unknown manuscript early in the eleventh century. Almost we lost him utterly.

But after all one need not devour a whole steer by way of knowing beefsteak; and the seven surviving plays are known to have been in high favor among the ancients. There have been numerous English translations of Aeschylus, most of them rather disappointing to those who have had some acquaintance with the original, though in all of them is to be felt much of the Aeschylean grandeur. There has been no adequate verse translation of any of the plays though Robert Browning, himself often Aeschylean in his greater moments, undertook a verse translation of the Agamemnon, perhaps the most powerful of the seven. It was not that Browning knew too little Greek. It may be said that he knew too much, or rather that he employed his great knowledge of the Greek tongue in ways that obscured the meaning of the poet, very often translating in accordance with his exhaustive knowledge of Greek etymology. For instance, what to the Greeks themselves meant "a net" he translated as "a wrap around." But it was as though the German word for a "corn" on the toe should be translated "hen's eye." Also, Browning used a jiggling eleven-syllable line for the dialogue by way of representing the twelve-syllable line of the original, and the difference in effect was vast. It is very doubtful if anyone unacquainted with the original, has ever been able to get out of Browning's version any very clear impression of what Browning was trying to do, though much of the work is admirable, being jagged, Titanic, like the original.

Blackie's Translation

Perhaps the best verse translation for those who approach Aeschylus for the first time is that by Blackie. It flows and sings; it is Tennysonian in manner, and being so, is more readily appealing than a faithful translation could be. But no one should stop with Blackie, and indeed those who are sincerely moved by Blackie's translation will never quite get over it. They will want more. The "more" is what H. Weir Smyth's prose translation is admirably calculated to give. It is among all the English translations of Aeschylus what the Lang, Leaf, and Myers prose *Iliad* and the Butcher and Lang *Odyssey* are among English translations of Homer. The meaning is rendered, and yet neither the spirit nor all of the sense of rhythm is allowed to escape. . . .

But why read Aeschylus at all in a world so full of recent books? Because we may be sure there is some good reason for the survival of a book through 2,400 years of constantly changing fashion. Perhaps those who are able to come upon that good reason may be the better able to judge the latest and loudest literary wheeze, the better able to hear the voices that endure.

Aeschylus boldly dedicated his work "To Time." And time has not forgotten.

An Admirable Translation

REVIEW OF *THE AENEID OF VIRGIL*, TRANSLATED BY HARLAN HOGE BALLARD (NEW YORK: SCRIBNER'S, 1930)

There has been considerable Virgil literature during this bimillennial year of the great Roman poet's birth, and doubt there will be more between now and the great date, Oct. 15. Thus far two distinguished translations of the *Aeneid* have appeared—that by T. H. Delabere May of Trinity College, Cambridge, which was noted in this column some months ago, and Harlan Hoge Ballard's, here listed. Both have been known to students of the classics for some years, but each is issued with revisions, and the very special occasion which their republication celebrates should give them the force of new works for a larger reading public than that which ordinarily cares about Virgil.

Of the two translations here noted, Mr. Ballard's is, for various reasons, easily the more satisfactory. Certainly a translation of poetry should give as much as possible the feel of the original, not only in its faithfulness to mood and idea, but in its form and movement as well. Owing to the very nature of poetry, this cannot be done with anything like complete success; and there never has been a wholly adequate reproduction of a great poem in another language. But there have been great differences in the degree of accuracy with which the poet's ideas have been conveyed and in the approximate suggestion of mood, manner and movement.

At the outset, Ballard's translation has the great advantage of being written in hexameters, the measure of the original, while May has employed pentameter verse. Although there is considerable difference in effect between Latin and English hexameters, the former being based upon the quantities of syllables and the latter upon accent, the movement of the original may be strongly suggested by accent, however much of the peculiar singing quality of quantitative verse may be lost in the necessary change of method. Indeed, in Ballard's skillful use of the English hexameter, what is lost will be little missed even by most of those who may have read the *Aeneid* in the original, for it is hardly likely that any large proportion of modern Latin students have ever come to read much of Virgil's verse for its intrinsic musical quality. The difficulties of grammar and syntax generally stand in the way of such appreciation, and it is likely that here, in Ballard's translation, for the first time, many a reader who found his Virgil lessons leaden in the old school days, will hear imperfectly as in a dream, the haunting music of that august singing voice that came into the world two thousand years ago.

Another excellent reason for preferring Ballard's version of the great Roman epic to May's is concerned with the matter of economy. In May's work, the Latin and English are presented on opposite pages, and regularly throughout the volume there are 46 lines of translation to 34 of the original. This very great difference in volume is due far less to the shorter length of the pentameter line than to a fundamental looseness in the translator's verse structure.

In Ballard's work, the number of lines is not only exactly that of the original, but so nearly do the Latin and English lines correspond that the numbered notes of any Latin text apply perfectly in all instances to the Ballard English version. This in itself is a surprising triumph of metrical skill as well as a great convenience to the reader who may sincerely desire to get the most out of the poem. And it is not only in the matter of verse mechanics that Ballard's version is admirable; if it were so, a "free" rendering might be in every way preferable, if done by a genuine appreciator. Ballard's version is remarkable for felicity of phrasing, and in turning to passages of more than usual Virgilian beauty and impressiveness, naturally not without misgivings, scarcely more than the inevitable minimum of disappointment is to be felt.

Though Virgil ceased singing 19 years before the beginning of the Christian era, there are good reasons why his great poem should appeal to us now, for no Spengler was needed to point out certain striking likenesses between our time and that in which Virgil lived.[6] As Ballard says, "Virgil, realizing the perils which threatened Rome—the loosening of the ties of loyalty, the arrogance of the rich, the restlessness of the poor, the growth of licentiousness and the decadence of religious faith—wrote the song of 'Arms and the Man,' that is, of courage and piety, in a supreme effort to save the state." In the *Aeneid* he crystallized the highest vision and aspiration of a great civilization already moribund.

In his essay on Virgil, the late George Edward Woodberry wrote truly as follows:

> Of all Virgil's loves, the greatest in power is the love of human life; and it is this that makes the poem so Christian-like, because it is embodied and conveyed in the forms of sorrow and especially of bereavement. Yet the burden of that sorrow comes as the burden of the Roman world running its long career of battle strife; here is the heart of Rome beating in the only Roman breast in which it had become fully conscious of itself. The world was ready to be re-born; there is no break; the premonitions of Christian feeling are natural to Virgil. It is this that makes him of all ancient writers the nearest to modern times, of all epic poets the nearest to all nations. The *Aeneid* is the dirge of Rome; majestic in its theme, beautiful in its emotions, sad in its philosophy, it is almost the dirge of life; yet many a modern mind still turns from the contemplation of human life in history, like the thousands of old days, to Virgil, and says with Dante, "Thou art my master."[7]

Greatness

REVIEW OF *SOCRATES*, BY A. E. TAYLOR (PHILADELPHIA: APPLETON, 1933)

Although this illuminating study of the great Athenian thinker who lived during the fifth century B.C. is published as one of the "Appleton Biographies," it is not to be correctly described as such. It is quite as impossible, in the strict sense of the term, to write a biography of Socrates as to write one of Homer, or of Jesus the Nazarene, or of Shakespeare. The necessary facts are lacking, which is not at all the calamity that it might be made to appear.

The author of this study, who is professor of moral philosophy in Edinburgh University and a distinguished authority on Plato, is himself careful to point out the impossibility of the task which, superficially, he seems to have assumed. He says: "It is certain that Jesus 'suffered under Pontius Pilate'; and no less certain that Socrates was put to death at Athens on a charge of impiety in the 'year of Laches' (399 B.C.). Any account of either which goes beyond such a statement is inevitably a personal construction." Immediately the question arises: Is it not, then, clearly foolish to write a book on the life of Socrates?

May not the answer be concerned with an ancient and stubbornly continuing misconception of personal importance, an almost universal delusion that must continue as long as there are egos to be blinded by their own desires—and (what is the matter of importance) to be stimulated into effort by those desires? Do not men ordinarily yearn to be "great" because they believe that thereby something will be added to them personally? Do not we, the admirers of alleged or real greatness, share this belief? And is not the excessive rarity of greatness in keeping with that very belief?

For human greatness is impersonal. It is the result of losing the self utterly in something far bigger than the self. This may be achieved at longer or shorter intervals throughout a life, or in a single burning moment. Very often, no doubt, perhaps in every case, men have had to be tricked into the way of greatness, through an initial conviction of vanity, that somehow something very much to be desired could be "gotten" for oneself. But whenever true greatness has resulted, the deluded self has been swallowed up in the vision pursued.

And in the end, it did not matter in the least what the effort or the torture may have been, nor what happened to the man. What mattered was the great deed done or the great vision of beauty and vital meaning made permanent for men to contemplate, or only the uplifting mood that endured about the otherwise meaningless name of one who lived to learn that after all no one can really "get," break his heart in trying as he may. Those who doubt the statement may consult the nearest undertaker.

With this view of the matter, the writing of such a book in the absence of biographical facts is easily seen to be justifiable. The author cannot say that on such a day this man was born, and continue, step by step, with those petty details of living which in reality at best could be of no more than curious interest now. But what the author can do, and does, is to rebuild out of all available fragmentary material the vanished world in which the greatness of the man developed and emerged; much as one might arrive at a clearer understanding of the nature of a concealed source of power by studying the action of its immediate impinging environment. The mood and manner and vital meaning of that enduring impersonal greatness are all that matter now or ever mattered.

"Socrates," through the long process of winnowing time, has become the distinguishing tag attached, for ready identification, to a great enduring tradition of essential sanity and wisdom and lofty moral heroism. Even if it could be shown that something or much of what is now included in the name was added by the ever-busy mythopoeic faculty of man, the resultant greatness, being still a human concept, would in no way be lessened for human uses.

It would be beside the point here to discuss the scholarly details of Prof. Taylor's golden little book; to show why he is inclined to believe that Socrates, in certain respects, was thus and not so, as some have contended, or that he may have done so and not thus at some doubtful point in his career; or to consider the question as to whether or not he was in truth very much the mystic in spite of his clear and uncompromising rationality, as the author contends. This may very well have been true, although it is now commonly assumed to be impossible, since "mysticism" is hardly likely to be respected in an age obsessed with "physical" things, whatever the doubtful term may mean.

What is to be realized by the sympathetic reader of the book is in the nature, not of detailed information, but of an emergent value that is wealth indeed. Those who, hitherto, may have been so familiar with the name of Socrates that they have never thought it necessary to go very far behind the name, might find Prof. Taylor's book a revelation. But it is to be hoped that such may not content themselves with what is only an introduction. They should take the trouble to read Xenophon's *Memorabilia*, together with Plato's *Apology* and *Phaedo*, in order as given. These constitute one of the supreme testaments of the human spirit.

Incidentally, it may be said here, and with a meaning greater than the words may bear, that it is precisely the Socratic spirit that our present world most direfully needs. There come times in history—and we are experiencing one of them—when the complexity of human follies has become so vast that nothing can solve the problem but a simple and direct approach to the root of folly. It is not difficult to know what Socrates would say about our fantastic social predicament, once the facts had been laid before him.

CHEERS FOR HUMANITY

REVIEW OF *THE PLATONIC LEGEND*, BY WARNER FITE (NEW YORK: SCRIBNER'S, 1934)

Nothing seems more sacrosanct than a myth that has been hallowed by centuries of uncritical acceptance, and to attack any hoary misconception or false appraisal is likely to strike many like a sin against the Holy Ghost. Plenty of evil may be justly attributed to the mythopoeic faculty in men; but more good, for without that faculty men could scarcely have achieved humanness, which is a matter, largely, of living by patterns in time that may withstand the assault of the visionless moments.

However faulty a myth may appear under critical scrutiny, the larger truth about it is that it has served somehow as a crystallization of higher aspirations; and, therefore, to disprove the myth is not equivalent to destroying its human value; for, in the final analysis, there is pitifully little that men can really know; and it is the human effect of what they believe they know that matters seriously.

For instance, there are those rationalists who are at pains to deny the historicity of Jesus of Nazareth, some of them seeming not to realize that the invention of the character would in itself remain a tremendous human achievement, and that the conception, even as an invention without historical foundations, would retain its human value.

But, "lest one good custom should corrupt the world," or perhaps, better still, lest we should be smothered in a clutter of old conceits no longer much more than empty forms, there come times when men must question what they have long accepted uncritically.[8] Such times are never the culturally creative ones; they are the times when self-consciousness dominates, that is to say, times of social disintegration. And always the destructive mood must miss the vital point, which is not one of mere fact, but of truth. Analysis inevitably destroys the life, the reality, of that which it dissects.

We are in such a time now, an overwhelmingly self-conscious time, far more critical than creative, given far more to the collecting of fact than to the apprehending of truth. The rage for "debunking" which dominated literature for some years has abated, through boredom, perhaps, if not because practically all the important heroic statues have, presumably, been knocked off their pedestals.

It is in no mere spirit of debunking in the sense of the recent rage that Warner Fite, professor of ethics at Princeton University, has taken the trouble to reconsider the Platonic legend in the volume here noted. Nevertheless, the foregoing remarks about myths in general and the nature of our time do seem to bear vitally, even though obliquely, upon his work.

For some years, it would seem, Prof. Fite has entertained a vague suspicion that the disciples of Plato have read into the writings of their master certain social and ethical conceptions that are not to be found there. As a result of a chance remark regarding Plato's ideal state, "warmly contested" by one of his Platonic colleagues, he decided to look into the matter.

"It occurred to me," he remarks, "that about the point in question I might perhaps be able to judge for myself. And so, having the next day clear, I spent all of it upon the 'Republic.' I found my impression confirmed. But I also found some other impressions confirmed; impressions, namely, of doubt and suspicion with regard to orthodox interpretations. This was then the beginning of what has since been a preoccupation, the outcome of which is the present volume."

The work is not addressed primarily to scholars, but rather "to the intelligent reader who has read some of Plato, or who perhaps knows him only at second hand, and who mainly wonders. . . . Platonic criticism seems to have a curiously Jesuitical effect upon the mind and character, and I wish the interested reader to be in a position to satisfy himself about the justice of the statements that may seem to him strange and doubtful!"

The book is so carefully reasoned, and such is the scope it covers, that its effectiveness can hardly be more than suggested here. But by way of indicating the general trend of the author's contentions, three of his more important points may be cited.

First, he undertakes to show that, far from being the ideal democrat and lover of all humanity, Plato was the perfect pattern of the uncompromising aristocrat. In the *Republic,* he finds that "all the means and opportunities of culture are to be concentrated upon the production of a supremely perfect guardian class," and that Plato's social and political theory, as revealed in that work, is "unique in the history of thought for devotion to the leisure-class ideal." In summing up a devastating chapter on the subject, the author says: "What it all comes to then is that Plato deliberately turned his back upon the civilization of Athens—upon what is still today regarded as the highest point in Greek civilization—and embraced the barbarism of Sparta."

Second, the author arrives, in vital particulars, at a complete reversal of the Socratic legend insofar as it may be based upon Plato. "The Platonic Socrates," we read, "seems to associate exclusively with the rich and well-born," and in the author's final appraisal this Platonic Socrates presents "a perplexing and not quite pleasing figure. The suspicion is suggested that the Socrates of Plato was a flatterer and a snob." It is further contended, after a careful presentation of the data involved, that "if we are to take Plato's picture as a true portrait, it will be absurd to say that Socrates died a martyr to free thought and free speech.

The third point is concerned with the true nature of Platonic love. "To the outsider seeking an acquaintance with Plato," says the author, not without sufficient data to support him, "it is usually, I imagine, a shock to discover that the dialogues of the master—of Plato, the stern moralist, high-minded and austere, preacher of an elevated sanity and wholesomeness, of classical measure and proportion, are full of the eroticism of perversion . . . and he may then find it amusing to note, in retrospect, how much of Platonic literature one may read, i.e., of literature about Plato, without making the discovery."

It's a devastating book, certainly; apparently, a scholarly book and carefully reasoned. It should arouse tremendous tempests in many highly respectable teapots. If, in truth, the castigation of sentimental pigheadedness be involved, there is no good reason why one should not enjoy the perennially needed spectacle.

But our oblique introductory remarks should still hold true. If, in keeping with the poet's dictum that man's reach must exceed his grasp, humanity since Plato has recreated him in the image of the highest it could dream, then may we not give three rousing cheers for humanity? And if the Platonic, or the Xenophontic, or any other Socrates was a climber and a snob, and did not, in literal fact, die a martyr to free thought and free speech, the legendary Socrates certainly did. It was men who made the legend; and so, hurrah for men!

As for "Platonic love"—

Now that we have arrived at that, let us talk about the weather.

THREE

Epic Landscape

In some of Neihardt's earliest writing he referred to the American West in epic terms and called for a poet to sing the epic songs of the American people. The first chapter of *The River and I* is entitled "The River of an Unwritten Epic."[9] In one of his earliest reviews for the *New York Times*, Neihardt refers to the opening up of trade on the upper Ohio River country as "the last lap of civilization's age-long westward journey" and wonders "that America has not produced a full-sized National epic."[10] Although he still directs the call to "some unknown poet," by the time he wrote "The Stuff of Our Unwritten Epic," he had already taken up the challenge himself.

Influences on Neihardt's concept of the epic came primarily from two writers. Lucile Aly credits Jane Harrison as the source of his epic theory, particularly a definition of the heroic spirit as "the outcome of a society cut loose from its roots, of a time of migrations."[11] George Woodberry's ideas were also an inspiration, and among the volumes in Neihardt's library were several collections of Woodberry's essays. In them one can see the seeds of Neihardt's view of the stories of America as epic material. Woodberry, too, called for an epic poet to celebrate the story of America's past, for although "Never since the Hellenes first looked on the Mediterranean has there been such a moment of beauty and power in the great human migration," no imagination had yet arrived to recast the story. "The field is open and calls loudly for new champions."[12]

Neihardt's casting of the western landscape in epic terms, celebrating, as it does, the actions of Euro-Americans responsible for the displacement and death of hundreds of thousands of original inhabitants, seems at odds with the eloquent portrayal of Black Elk's vision. Indeed,

there was much about his race that Neihardt deplored: a headlong
rush to embrace technological "progress," a poverty of spirit, and an
individualism that forsakes the good of the group for individual gain.
He recognized that, even at its height, ancient Athens enslaved fellow
humans and that the Indo-Europeans were a predatory people who had
planted the seeds of their own destruction in their machine technology.[13]
He acknowledged the contributions of other cultures, such as the ancient
people of the American Southwest, who left evidence of a wisdom and
richness of spirit that his culture sorely needed. He distinguished,
however, between learning from another culture and claiming it as one's
own. His particular heritage, and the heritage he considered America's,
had its roots in the ancient lands of the Mediterranean.

In addressing what lay ahead for indigenous people, Neihardt began
with the premise that it wasn't possible to return to the past. For him
assimilation was inevitable, assimilation into a culture defined by a male,
western European tradition that could point to the epic as part of its
tradition. In his belief that the good of the group overshadows the good
of the individual, he hoped for a "homogeneous people, cherishing in
common all our great traditions," relying on a Western male tradition
for his definition of "our."[14]

As an inheritor of that tradition, Neihardt celebrated the heroic
spirit of the epic adventurer. While acknowledging human failings, he
chose to focus instead on the noblest attributes of humanity. In looking
at the legendary figures of human history who have gained mythic
proportions, whether Achilles and Arthur from centuries past, or Jed
Smith and Hugh Glass from his own, Neihardt argued that it is the
human spirit that built the myth that matters, and it is that spirit that
is embraced when we celebrate our heroes.

THE STUFF OF OUR UNWRITTEN EPIC

REVIEW OF *ECONOMIC BEGINNINGS OF THE FAR WEST*, BY KATHERINE COMAN
(NEW YORK: MACMILLAN, 1912)

Just now, when new interest is being aroused in the history of the West,
the publication of Katherine Coman's scholarly work is particularly timely.
Being entitled "Economic Beginnings," it is probable that those who have
not already a deep interest in the subject will form a false idea of the nature
of the work. It is far from "dry." The movements traced by the author
are economic in the sense that all great human movements are primarily
economic movements. No more absorbing story could be written than that
which is set forth and suggested in these volumes. If America has a great

unwritten epic, that epic is to be found somewhere in the period of time here treated.

What the Arthurian era was to England, the time of Charlemagne to France, the period of the Vikings to the north, and the Trojan war to Greece, that is the period considered by Katherine Coman to America.

We have often heard it said that America lacks fine old traditions. Nothing could be farther from the truth. We have a cycle of hero stories—no less heroic for being true—that easily equals Malory's *Morte D'Arthur*. Considering merely the fur trade era, we find men that Homer would have turned into demigods. What of old Hugh Glass and John Colter and Rose and Kenneth Mackenzie and Manuel Lisa and Mike Fink and Alexander Harvey and Yellowstone Kelly and Etienne Provost and Henry and Larpenteur, to mention only a few?

Naturally our author treats this particular period only as a proportionate part of the grand movement that began with Coronado; but not one chapter of the work is dull. It is upon such works as this, as well as upon the records left by many of the chief actors in the huge western drama, that our not impossible epic poet may build the work that shall interpret us to future ages.

To a large percentage of our reading population, the word "western" means cowboys and gun-play. But when the cowboy and the six-shooter appeared in the West, the true heroic age—the age with the stuff of epics in it—had already passed away.

In producing these two volumes Katherine Coman has performed a patriotic as well as a scholarly task.

Valuable and Enthralling

REVIEW OF *INDIAN HEROES AND GREAT CHIEFTAINS*, BY CHARLES A. EASTMAN (BOSTON: LITTLE, 1918)

One of the most stirring periods in American history is that in which the Sioux and Cheyenne tribes were making their last stand against the tide of the white man's civilization. Everyone has some more or less vague ideas concerning this genuine epic period, but few indeed are those who have a correct conception of what took place then or of the Indians themselves. Victors write the history that we accept as orthodox; and for this reason it is a safe guess that history, as we learn it, is largely fiction, so far as the interpretation of movements and motives are concerned.

Dr. Charles A. Eastman, author of the valuable and enthralling volume before us, is a Sioux Indian and has had every opportunity to know the heroes of the Sioux and Cheyenne wars as they really were and not as most white men think they were. Through personal acquaintance with many great men of his tribe and through intimate contact with the old Indian veterans, Dr. Eastman has been able to recover the chief incidents in the lives of 15 of the famous men of the Sioux and Cheyenne nations, as follows: Red Cloud, Spotted Tail, Little Crow, Tamahay Gall, Crazy Horse, Sitting Bull, Rain-in-the-Face, Two Strike, American Horse, Dull Knife, Roman Nose, Chief Joseph, Little Wolf, Hole-in-the-Day.

The volume is issued as a juvenile; but it should not be inferred from this fact that Dr. Eastman's appeal is solely to immature minds. His is a capital book for boys and girls from 10 years on to 14 or 18, but it is also a valuable book for any man or woman who might care to know the truth about Indian character and Indian warfare. Many interesting incidents in the old Indian wars of the plains, such as are not to be found in government reports or in books written by white men, are given here.

Dr. Eastman appears to have fallen into two slight errors which ought to be corrected in the next edition of the volume. He states that at the time of Custer's last battle on the bluffs above the Little Big Horn, Reno "was intrenched in a deep gully," where he was able to remain until Terry came up. The present writer is familiar with both Custer's and Reno's battlefields, and can say with certainty that Reno intrenched himself upon a high and ragged hill to the east of the river valley. Again, Dr. Eastman states that Sitting Bull was buried outside the graveyard at Fort Yates, evidently as a mark of disrespect for the great chieftain. The writer of these paragraphs has himself sat in the moonlight upon the grave of Sitting Bull, burning good tobacco to the memory of that great chieftain. The grave was by that time well within the northwestern corner of the burying ground.

But these are trifling matters, while the book itself is admirable in many ways.

WE FORGET THEM

REVIEW OF *JOHN COLTER*, BY STALLO VINTON (NEW YORK: EBERSTADT, 1926)
Israel Putnam rides his horse down a stairway; Paul Revere takes a nice little nocturnal gallop in the vicinity of Boston. Millions of school children know practically all that is to be known about these heroes—which really isn't very much.

Jedediah Smith leads the first body of Americans overland to the Spanish settlements of California in the 20s; is the first white man to cross the desert region between San Francisco and Salt Lake; covers practically the entire country west of the Rockies and between the Columbia and the Colorado, doing this mostly on foot, at a time when that vast triangular wilderness was a white space on the map, save for the tracing of a mythical river; [loses] two bands of men by massacre and is killed on the Cimmarron River when still in his thirties—altogether a marvelous career. Millions of school children do not know his name, though he discovered and explored the great central route from the Missouri to the Pacific—the route over which the westering tides of migration flowed. He was the greatest of our continental explorers after Lewis and Clark, and in certain respects, more important than they. Orthodox historians, writing for the general public or for schools, make little or nothing of him; generally he is ignored. It is the same with most of the great heroes of our West.

This state of affairs is not to be explained by the assumption that orthodox historians of the United States live in or east of Hoboken both geographically and intellectually, though there may be some slight adumbration of truth in the exaggeration. It is due to the fact that the East had time to fix its heroic traditions in its culture—and pass both on to us—before the great world-wave of modern commercialism struck us. That wave reached us just when the western frontier was disappearing. We of the West had not time to become self-conscious, to formulate and enshrine our heroic traditions in story. As a people, we do not even now know what they are. And yet it can be shown that during the nineteenth century there developed in our American West one of the greatest epic periods in the long story of the Aryan peoples.

Specialists in Western history have been doing very remarkable work in their field, and it is to be hoped that some day it will be considered impossible, even by historians living in Hoboken and beyond, to write a history of the United States either for schools or for the general public, that does not give as full and accurate an account of the development of the West as is now given of the East. That time may be far off. It may never come; for we may never become a homogeneous people, cherishing in common all our great traditions. Perhaps our country is too large; perhaps too many unassimilable people have swarmed already upon our shores.

Nevertheless, it is something worth hoping for, and it is in this hope that such contributions as that here listed should be welcomed.

The story of John Colter is one of the most heroic in our annals; and if his exploits had been no more than a revelation of human courage, he would still deserve well of his countrymen in all generations, for is not courage the fundamental virtue after all? But Colter has other claims upon the memory of men, as those who shall read Mr. Vinton's very interesting book on the subject must agree. References to Colter are to be found in many early books of Western travel, beginning with the *Journals* of Lewis and Clark; and ever since Bradbury and Washington Irving told of his thrilling escape from the Blackfeet, that episode has been retold in many versions.[15] It has remained for Mr. Vinton to undertake the first connected account of the man's career as an adventurer and his achievements as an explorer. For the first time an account of the Colter family is given, and there is a good deal of original and revealing comment on Colter's trails. Otherwise, there is naturally not much to tell that is new to students of Western history, for records say little of this remarkable man who, in his own lifetime was scarcely credited and who died into a vague legend 113 years ago last fall. But even close students of Western history will feel that Mr. Vinton's synthesis of hitherto scattered fragments, enriched by some very pertinent comment, constitutes a new and worthy contribution.

It will be remembered that a grave, said by old-timers to be that of John Colter, was scooped up by a steam shovel near Dundee during June of last year. So little did even his home country know of him!

A Magnificent Story

REVIEW OF *THE SANTA FE TRAIL*, BY R. L. DUFFUS (NEW YORK: LONGMAN, 1930)

Heretofore anyone wishing to inform himself upon the history of the Santa Fe Trail, but having neither the inclination nor the opportunity for laborious research, generally found his attention directed to but two volumes—Josiah Gregg's *Commerce of the Prairies* and Col. Henry Inman's *The Old Santa Fe Trail*. The former was written at first hand and published in 1845 by a Santa Fe trader who first traveled the trail in 1831. It still holds a lonely place as the classic in its field, and will continue to do so. Inman's book, first issued in 1897, makes fairly pleasant reading, but it contains curious errors, some of which are so glaring as to be obvious to almost anyone. Inman's book is, deservedly, out of print. Gregg's, reprinted in Thwaite's monumental series of *Early Western Travels,* is pretty much a public library book, not commonly to be seen in private collections. Furthermore, it was impossible for Gregg to view his subject as from a height of time. He could not know toward what truly astonishing consummation the great movement of which he was a part, and a portion of which he described, was tending.

Now that popular interest in Western history is on the increase, a comprehensive and easily readable account of the whole southwestward movement from the beginning was very much needed, and the need has been met in an admirable way by R. L. Duffus in his volume just published.

There is plenty of evidence that Mr. Duffus knows the authentic sources and has striven for accuracy in the marshaling of his facts, so much so that serious errors are out of the question; but more than accuracy is desirable in the presentation of a period so stirring and so important. To be effective for general reading, the assembled data must be fused by the creative imagination into an organic whole, must be transformed into a flowing story, factual in its details, but, what is vastly more vital, with those emergent meanings which constitute the truth about men's doings. Though scientific in the assembling and winnowing of his material, Mr. Duffus has wrought his story in the mood of art and his evident enthusiasm for his subject is contagious. The whole magnificent epos comes alive in his narrative, beginning with the first eastward ventures of the Spaniards of New Mexico in the sixteenth century and ending with the construction of the Atchison, Topeka and Santa Fe Railroad. What lies between is, aside from its value as American history, one of the most compelling tales imaginable. Its hero is no less than a Race, and the action is concerned with the last major phase of a westward migration of peoples that began thousands of years ago beyond the Danube, beyond the Hellespont, and only in a day still remembered by very old men reached the Pacific Ocean and shocked the Orient awake.

A BOOK WITH LIGHT IN IT

REVIEW OF *ANCIENT LIFE IN THE AMERICAN SOUTHWEST*, BY EDGAR L. HEWETT (INDIANAPOLIS: BOBBS, 1930)

Edgar L. Hewett is one of the foremost archeologists and anthropologists in the world. Although he has done important work in the deserts of Western Asia and Northern Africa, it is for his explorations and discoveries in the American Southwest, Mexico, Guatemala, and Yucatan that the world is most indebted to him. The present interest in Mayan civilization is due largely to his excavations in the ancient city of Quirigua, Guatemala. It was as a result of his reports that the Mesa Verde National Park was established, and it was he who prepared the existing laws for the preservation of American antiquities. His explorations among the ancient cliff dwellings and pueblos of Colorado, Utah, New Mexico and Arizona during the past 20 years or more have resulted in many important discoveries. He is head of the Department of Anthropology at the University of New Mexico and Director of the School of American Research and of the Museum at Santa Fe.

It may safely be taken for granted by any reader approaching the work here noted that what its author does not know about ancient human society in our Southwest is not yet known by anyone; and, what is better still, very early in the book it will become apparent that only what is definitely known will be presented as fact.

So much and no more about the author and his book might give the impression that what we have here is a "dry" scientific treatise calculated to interest specialists only; but if a more intensely human book has appeared this season, or one in which a more profound romantic appeal is potential, this writer has not seen it. It's the "just-one-more-chapter" sort of book that carries you on into the still hours when you know you ought to be in bed.

The reason for this is that Dr. Hewett is quite as much the seer as the scientist. To him, archeology is not an end, but merely a means of extending our understanding of human beings on this planet. In his pages an essentially great people comes to life out of the desert ruins of the Southwest, and far more than mere curiosity is aroused by the revelation. It is natural for us to assume that our own way of regarding life and the characteristic aims that we pursue with so much energy are somehow inherent in the abiding scheme of things. But here we are afforded the opportunity to realize—many of us for the first time, no doubt—that life has been differently and admirably lived by great numbers of men and women who preceded us on this continent, and that, in some very important respects, their lives may have been saner, happier, nearer to the great realities than ours can be in the complex world that we have created with, perhaps, somewhat more ingenuity than wisdom.

If only the first three chapters of this volume had been published it would have been in its many implications a remarkable contribution to social philosophy that is still obviously in its infancy. It is not that anyone would contend for the adoption by our world of a way of life successfully developed by an ancient people alien in spirit to us; it is that we sorely need a vantage point, outside our familiar and sadly erring world, from which to consider the ultimate human significance of our characteristic aims and activities and the very foundations of our society that we take blandly for granted.

No reader who is eager for more light upon the questions that vex our world should miss this book. But so little obtrusive is the social vision involved that those who may wish to read only for the romantic satisfaction of curiosity will be amply repaid for their effort.

REVIEW OF *THE PONY EXPRESS GOES THROUGH*, BY HOWARD R. DRIGGS
(NEW YORK: STOKES, 1935)

One of the greatest stories in history is that of the conquest and settlement of the American West. So astonishing is it in many particulars that at moments it seems almost as though some Gargantuan raconteur, full of meat and exuberant imagination, had made it up in his most expansive and irresponsible vein.

Consider, for instance, such matters as the all-but-incredible Mormon adventure, the bison herd men traveled through for days, the years when all summer long the westward-flowing stream of emigrant wagons smoked along the Platte, the quite preposterous verities of the gold rush days. So much of it was the sort of thing that couldn't be and was—all of it conceived in keeping with the sublimely extravagant spirit of vast, empty distances and wearily creeping time and unconquerable hope and the accumulated racial courage of 10,000 heroic years. Much of it makes one proud to be a man.

In this magnificent story, not the least striking episode is that of the Pony Express. It has often been told, and so far as historical fact is concerned, there is nothing new of importance to tell. All those who are acquainted with the history of the West are aware that in April, 1860, the firm of Russell, Majors & Waddell inaugurated a fast mail service by relay riders between St. Joseph, Mo., and California, covering in 10 days the distance that had formerly required months.

Howard R. Driggs here tells the familiar tale again, but happily he has something vital to add. He has long been interested in the subject, and years ago he began hunting up the old-timers who, as boys, had helped to carry the mail for the Pony Express. Each of these recalled his adventures for Dr. Driggs, and they are all to be found in the volume listed above.

If little or nothing of great factual importance is added to the story, these recorded memories of those old boys, all of whom have now crossed the divide for good, certainly do serve to vitalize the well-known facts; and students of Western history, as well as youngsters who care only for good stories, will be grateful to Dr. Driggs for what he has done.

2
TROUBLED PLANET

FOUR

Tremendous Mood of War

Neihardt was particularly interested in books that examined the world political situation. However, he saw most explanations of the world's woes as simplistic and self-serving. The underlying cause of war is economic, he argued, and even before the "war to end all wars" was over, he anticipated another to follow it. In 1935 he wrote that it is obvious that there is "more tremendous reason for war now than ever before in the record of mankind; it is the reason for the last one and for the one that is brewing." The reason? The fact that the very makeup of the world's societies is based "upon the idea that the many things men need and desire are produced not primarily for use, but in order that a relatively small owning minority may grow richer and richer."[1]

Even those leaders who had the best interests of the citizenry at heart (and they were few, as far as Neihardt was concerned), engaged for the most part in naïve and fuzzy thinking, mistaking the symptoms for the disease and fine feelings and good intentions for clear thinking. Neihardt showed particular impatience with sentimental hand-wringing that served merely to absolve the sentimentalist of responsibility. Neihardt gave particular prominence in his column to those books that he thought offered "luminous sanity" to the discussion of complex social problems.

WAR AND SOCIETY
REVIEW OF *SOCIAL PROGRESS AND THE DARWINIAN THEORY*, BY
GEORGE NASMYTH (NEW YORK: PUTNAM'S, 1916)

It is the contention of Dr. Nasmyth that the philosophy of force is the real cause of "the breakdown of civilization" in Europe; and his purpose is to show from whence sprang this philosophy and how it came to dominate the modern world, as it undoubtedly does.

What is the philosophy of force? It is, Dr. Nasmyth tells us, the belief that human progress is the result of natural selection operating in the social realm through the agency of war. The theory has been eloquently expounded, not only by such men as Nietzsche, Von Moltke, Bernhardi and Theodore Roosevelt, but also by such men as Herbert Spencer, Ernest Renan and Ruskin. The source of the theory, we are told, is to be in the misconception of the Darwinian theory of evolution, due to an illogical application of definite biological analogies to human society. It is Dr. Nasmyth's chief purpose to show that Darwin himself did not push his theory so far, and that the struggle by which mankind has advanced was the struggle of man against the external universe, and not of man with man and social group with social group. Without a doubt, this point is well sustained by the author, and for that reason alone, if for no other, the volume should have the careful attention of thinkers.

It would seem, however, that Dr. Nasmyth, after successfully confounding those who defend the philosophy of force on the grounds of biological evolution, proceeds to push his own contention too far. No one can doubt that modern militarism, reaching its maximum development in imperial Germany, is truly the result of a misapprehension of the Darwinian theory. Nor can one doubt, as Dr. Nasmyth states, that the geographical position of Germany and the Franco Prussian war were largely responsible for the practical application of the theory by the German empire. This much seems clear. But we begin to question Dr. Nasmyth's argument when he makes this philosophy of force the cause of all modern social ills.

The present war is not, as is generally supposed, of dynastic, but of commercial origin; and it is to the same source that the ills of society must be traced, and to nothing else. The philosophy of force, far from being the cause of modern social ills, is, in fact, merely the technic of world competition for markets, and quite properly so; for competition, however veiled by custom, is a form of violence.

Dr. Nasmyth himself seems to suspect something of the kind in his later chapters, although he still maintains that the philosophy of force is a cause, and not, as it seems to us, a logical result of the social disease. He makes a strong and, at times, convincing plea for the establishment of a world federation in the interest of universal peace; and since it is undeniable that society tends more and more toward the larger unit, his argument is of great significance. But he does not seem to grasp the fact that only by destroying our present competitive system of economics and instituting universal co-operation could his dream become a reality.

EXCELLENT INTENTIONS
REVIEW OF *THE FIGHT FOR PEACE*, BY DEVERE ALLEN (NEW YORK:
MACMILLAN, 1930)

The world peace movement, according to Devere Allen, editor of *The World Tomorrow,* is now 115 years old.[2] During that time hostilities have not ceased upon this planet, there having been nine wars of great magnitude, 49 large-scale conflicts and 194 minor conflicts. Also, wars have grown steadily more terrible, and it is rumored by the experts that the next one will make old-fashioned hell look like a jolly family reunion down on the old home farm.

While granting, as he must, that there is far more social dynamite lying scattered everywhere about the world just now than ever before in history, Mr. Devere Allen is somewhat hopeful in view of the fact that the peace movement is growing, and while he is no sunny optimist, he is sufficiently impressed by the possibilities of that movement to write an exhaustive history of it, beginning in 1815 and ending with last year. In addition to the history of the movement, he discusses the various agencies now working for peace, their accomplishments, and the various gloomy, as well as hopeful, aspects of the peace question.

If the reader is able to regard modern war as the world-disease itself and not as an acute symptom thereof, this will seem a masterful book. It is evidently based upon wide and careful research and the material is ably presented. But after all the earnest discussion, that in every particular does the author great credit as a humanitarian and often even as a realistic thinker in the minor mechanics of the problem, we seem to arrive at nothing more useful to us in our tragic predicament than is to be found in the following quotations:

War abolition can never be accomplished until the minds of people by millions all over the world have made the transition from a refusal to sanction war in general to oppose all wars concretely, in particular. That opposition will have to be like granite. At every point where the appeal of war is plausible, where the war method wears away resistance, we must erect Gibraltars of conviction.

The corner stone of these foundations is love. Let those scorn who will, or cry out 'sentimentalism,' love is an art, which can create its artists out of those who try to practice it, however humbly and inadequately. A fine, transcendent cause must always be its own supreme reward to those who labor for it; there is no worthier, higher cause than pacifism.

Certainly no one should question the good intentions and fine feeling of the genuine pacifist; but are good intentions and fine feeling necessarily enough? Might not understanding be a bit useful even to the best intentions? And is it not a fact—pathetic or amusing, according to one's temperamental bias—that many an ardent and distinguished pacifist, who no doubt sincerely wishes to abolish war, is nevertheless uncompromisingly loyal to the economic scheme out of which the last war grew inevitably as will the next one? And is there not something childish about the very common assumption that war is more to be deplored than is a peace of exploitation in which millions upon millions suffer want because too much of everything has been produced by them?

Hitler's Book

REVIEW OF *MY BATTLE*, BY ADOLF HITLER BOSTON: HOUGHTON, 1933)
Whatever else may be said of it, this is a book of very great importance; and those who wish to know what kind of world they are living in just now cannot afford to ignore it. *My Battle* is described as autobiography, but it is scarcely that, in the strict sense of the term. Rather, it is the passionate statement of a world view, of a social and political creed with which the man is obsessed; and the story he tells is that of the development of the creed, the growth of the obsession.

The first half of the book was written and published in 1924, while Hitler was in prison after the failure of the Munich "putsch" during November of the previous year. The last half of the work appeared in 1927. In the spring of the present year, shortly after the author was appointed Chancellor, the whole work was published in Germany.

What we have here is an abridgment; but we are assured that only matter not of general interest has been omitted, and that all the author's "sentiments and ideals of government" are fully expressed in this English version. Whether this assurance is true or not, surely few leaders of nations have ever spoken to the world in so direct and unmistakable a manner.

Accustomed as we are to the fogs of false idealism and the foxy utterances of statesmen, the brutal directness and utter simplicity of this man's message to the German people, and now to the world, cannot but have a rather terrifying effect. For what we have here is something more than the utterance of a fanatical individual who has managed somehow to gain control of a desperate and powerful people. There are reasons for believing that a major world trend here finds extreme expression. It is the trend against all that liberalism meant to us in the heyday of a regime that is dying.

Although the original work contained 800 pages, here abridged to 300, Hitler's world view and political and social creed, as set forth here in unequivocal language, can be stated in relatively few words.

He frankly views world affairs as a great dog-fight; and in the short-sighted view, which is the most persuasive to the masses, who will contend that he is not realistic? He regards democracy and parliamentary government with contempt.

"Do we believe," he asks, "that progress comes in this world from the combined intelligence of the majority and not from the brain of an individual? . . . One thing we must and may never forget; a majority can never be a substitute for the Man." The world is left in no doubt as to the identity of the Man he has in mind.

His movement "is in its essence and organization anti-parliamentarian, i.e., it rejects in principle any theory of the majority vote, implying that the leader is degraded to being merely to carry out the orders and opinions of others." The purpose of the movement is "to create a German state" more powerful than all others. The strength of his movement lies "in the spirit of religious fanaticism and intolerance in which it attacks all others, being fanatically convinced that it alone is right."

There must be no compromise, no alliance with any group differing in outlook ever so slightly. Deadly hate for the enemy is a prime essential, and the hating must begin with the Jews, from whom, in the last analysis, according to Hitler's conviction, flow all political and social evils.

Germany must have more territory on the continent, and "when we think of new lands in Europe, we are bound to think first of Russia and her border states. . . . The immense empire is ripe for collapse; and the end of the Jewish domination will mean the end of Russia as a state." In other words, Germany must spread over European Russia. But first, the ancient strife with France must be ended forever. France must be "isolated" diplomatically, so that when "the Day" shall come again, she will have to fight alone, and with a very different result from that of the last encounter.

To those who still put their faith in the old liberalism, failing to realize what has happened and is happening in the world, such boldly mouthed doctrine may sound like a madman's raving. But we shall probably not get far in understanding the phenomenon that is Hitlerism if we consider it in terms of the individual called Hitler. Hitlerism is a social phenomenon, a locally intensified symptom of a stage of the social breakdown throughout the world; and, conceivably, we may live to experience it in some form euphoniously named and far less frankly stated.

We liberals of a less troubled day placed our faith in political democracy, failing to realize that we had entered upon an age when, in order to have reality, the democratic concept would have to be extended into the economic realm. There is now a strong and growing urge in that direction all over the world, and Hitlerism is a locally modified and peculiarly rabid form of Fascism, which is the last defense of a dying regime against the growing forces of the future.

There is nothing in this book of Hitler's to indicate that he understands the underlying causes of the present tragic world muddle. For the moment, he is undoubtedly a more effective leader because of his very lack of understanding. His naively simple doctrine, engined with hate and intolerance, is of a sort readily communicable to masses, and especially to the desperate masses of Germany.

BURNING CONVICTION

REVIEW OF *"HALT!" CRY THE DEAD*, EDITED BY FREDERICK A. BARBER
(NEW YORK: ASSOCIATION PRESS, 1935)

During the late sixteenth century there sprang up in various parts of Europe flourishing crops of tales about communities of men who did everything backwards, serenely unaware that effects may have definite causes, and always concocting fantastically ingenious answers to the wrong questions. In Germany, such tales concerned the "Schildburgers"; in Holland, "the people of Kampen"; in England, "the wise men of Gotham," "the gewks of Gordon," etc.

There is the tale of the Schildburgers, who built a community house without windows. Finding themselves in darkness, they removed the roof, and lo! there was light. There is the tale of the burning down of all the people's houses by way of killing an elusive cat, which got away, after all, in the universal excitement. There is the tale of the villagers who stood with joined hands about the thorn bush that a cuckoo therein might not escape, but abide there singing all the year.

Then there was, or should have been, let us say, the tale about the time when millions of the Schildburgers, having raised too much to eat and made too many shoes and clothes, found themselves barefooted, in rags and starving. And so they said: "Clearly our grievous lack grows out of our super-abundance." And thereupon they fell to destroying their food that they might be fed, their clothing that they might be clothed, their shoes that they might be shod. Nor did they lack excellent reasons for their acts, being Schildburgers.

Likewise, there was, or should have been, the story of how the Schildburgers were in the habit of periodically murdering their neighbors in a big way and being murdered by them in a way equally big; and since it was clearly the weapons with which the murdering was done, they very sensibly proposed to their neighbors that the quantity and sharpness of the weapons on both sides be limited by a gentlemen's agreement. This proved how humane they were, as well as how masterly in the doctoring of symptoms.

And while making weapons of an excessive sharpness faster than ever, they further proposed to their neighbors that all murdering be ended forever by decree. But not one word did the Schildburgers have to say about the underlying cause of their desire to commit wholesale murder in the first place; for the cause was a holy thing and therefore not to be questioned.

In consideration of precisely what, then, may these oblique remarks be apropos? Precisely nothing, if the blind so wish it!

Well, here is a book about the cost of war and its horrors—an intensely humane book, full of pity for suffering humanity; a book produced with an indubitably noble purpose. More than a dozen lovers of humanity, men and women of the finest character, of very exceptional intelligence in most matters, beyond a doubt, here hold forth with burning conviction to the effect that war is to be regarded as criminal insanity on a tremendous scale. They are right; they are so obviously right that an occasional individual in the audience might well wonder why they pitch their voices so high. They prove with figures that the cost of war is almost, or quite, unthinkable—cost in both money and suffering.

So they want to end war; and certainly the burning desire to do so does them great credit. Their hearts are as right as rain.

But as one reads on, it becomes distressingly clear that some indispensable Hamlet is being left out of this drama of thoroughly righteous emotion. They all want to stop war by amicable agreement, while ignoring the vital core of the matter—the deep determining cause of the last war and of the next one.

In the matter of causation, we arrive at nothing better than the following, quoted from the book: "The hold of war on men's minds, which is the hold of tradition and ignorance, must be broken. There is today no reason for war (!!); there is only the habit of war which the world has so far not overcome."

So it was only the ancient habit of war that flung our millions into Europe! "There is today no reason for war"! A happening so tremendous without a reason! Could a Schildburger do better?

As a matter of obvious fact, there is a more tremendous reason for war now than ever before in the records of mankind; it is the reason for the last one and for the one that is brewing. The reason should be looked for in the very constitution of our acquisitive, and therefore necessarily predatory, societies, based as they are, in true Schildburger fashion, upon the idea that the many things men need and desire are produced not primarily for use, but in order that a relatively small owning minority may grow richer and richer.

In this whole passionately written book of estimable intentions, not once is there any intimation of a vital relationship between the bloodless, unspectacular atrocities of the "depression" and the bloody, spectacular atrocities of war.

Yet the deep-seated cause is the same in each case. The raising of high tariff walls is only modern war without the marching and the guns and the gas, and the results of the bloodless social situation involved are as terrible as war for the dumb, suffering millions in the countries that raise the walls. If casual readers or the good people who contributed to this book are puzzled by these remarks, they could do worse than study *The Open Door at Home*, by Charles A. Beard.[3]

There are many pathetic passages in this book. The following, by a very eminent divine, is an illustration: "If I blame anybody about this matter (the last war) it is men like myself. We went out to the army and explained to those valiant men what a resplendent future they were preparing for their children by their heroic sacrifice. O Unknown Soldier, however can I make that right with you?"

He can't make it right by sentimentalizing about it and passionately "renouncing war," as he does. He shall have to do a bit of clearer thinking about the cause of that which he renounces. It was not his heart that was wrong before; it was his head. And there's nothing in his "ringing" renunciation of war to indicate that the head is working any better now than formerly.

FIVE

Breadlines and Bursting Granaries

Neihardt insisted that a political and economic system able to provide for the basic needs of all human beings is possible. Once these basic needs have been met, then people can "cultivate values beyond materialistic goals and acquisitive instincts; trust the poetic impulse that enables people to understand each other and become better through respecting in themselves the urge to compassion, to magnanimity, to love."[4]

Humanity's needs were still unmet, however, and Neihardt wrote against an "economic system that is not self-sustaining [and] is kept going by enormous debt (steadily increasing), subsidies, waste."[5] Encompassing the 1930s, Neihardt's writing for the *Post-Dispatch*, not surprisingly, dealt with one of the most devastating of economic calamities, the Great Depression.

Once again, Neihardt had sharp words for complacent writers who trivialized the suffering of their fellow citizens by offering patronizing platitudes instead of genuine solutions. In reviewing a book by H. M. Reymond promising to permanently cure economic depressions, Neihardt challenged the author's claim, and suggested that the twelve million men Reymond dismisses and their sixteen million ill-fed or starving children might challenge his assertions as well. Neihardt likened the schemes of the champions of the dying order to something out of Alice's Wonderland, was harshly critical of an economic system built on the creation of artificial demands for more and more goods, and scorned the Hoover administration's "ruling class mentality" that blamed the problem of the ill-nourished child on "ill-instructed children and ignorant parents."[6]

Neihardt insisted that an attack on the problem must begin with clear-headedness, and he worked to bring clarity to the issues. He featured books that dismantled prevailing myths, scrutinized "official" reports, and reexamined the measures used to justify current policies, weaving into the discussion his own layer of interpretation and insight.

DISSERTATION ON FEAR
REVIEW OF *CASTING OUT FEAR*, BY FLORA BIGELOW GUEST
(NEW YORK: LANE, 1918)

Ladies and Gentlemen—Allow us to present the Honorable Mrs. Lionel Guest. (Cheers from the Snob's Gallery.) The Lady has an important message to deliver. It is all about Fear. She has made the discovery that nothing whatever is wrong with this world but Fear! You can all be just what you want to be, do exactly what you want to do, and become as rich as you wish to be, if you will only cast out Fear. But if you are chuckle headed and persist in entertaining Fear, then it is only reasonable that you should bear the consequences. That, in brief, is the Lady's thesis.

She is a great believer in the power of Love, and gives us a beautiful and touching illustration. Once, she tells us, she saw a dear little mamma birdie striving to protect her darling little ones during a terrific rainstorm. The Hon. Mrs. Lionel Guest sat at a window and watched the whole beautiful demonstration of Love. The mamma birdie sat there within a few feet of the Hon. Mrs. Guest and drowned. Mrs. Guest saw it all taking place—but kept to cover. This was doubtless a fine display on the part of the dear little mamma birdie, but how about the Hon. Mrs. Guest? Can it be that she was withheld from demonstrating her own exceeding Love through Fear of getting wet? Banish the thought!

A short while ago we were reading in the papers about children dying in the slums of New York for want of milk. Now comes the Hon. Mrs. Lionel Guest with the assurance that "the pinched bodies and souls of millions of children in the world today are the result of education in Fear, which can only be counteracted by the positive education of love and understanding." You see, the babies didn't really need milk; they simply needed love and understanding, which, we infer, is very fattening. It is all delightfully simple, when explained.

The Hon. Mrs. Lionel Guest is ingenious and illustrates her thesis in many ways. There's swimming. Why, she asks us, can the horse and the cow and the dog swim right off without being taught, and why can't men do the same? The answer is simple, for Mrs. Guest is an exceedingly simple lady. Cows and horses and dogs don't fear water! Men do! There you are! We wouldn't for the world contradict a lady, but somehow we seem to remember something about specific gravity. Now, there's something—specific gravity! Has the lady ever looked into the matter?

Among many other things, the lady tells us of the great advantages that accrue to one who lives in an attic—nearness to the beautiful stars and the dear blue sky, and all that sort of thing. The Hon. Mrs. Guest, however, does not live in an attic.

But perhaps the lady's supreme revelation is the following: "Poverty is unintelligent and unnecessary. There is plenty of money in the world, and we share equally the time to earn it." Doubtless now that the secret is out, everybody in the world, except the extremely indolent will become millionaires. At $5 per day, one can easily become a millionaire in 548 years, providing one doesn't spend a cent and is never out of employment, even on Sundays! If one is getting $2.50 per day, and can work every day, living on love, one can easily become a millionaire in a little over a thousand years. So what the Hon. Mrs. Lionel Guest says is very illuminating.

The Hon. Mrs. Guest is a sworn enemy of Fear and can say nothing good of it—which seems a bit uncharitable and also ungrateful. Is she not aware that nothing but Fear is now holding the unreasonable masses in check? Were Fear suddenly to vanish from the world—fear of hunger, of the police, of the army, of death by these agencies—would we not have a state of unthinkable anarchy within 24 hours? Perhaps the Hon. Mrs. Guest has not been reading the papers of late.

PERPETUAL MOTION
REVIEW OF *OUR BIGGEST CUSTOMER*, BY GEORGE HARRISON PHELPS
(NEW YORK: LIVERIGHT, 1929)
Mr. George Harrison Phelps is at great pains to explain in a preface to this new discussion of the labor problem that positively he is not a "red." On the contrary, he assures us he has "a capitalistic distaste for words, as well as figures, that register red."

The statement hardly seems necessary, considering the fact that, from the very beginning, Mr. Phelps divides the human race into two distinct classes—"we" and "the laboring man," "we" quite clearly signifying the industrial masters and their lieutenants. A dairyman could scarcely be more explicit in discussing his herd.

What should be "our" attitude towards labor? How should "we" approach the problem of unemployment? These questions are discussed, not in the interest of the laboring man but from the viewpoint of greater profits for "us," as Mr. Phelps needlessly insists.

Mr. Phelps has hit upon a new but not an original idea, since one Mr. Ford has been expounding it for some time. He has come to realize, with something of the force of an apocalyptic vision, one gathers, that there are a great many more laboring men in this world than other people. In fact, laboring men constitute 86 per cent of the buying public. Now how are "we" going to prosper if we do not sell in ever increasing amounts to these same laboring men? And how can these people buy back in steadily increasing amounts the product of their labor if many of them lack employment and if those who are employed have not money enough to turn the trick? Obviously, it can't be done.

What, then, must be done? Mr. Phelps makes it all clear. Everybody in the laboring class must be employed, and this desirable state of affairs can be realized by decreasing the number of hours of labor per man per year. But merely shortening the work day and instituting the five-day work week will not increase the total purchasing power of the laboring class. Wages must be raised at the same time. Then more and more strenuous publicity of every conceivable sort must be directed at this fellow with his increased pay so that he will spend all of it. Furthermore, every effort must be made to invent more and more things that the laboring man could possibly be induced to buy. The increased leisure will, as Mr. Phelps points out, give the laboring man more time to acquire new desires under the steadily increasing stimulation of publicity schemes. Installment buying must be encouraged as much as possible, so that not only will the laboring class spend all it has as fast as received, but it will constantly be in debt to "us."

Thus, as anyone can see, a sort of economic perpetual motion will be set up, the laborer producing more and more as machines develop, and consuming more and more and more, and producing more and more and more and more, and consuming more and more and more and more—right on into the twentieth century Utopia.

Utopia is right, for with the invention of more and more ingenious labor-saving machines the time is sure to come—isn't it?—when labor will be almost wholly "saved" and the world will be nearly automatic. "We" shall, of course, keep on increasing wages as a means of increasing purchasing power for our increasing industrial output, and so, by and by, the laboring class shall be only a consuming class with nothing to do but to study publicity, acquiring new desires and satisfying them all day long, year in and year out. That will be the life!

It seems that there might be something wrong about all this, but why be a crab?

In the meanwhile, "milk from contented cows" is "our" slogan.

REVIEW OF *CRIMINALS AND POLITICIANS*, BY DENIS LYNCH
(NEW YORK: MACMILLAN, 1932)

During our latest quadrennial sham battle, we heard high praise of our "rugged American individualism" and were importuned to rally in defense of it. Apparently the "forgotten man" was not greatly impressed by the fine mouth-filling phrase. Perhaps he yearned for cheese and crackers with his "beer by Christmas." Possibly the thought of starving, both ruggedly and individually, was too much for him. But had he understood the now obsolete, though still dominant, social principle concealed beneath that phrase, and had he been aware that his choice of answers was being limited automatically to an essential "yes," he might have answered "no"—and started something vital to his interests.

The above oblique remarks may seem quite beside the point in any comment on a serious study of triumphant gangsterism and racketeering in America, such as that here listed; but anyone who may take the trouble to read Mr. Lynch's volume with care should be able to see the connection. For what is gangsterism in America but the logical, extreme result of this very social philosophy of "rugged individualism" that has been praised so highly? A social doctrine, involving a glorification of the predatory and acquisitive instincts in the human animal, leads inevitably to anarchy; and we have arrived.

Those who think complacently about gangsterism as merely a detached phase of crime, to be suppressed somehow, are kidding themselves. This social phenomenon is integral in our existing social structure. Already the annual cost of gangsterism to the American people, according to the official estimate, exceeds the cost of running the Federal Government. A state of open and successful armed rebellion exists in America. Nowhere is anything really done about it, for the very good reason, as Mr. Lynch shows and most people already know, that government, itself, has become pretty much a racket.

Let the hunger marchers—potentially useful citizens, empty in the midst of plenty—throw a few pathetic bricks in Washington if they want to learn just how "rugged" our "individualism" can be! The army attacked the bonus rabble, which had no profits to share with politicians; but the army has not yet been summoned to rub out gangsterism.

FOR THOSE WHO CARE

REVIEW OF *HUMAN ASPECTS OF UNEMPLOYMENT AND RELIEF*, BY JAMES M. WILLIAMS (CHAPEL HILL: UNIVERSITY OF NORTH CAROLINA PRESS, 1933)

In his opening address at the White House conference on child health and protection in November, 1930, President Hoover remarked: "The ill-nourished child is in our country not the product of poverty; it is largely the product of ill-instructed children and ignorant parents." In May of last year, Secretary Wilbur, addressing the National Conference of Social Work, stated that the depression is "not so serious as many suppose," that "civilization is broken out with hives which irritate and bother us."

It is the ruling class mentality that is vocal to these utterances, and anyone who cares to know how much that mentality lacks for competent leadership in the present crisis should read the volume listed here. The book will not be conspicuously displayed on news stands, and even if it were so, those who need most to read it have not the $2.50 that it costs. It can be had at the Public Library, no doubt; and if the general public could know how deeply vital to its interest the subject matter of the work really is, the Public Library would be overwhelmed with requests for the book. But this will not happen for various reasons, all of them pathetic.

All that can be done for this truly precious book is to urge its vital importance upon that minority which, in no spirit of condescension, sincerely cares about all human beings; which keenly desires to know and understand; and which must give us our leaders when the time comes.

Dr. James M. Williams is professor of economics and sociology at Hobart College; but, what is far more important in considering the work here noted, he is a relief worker with wide experience. What is more important still, in the preparation of the present work he has had the assistance of various Federal and state departments, of numerous national and state organizations devoted to social welfare work, and of a large number of individuals engaged in such work. There can be no question that his presentation is authoritative. Furthermore, little or nothing of the polemical spirit has been allowed to creep into the work, which is, by its very nature, and without recourse to commentary, a most terrible indictment of our planless society and its putative leaders.

So long as a work bearing on the social question involves abstract thinking, it is possible for readers to escape the most cogent argument by fleeing into the foggy realm of personal opinion. They just don't agree with the author, and that's all. But here we are confronted with the well-attested brutal fact about the unemployment situation and its ghastly meaning to millions upon millions of men like the luckiest of ourselves, of women like our mothers and wives, of children like our children, kid ourselves as we may.

Case after case, each well attested as representative and not at all exceptional, is set forth by way of forcing into the consciousness of the reader a burning awareness of the fact that millions of potentially useful people are now living in hell by no fault of their own; that no amount of charity can save them, even though charity were adequate for physical needs, since even the poverty-stricken human being is rather more than an empty belly and a coatless back.

If the book were written with less reserve, as it well might have been, considering the outrageous character of the subject matter, its effect would have been less overwhelming. But there is an impressive moderation in the author's manner that gives to his utterance the character of a fateful whisper in a vast silence.

If anyone who reads this book shall feel even briefly, in a flash of understanding, that each of the 16,000,000 children it considers is in very truth his own; if sleep does not come to him so quickly that night; if the meals he eats thereafter and the common decencies of life that he usually accepts without thought seem to leave an unfamiliar lack; then he may know that he is at least beginning to qualify for a fellowship in that minority that one day must rescue us.

Do They Know Enough?

REVIEW OF *FINDING A JOB*, BY ROGER W. BABSON (NEW YORK: REVELL, 1933)

We have with us this evening, as chairmen say by way of presenting the speaker, one who needs no introduction. Roger W. Babson is universally known as a great business wizard, and when he consents to speak on a subject so near to the hearts of multitudes as that which he has chosen— "Finding a Job"—one can almost hear the world-wide rustle of uncounted ears pricked up.

Now, when Mr. Babson began writing this book, so he tells us, his sole purpose was "to help young people to secure a job." Not that he really knew specifically where the jobs were to be found, as the text at long last reveals, but rather in the loftier sense of stimulating, by the administration of appropriate homilies, "those great qualities of initiative, self-control, courage and persistence which are spiritual and which come only through right living, prayerful meditation and service for others."

But, as Mr. Babson proceeded, an illuminating revelation came to him. He noted that "the nation was bulging over with raw materials and manufactured goods of every kind," while millions were in dire need. Being a business wizard, he could see quick as a flash "the great importance attached to distribution." Our distribution system "had entirely broken down"; therefore, the "greatest immediate opportunity open to young people" was not in the field of production, but of distribution.

"The return of good business and employment under our present system," he observes, "is not awaiting a quack cure-all or the adoption of some economic fad, but an increased expenditure on research, salesmanship and advertising, to bring distribution in line with production."

In other words, the millions of young people in need of a job should go into the high-pressure selling game, that the jobless and moneyless millions may be awakened to their long-neglected duty as buyers and consumers. "The nation needs only orders for good," we are assured. "Business is waiting only for more sales," we are told, and, "If the millions of unemployed would start out today to sell the products of factories which are running on part time, prosperity would return tomorrow." That is to say, if the millions of unemployed would only have the push and enterprise to sell each other what they have not the money to buy, soon everybody would have plenty.

It is, one gathers, a matter of very stubborn "sales resistance"; but "certainly," says Mr. Babson, "business is never made better by people loafing. If everyone would be willing to work harder in times of depression, the depression would soon be over." Work harder at what, Mr. Babson? Why—uh—just work harder to find some work to work harder at, and, failing in this, work harder to overcome your own "sales resistance" and that of your equally stubborn and moneyless neighbors. What the nation needs is "more orders for goods"; and if the moneyless millions would only begin to buy with all their might, they would soon have jobs and plenty of money.

Nothing so thoroughly establishes the truth of a matter as statistics, and Mr. Babson is not only a statistician himself, but employs a large staff of statisticians. We may well, then, be impressed when he remarks that "statistics show there are more opportunities for young people today than ever before in the history of our country."

"The number of unemployed," he continues, "is no criterion of the number of opportunities. The number of unemployed is rather a barometer of the character, industry, initiative and courage of the people." Furthermore, "Unemployment—like crime—is due largely to the wrong motives and ambitions which young people get from pernicious movies, irresponsible newspapers and cheap magazines."

Mr. Babson, the economic expert, has no patience with those theorists who see a direct relation between the development of labor-saving machinery and the great economic breakdown, and he has his statistical reasons. "Statistics show that far less automatic machinery is used during periods of unemployment than during periods of employment," and, indeed, quite obviously, they should do so, if they don't.

But, getting right down to brass tacks, Mr. Babson sums the whole matter up in one swift and masterly sentence: "The only solution (of the unemployment problem) is the elimination of unemployment through putting more people to work."

But even if working harder to find some work to work harder at should prove unavailing, "Remember," says Mr. Babson, "that now, while unemployed, you have a great opportunity to build yourself up physically, mentally and spiritually." (With the wife worried sick at home, the rent long over-due and the children hungry!) "Go to a free clinic and get examined. Ask for some advice as to diet." (But where to get the diet, Mr. Babson!) "Spend an hour a day just storing up your physical batteries." (With what, Mr. Babson?) "Breathe deeply, drink much water, chew your food." (What food, Mr. Babson!) "Remember that you have as much time as President Roosevelt or Henry Ford. The difference between you and them is in the way you use this time." (Applesauce, Mr. Babson!)

Having exhausted the subject of the necessity of concentrating on distribution through high-pressure sales methods, production being already overdone, according to the argument, Mr. Babson discovers another vital necessity, as follows: "I am appealing, therefore" (Wherefore, Mr. Babson?) "to parents and young people that they assume the risks of starting new industries—" What! Still more industries with so many shut down or only limping along on part time? This hardly seems in keeping with the voluminously labored thesis of the book!

Can it be that our business wizards and our economic leaders really don't know enough to save us?

BEWARE OF SUBSTITUTES!
REVIEW OF *LET'S GET WHAT WE WANT*, BY WALTER B. PITKIN
(NEW YORK: SIMON, 1935)

Walter B. Pitkin, than whom, as the introducers say, there is certainly none whomer, has been frightfully busy of late telling the world various strange things, all of them intensely interesting if true.

Eight or nine years ago, he wrote a book the purpose of which was to warn the world that it was in very grave danger of having far too many "best minds." He was then deep in the matter of intelligence testing, and if subsequent events have not tended to support his thesis, he did make it clear that a "best mind" was best for the intelligence test, if for nothing else.

Since those days, he has become a veritable book factory, not to say a fount of inspiration. He has told youths how to go at the business of getting jobs, and if they haven't done as he said, how can he be blamed?

He has told everyone how to improve himself without delay. He has given "marching orders" for the "lost generation." He has informed the world that life begins at 40, and for a brief season, goodly crowds of wistful thinkers were surprised and delighted. After that, he assured the poor broken-down world that capitalism is carrying on. Also, he gave us the secret of happiness ($3.50, please, and cheap at the price). There was also a fairly voluminous history of human stupidity (all for five bucks).[7]

And here yet another important secret is divulged! How in the world does one man do it all? It's nothing short of marvelous. "Let's Get What We Want!" this time! All right, let's do! Won't it be fun? And what is it that we want? We don't know, but our mentor does, and he tells us. We want a decent life for everybody. And why haven't we been getting it? Because we don't know what's the matter with the world. And what is the matter?

You'll be surprised! Probably you have supposed that maybe there was something fundamentally wrong with the present economic system—something about the private ownership of the means of production and distribution for profit in an age of machine industrialism. But that is a pitiful error, it seems. The real trouble—the only trouble—is the manufacturing and selling of inferior products by the smaller concerns that "chisel" in on the big and efficient industries!

There is a large class of "American coolies" and criminals who do this. And so we must awaken to the cause of our trouble and demand that these coolie chiselers and sharpers be eliminated. That's the way to save us. There's a bookful of expatiation on the subject, but that's the heart of the secret.

"If this country could be spared the losses incurred through the machinations of the underlings," declares Mr. Pitkin, "all the decent folks could have good homes, the best of food and ideal medical service."

So now we know. (Two dollars, please, and a real bargain; it's a thoroughly modern factory job, quantity production, with hardly any overhead, making the quality and the price possible. Always look for the Pitkin trademark on the package.)

SIX

Social Turmoil

Although Neihardt believed that most of the world's ills could be traced to a common source, he had ample commentary on the manifestations of the disease. The profusion of books chronicling a variety of social problems provided him with plenty of fodder: disregard for law, suspicion of authority, eagerness for more and more exciting pleasures, a tendency to regard luxuries as necessities, a growing distaste for hard work, cynicism, and a sordid materialistic view of life. His opinions were wide-ranging, and he explored such issues as education, feminism, socialism, the criminal justice system, and Prohibition.

Neihardt encouraged his readers to examine these issues critically and to look beneath superficial symptoms to find the root of contemporary problems. He asked them to think independently and to make conscious choices in their lives, reminding them that rarely are complex questions patterned in definite blacks and whites, nor are they answerable with a "yes" or "no," for "the fact remains that the possible good comes mostly in varying shades of gray, while those who insist stubbornly upon white or nothing are likely to get black for their pains."[8] Indiscriminate acceptance of the mob mood won't do, nor will complacent self-assurance that the wonders of "progress" will solve all social ills. Neihardt's fellow Americans had marvelous technological gadgets in their hands, but those gadgets demanded a high level of responsibility, since "Chemistry will slay fathers and husbands and brothers by the million as readily as it will save a baby's life or make the earth more fruitful."[9] The great question of the day, Neihardt believed, did not involve what great invention lay ahead. The vital question was, rather, "How shall we become more human?"

A Plea for Education

REVIEW OF *COLLEGE SONS AND COLLEGE FATHERS*, BY HENRY SEIDEL CANBY
(NEW YORK: HARPER, 1915)

One of the most hopeful signs to be noted amid the present day glorification
of utilitarianism is the increasing number of books that deal with the higher
education as a necessary factor in the building of a genuine civilization.
This growing championship of the humanities is one phase of a strong
reactionary tendency that has been setting in against a blatant democracy
during the past three or four years and which is probably destined to
serve as a necessary check upon social evolution in America, lest that our
highhanded "liberty" arrive at the worst of all tyrannies, that of the little
thinking and highly emotional people.

Professor Canby, of the English department at Yale, here treats of
university education from the three angles of the student, the professor and
the results achieved. His purpose has been to meet the prevalent popular
criticism of universities, to note wherein it is just and to place the blame
where, in his opinion, it properly belongs. He grants that in general our
universities have not been turning out men of real culture; and by culture
he means "no mere affection of knowledge, nor any power of glib speech or
idle command of the fopperies of art and literature, but rather an intelligent
interest in the possibilities of living."

He denies the imputation that the universities are primarily to blame
for this fact, and affirms that the community has merely gotten what it has
demanded. America is obsessed with the idea of the necessity of "getting a
living," which, to the poor man, means a few dollars a week, and, to the rich
man, any amount that can possibly be acquired. In either case the emphasis
is laid almost entirely upon getting the means of life, and little thought is
given to what shall be done with life when one has made it secure. In other
words, we are, as a people, rank materialists. Boys are sent to school, not with
the impression that they are to be developed mentally and spiritually, but
that they may be "efficient" in business when they come out. They therefore
seek the shortcut and scorn those studies that do not seem to promise direct
financial returns. To become educated in the true sense, a man must be
convinced that the end is desirable; and the necessary desire, save in highly
exceptional cases, cannot be generated in a home atmosphere characterized
by indifference to all but material prosperity. "If you wish better education,"
says Professor Canby, "ask for it as strenuously and as intelligently as you
ask for dividends; pay reasonably for it; and you will get it."

In discussing the state of American literature, the author finds the same
source of mediocrity—lack of intelligent popular demand for the best.

At this point one is moved to ask how this dearth of popular intelligence is to be supplied, if not by the schools; for surely if they are not to be the bearers of the torch, we face a great darkness. The populace can not lift itself; the lift must come from above. Then one remembers that this is a country in which popular opinion, however misguided, is king in all final appeals, and that universities cannot exist without financial support. Thereupon the question is resolved into one of the general lack of discipline and disrespect for authority which is undeniably characteristic of this land of the free—free to be ignorant, in this particular instance.

In a nation characterized by a strong centralization of governmental power, universities might possess more authority, and so be more efficient to the end for which they were established. But in America they must indulge in wheedling. And, to be frank, it seems to us that Professor Canby is doing just that in the volume here considered. But even so, the sign is a good one; and we heartily recommend the book to thoughtful people.

CIVILIZATION AND MRS. SHIMMYALL (1926)

A short while ago some attention was given in these columns to Oswald Spengler's great and gloomy book, *The Decline of the West*. Elsewhere on today's page will be found some appreciative remarks on what we have ventured to call one of the funniest books of the year, Ethel Harriman's *Romantic, I Call It!*[10] At first glance, it might seem like drawing a rather long bow even to suggest a possible relation between the two; and yet things that are apparently the most diverse are very often the most intimately related.

The question here involved is one of culture, by which is to be understood a creative preoccupation with the higher human values based upon a profound belief in the reality of those values. A man may be said to be "cultured" in proportion as he has realized creatively, in the development of his own personality, the high moods of understanding that have been achieved cumulatively by the finest spirits of the race. A race that has not achieved a culture in this sense, is a race soon lost in time. A classical example is that of the Carthagenians, whose dominant values were material, that is to say, of the moment and place. Several years ago, Count Korzybski pointed out in his *Manhood of Humanity* that the essential difference between man and brute is the difference between space values, which are material, and time values, which are cultural.[11]

The volume had light enough in it, by implication, to illuminate the world; but light exists for the receiving eye alone. It is no doubt highly significant that the word culture, as ordinarily used, has lost its old rich meaning. One hesitates to use it in most conversations for fear of being regarded as an effeminate poseur. And it must be granted that by far the greatest portion of the really powerful men of our time are engaged primarily in the manipulation of material values. To deplore this fact or to point it out in a spirit of detraction would be foolish and unfair. In general, men do pretty much as they must in keeping with the prevailing direction of the world in their time. The important matter is never to deplore but to understand if possible.

The word culture, in its most common current significance, seems to refer rather to certain superficial matters that were formerly mere by-products of culture in its original meaning. What were formerly only superficial indications of an inward state of development are now pretty generally substituted for that inward state, being put on from the outside like powder and rouge. A lifetime is not too long for the achievement of culture in the fine old sense of enriched personality. To assume the pathetic outward symbol of a non-existent inward grace, is much more expeditious; and "time is money," as we say.

Spengler's Thesis
If there be any suggestion of truth in the foregoing remarks it might seem to be in support of Spengler's theory of cultures and civilizations as set forth in *The Decline of the West*. As will be remembered, it is Spengler's thesis that the culture of the Occident is dead; that our Western society has entered upon the final phase of our Western culture cycle, that of an uncreative, materialistic, cynical civilization to be concentrated in a few huge "autumnal cities." It is not the purpose of this article to defend that extremely depressing theory. It may well prove false, for who can tell what new and powerful currents of social tendency may cut across the stream in which we now seem to be drifting, changing the direction of the world-flow?

It is quite conceivable that our headlong 20th century plunge into materialism may produce results in the economic realm that may start us off in the opposite direction, and with the marvelous system of communication that we have developed, we would move fast and far in any direction we might be forced to take. But if we assume that Spengler is right (and certainly his argument seems well calculated to overwhelm), does not Ethel Harriman's burlesque characterization of Mrs. Shimmyall take on a more facetious significance? May not Mrs. Shimmyall be conceived in the spirit of sublime folly that has made Don Quixote a lord of tears and laughter for more than 300 years?

Culture Left to Women

It is a commonplace that culture, in our time and country, is left largely to the women, and not a little fun has been poked at them for the alleged way they have of "making culture hum." In thousands of little towns all over the country, it is they who keep burning the race-old torch of culture—and very often it is pathetically smoky. Nevertheless, many of them truly believe in the value to mankind of that light of the ages; and not a year passes but that Browning or Shakespeare or Dante or Plato are discovered with an excited cackling in many a small town woman's club. But their menfolk stick strictly to business. They are mildly amused, though they are willing to grant that "culture" is all right for the women.

Can it be that the women are cherishing a thing that is dead, and that their menfolk, who have been caught in the swirl of the living world, instinctively know this?

Don Quixote cherished the dead culture that was chivalry; but Sancho Panza knew better.

According to her light, which was hardly to be called brilliant, Mrs. Shimmyall pursued "the true and the beautiful" while Mr. Shimmyall stuck to his buns.

Is it possible that Ethel Harriman presents a low burlesque version of a new Cervantean comedy?

At first glance, the question may seem scarce reverent toward the ladies; but anyone who shall read into it a spirit of derision has lost his way in the little forest of these words. For what is Don Quixote but a symbol of man's reach and that must always "exceed his grasp"? And surely all the beauty and wonder of our human world are to be sought only upon the Quixote side of Sancho's visionless reality.

How Shall We Be Saved?

REVIEW OF *THE ESCAPE FROM THE PRIMITIVE*, BY HORACE CARNCROSS
(NEW YORK: SCRIBNER'S, 1926), AND *THINKING ABOUT THINKING*,
BY CASSIUS J. KEYSER (NEW YORK: DUTTON, 1926)

Are there any indications that the human race—or, let us say, that portion of it that inhabits the Occident—is beginning to grow up?

To a great many people such a question is likely to seem preposterous, for there is a pleasing assumption abroad to the effect that ours is the only generation that has ever been "modern"; that we have long since grown the full beard of wisdom, and that we are to the people of past ages as men to children. If this be an illusion, as many of our thinkers contend, it may be attributed to the primitive ego's natural over-estimation of its own, to diminishing perspective in time, to the particular standard of values by which we as a mass are persuaded to appraise everything, and to the obviously brilliant triumphs of modern science in conquering our physical environment. We are likely to forget that we of the great multitude have had nothing whatever to do with the winning of scientific victories over certain physical forces that now serve us. Compared with the mass of us, it is mere handful of specially gifted men who have made all the "progress" of that sort.

An essentially inhuman message may be sent by radio. A man may step into a limousine without altering his ethical conceptions, for many are doing so daily. A savage or a child may press an electric button. An airplane does not care who rides it or for what purpose. The scientific marvel of moving pictures may be made a pander to the primitive lusts of men. Chemistry will slay fathers and husbands and brothers by the million as readily as it will save a baby's life or make the earth more fruitful. A mass of people milling about an electric scoreboard—itself the product of rare genius—may give an astonishingly correct representation of a savage tribe on the warpath.

Though no one will question the general proposition that it is better for men to control than to be enslaved by natural forces, it must be remembered that the value of the power to do is conditioned wholly by the purpose of doing and its social result. And we should not forget that for four terrible years, not so long ago, the whole world directed its marvelous powers to distinctly anti-social ends—apparently without learning much, if we may judge by the horse-trading methods that seemed to prevail at Versailles.

Increased Power Not Maturing

So it cannot be solely to the magnification of our power that we can safely look for indications of a generally maturing humanity, if there be such. We must look, rather, to the quality of the habitual mental processes by which our increasing power is directed, not only in the larger relations of society as a whole, but in the private matters of every day.

In his *Kyra Kyralina*, recently published, Panait Istrati remarked, what many before him must have noted and some had said, that the percentage of human beings in the great mass is very much smaller than is commonly supposed.[12] It is a hard saying; nor can any one of us afford to gloat over it in a self-approving mood, since all of us are descended from the same brutal ancestry, and there has scarcely been sufficient time and opportunity as yet to live it down. It may be that the most highly developed among us are human only under favorable circumstances and that the rest of us are so only in spots.

How shall we become more human? is the great inclusive question of our time. It is the one that, more and more, is being substituted by our intellectuals for the dominating question of former times, How shall our souls be saved? Many believe that the two are essentially one, in original intention; but that the older form was based upon a primitive conception of the problem involved; and that a scientific understanding of the problems demands something more dependable than a primitive technique in the solution.

Attack Problem Variously
The problem has been discussed from many angles in recent years, and the number of books bearing more or less directly upon it is rapidly increasing. All the works of the several schools of psychoanalysts have been offered as contributions to a possible solution. The behaviorist attacks the problems from the mechanistic viewpoint, in keeping with the prevailing vogue of materialism. An idealistic philosopher, like Ouspensky, in keeping with an ancient Oriental persuasion, approaches it through the conception of multiple dimensionality and rising levels of consciousness.[13] In his *Manhood of Humanity*—a work glowing with diffused light that stimulates but is difficult to focus—Count Korzybski discusses the question in terms of values that are of time and that are of space, arguing that the former are human, the latter brutal, and that in proportion as time values are made to take precedence over those of space shall our human social problems be solved. Robinson's *The Mind in the Making* and Randall's more recent work, *The Making of the Modern Mind,* attack the question from still other angles; and Browne's *This Believing World* presents in a popular manner certain important material for those for whom independent thought about the problem may be a possibility.[14]

Even Spengler's tremendous devastating work, *The Decline of the West,* is a consideration of the problem with a negative answer, for he says in substance: A race attains its highest human level during the creative period of the culture, which finally crystalizes into the barren, materialistic and cynical civilization of great autumnal cities. In support of his contention that we of the Western world have already passed our cultural prime, he summons a mass of learning and an intellectual power such as have seldom been combined in a single personality.

Gloomier Answers from Europe
Significantly enough, it is from Europe that most of the gloomier answers seem to come; for Europe is old and hard hit by her rude awakening from

impossible dreams; and even philosophers are unable wholly to escape the influence of their social atmosphere.

Our American philosophers seem distinctly more hopeful. Unlike Spengler, who sees in the history of mankind no steady general progression of the human spirit but only a lengthening series of closed cultural cycles, racial genius flowering that it may bear the seed of its doom, it would seem that a majority of our thinkers make much of the great Victorian hope that came into the world with the theory of evolution and the bright promises of modern science. Both books listed above deal in a spirit of scientific hopefulness with the question: What is it to be human, to what extent have we become so, and how shall we achieve more humanity? Though one is by a practicing psychoanalyst and the other by a mathematician, each book admirably supplements the other and the two may well be read together.

Subhuman and Human Thinking

In *Thinking about Thinking,* the general problem of becoming more human is stated and discussed from the viewpoint of an expert logician. The author, Dr. Keyser, considers three modes of thought, their relation to each other and their relative value in the important business of striving to understand ourselves, each other and our environment, to the end that we may live the more happily together on this not unfriendly planet.

The three ways of thinking are termed organic, empirical, and autonomous; and anyone who shall master the distinctions pointed out and strive with some success to apply the understanding thus gained to the consideration of every matter that concerns him, will be in a fair way to become one of the few really civilized people of his neighborhood. Also, he will be lonesome; for not only will he be likely to outrage the well-meaning primitives of his acquaintance; he will also be obliged to cast away many a hallowed prejudice.

Organic thinking, as Dr. Keyser uses the term, signifies an automatic mental reaction to a given stimulus in keeping with the instincts, prejudices, and peculiarities that, taken together, make up the consciousness of the person concerned. By way of illustration, he cites the case of a kitten pursued by a dog and defending herself by what appeared to be a masterpiece of deliberately planned tactics. The action of the kitten, he maintains, was not the result of independent thinking, but merely a mobilization of the kitten's potentialities under the stimulus of fear. The author argues convincingly that by far the greater portion of mental processes in which the vast majority of people indulge never rise beyond the level of such "organic thinking." Present a new idea to most men—one that conflicts with those already accepted—and the immediate reaction is one of violent defense, a hostile and automatic mobilization of the assorted collection of instincts, prejudices, private interests, hatreds, loves and hopes which the individual identifies with himself and by which he has been accustomed to live.

Organic Thinking in Man

The following is given as a readily recognizable example of organic thinking in a man. One who had lived among the Mormons remarked to the author that "these people actually regard themselves as the chosen people of God," whereupon he laughed heartily at a proposition so manifestly absurd to him. "But," remarked the author, "they are not the only people who have so regarded themselves. The Jews, for instance, regarded themselves as the chosen people." Immediately the critic of the Mormons became serious. "Yes," he said, "but they really were!"

Organic thinking, as Dr. Keyser uses the term, is subhuman thinking.

Now if an unfamiliar and apparently revolutionary idea were presented to a Socrates, he would examine it dispassionately, eager to know if it were false or true. Truth to him would not seem a permanent possession to be identified with self and so jealously defended; but rather a thing to be sought without ceasing in a world where it is no advantage to receive the wrong answer to any question. His procedure would be somewhat as follows: "It may be true," he would say; "let us examine it." He would then seek for the assumptions upon which the proposition had been based, and he would insist upon a careful examination of those assumptions. Behind the simplest proposition many assumptions upon which it is based are one being based upon the other in a lengthening chain. And the utmost that Socrates himself could do with the proposition would be to reach this decision. The proposition is true if the assumptions upon which it is based are true. This "if-then" mode of thinking the author terms autonomous; and in proportion as men employ it in the solution of their problems they rise from the brute and achieve humanity. The idea is far more fruitful than appears at first glance. Let the reader test it for himself and learn how much of the world's woe would disappear if it could be universally employed. Empirical thinking is a step in advance of the subhuman variety. It is the extremely useful trial and error method by which science has developed, but it requires the constant critical supervision of the autonomous thought for the detection and examination of assumptions.

Note of Hopefulness

As to the note of hopefulness in his discussion, Dr. Keyser points out what seems to him a definite indication of human progress. Only twenty-two centuries ago, he maintains, there was but one outstanding example of autonomous thinking in the world—Euclid's Elements. Not until the seventeenth century did the second appear in Spinoza's philosophy; and in the eighteenth century a third appeared in Saccheri's non-Euclidian geometry. Thus during the first half-million years of man's existence, not a single great example of autonomous thought was produced. Two thousand years ago there were two. But during "the present generation scientific doctrines of the autonomous type have arisen by the score." This would seem to be a very hopeful sign, and it is undoubtedly true that the increase in such thinking is working a revolution in the beliefs of the masses, for the old faiths can hardly be said to have the power over men that they once had.

But in considering the proposition that mankind is gaining in humanity by virtue of an increase in autonomous thinking, we must employ the "if-then" method, which compels us to examine the underlying assumption. It is assumed as self-evident that reason is the only or the most efficient human means of arriving at the workable "truth." Is this assumption merely the outgrowth of the materialistic persuasion of our time and hemisphere? Oriental thinkers would not accept the assumption. They would doubtless insist that by the methods of reason, however highly developed, we achieve merely an intricate system of illusions. But for that matter, our author himself insists on the fact that not one of the propositions by which we live can be absolutely proven. All rest upon assumptions that are neither capable of proof nor self evident. The most that we can say, he tells us, is that a proposition is true if the underlying assumptions be true.

Spengler's Statement

At this point one remembers Spengler's statement to the effect that our Western thinking now tends more and more to resolve all knowledge "into a vast system of morphological relationships." And the question arises: Can men live creatively without the illusion of at least a few absolute certainties?

Is our present faith in reason only another passing vagary—a fashion that has triumphed for the moment and so seems good to us?

However that may be, autonomous thinking does make for tolerance and a greater kindliness in human relationships. As much can be said of other doctrines in no way based on autonomous thought—those taught by Jesus of Nazareth and Buddha, for instance. There is here no reference to dogmatic forms that have grown out of and away from the original simple teachings.

Escaping from the Brute

Dr. Carncross, a practicing psychoanalyst, discusses the state of the world and its possible betterment from the viewpoint of his own specialty. It may be said that he offers a technique whereby it may be possible for a given individual to achieve the "autonomous thinking" of Dr. Keyser's discussion. The organic thinker is the primitive thinker with no knowledge of the mechanism of his thought. Dr. Carncross analyzes that mechanism, and in doing so throws much light upon individual and social problems. It is his contention that, although the world has come a considerable distance from the savage state, it still has far to go before it can become "even nearly civilized." Individuals make up the world, and the vast majority of individuals are still in the grip of inherited attitudes, fears, prohibitions. Decisions are not reached by independent creative thought, but in keeping with those inherited attitudes, fears, prohibitions, much as Dr. Keyser's kitten "decided" in her affair with the dog. He points out the origin of the various complexes that do so much of our thinking for us and points the way to escape.

Scientific Occidental Conception

It is a matter of curious interest to note, in following Dr. Carncross, how the scientific Occidental conception of the ego, its illusions and the ills that spring therefrom, seem to lead to the same method of escape that was pointed out long ago by unscientific Oriental seers. Escape from the thralldom of the self regarding ego is the purpose of psychoanalysis as it has been the purpose of every great religion. The infantile conception of life is egocentric. Adolescence is the process of losing the ego in larger and larger relations. Health, happiness—salvation, shall we say?—is the result of a merging of the self in the whole vast process of which we are a part, in so far as we can understand it. If this be the meaning of adolescence, our society is certainly far from grown up and Dr. Carncross points many symptoms of a clinging infantilism in our individual and social views and acts.

Is it not possible that all sincere methods of approach to the questions—How shall our souls be saved? How shall we become more human?—lead inevitably to one answer, the apparent difference being merely one of terms? And who knows how many different approaches may be tried in keeping with the changing persuasions of the world before we shall accept as truth the answer to which all methods of inquiry seem to lead?

STRAWS IN THE WIND

REVIEW OF *THIS UGLY CIVILIZATION*, BY RALPH BORSODI (NEW YORK: SIMON,
1929), AND *OUR BUSINESS, CIVILIZATION*, BY JAMES TRUSLOW ADAMS
(NEW YORK: BONI, 1929)

Aside from the rapidity with which one literary fad follows another and the
general wild confusion of values that prevails in literary circles, perhaps the
most important single fact to be noted in recent literature is the increase
each season in the number of unhappy books dealing with the trend of our
industrial civilization. We may laugh them off, if we like, saying something
modishly flippant about this business of "viewing with alarm"; and without
doubt some of them justify a chuckle. Nevertheless, they are, at least, straws
in the world wind, and a surprisingly large percentage of them are certainly
not the product of fools. Neither are the great majority of such books
being written in response to a fashion, as most outlines, biographies and
sex-books obviously are; and this for the very good reason that no crowd-
minded writer could even wish to oppose what is precisely a crowd-minded
affair. Surely no class of contemporary books is being produced by more
cultivated men, and almost always the world-view they defend is a distinctly
humane one, taking into consideration the whole range of human values.
The so-called poets, as a class, are manifestly far below the intellectual and
spiritual level of the majority of such writers.

These books seem to attract a considerable number of readers, and many,
no doubt, for intelligent reasons; but, considering the temper of the time,
it is probable that they are read more often by sensation-hunters who live in
the moment and whose slogan is, "I should worry." Nor can such books be
expected to have anymore effect upon the world-trend than the pointing
straw can have upon the gale.

To the writers of such books and to those in all civilized nations who hold
the same view, the situation must seem somewhat as follows: A boat-load of
people is drifting smoothly and with steadily increasing speed down a great
stream. All but one or two are loudly congratulating themselves, each other
and the universe in general upon the amazing progress that is being made
and the marvelous smoothness of the ride. Here and there in the boat one
who has looked behind and ahead and knows of other boat rides in other
times strives to get a word in edgewise. "Can't you see," he says, "that our
speed and the smoothness thereof are the speed and smoothness of a terrific
current that is approaching a cataract?" A few lean to listen and some of
these are made thoughtful by what they hear, while some only haw-haw
and resume their shouting. But most hear not at all.

And maybe it is better so, for talking in a drifting boat can hardly stop the river. And then, who knows what unforeseen cross-current may send the craft ashore? Or, better still, what deep, smooth rapids may break the sharp descent and lead to lakelike calms no man can see?

Though the two books here listed deal with the same theme—the standardization and dehumanization of society as the result of our industrial madness—they are written from different points of view. James Truslow Adams' approach is that of the humanistic scholar and educator, while Borsodi writes as one with business experience, as an economist and a statistician. That they reach the same general conclusions should be considered, at least, as curious; and it would be well for those who are interested to read both books—*Our Business, Civilization* first, since it serves admirably to present the general background for Mr. Borsodi's more direct, because more personal and factual, discussion.

Happily, neither writer betrays any Messianic notions, and neither assumes that the drift can be checked save by catastrophe or by economic forces that may be latent in the drift; and this fact alone should win the respect of intelligent readers. Nevertheless, Mr. Borsodi has some constructive suggestions to make—not to society as a whole, but only to the occasional individual who may have both the desire and the ability to escape the mad economic whirl of our time. What most distinguishes his discussion from others is his insistence upon the necessity of making a distinction between domestic and factory machines. Unlike many, he does not deplore "the machine age"; he glories in it. It is the factory system and its tendency to make men merely "herd-minded" manufacturing and consuming mechanisms that he deplores while pointing out how individuals here and there may escape by the aid of domestic machinery. "The right kind of machinery," he says, "must be used to free men from the tyranny of the wrong kind of machinery." This portion of his argument seems to be based upon his own experience, and he urges others to undertake the "adventure for freemen," the nature of which is indicated by his closing paragraph. "I, at least, can say to the factory: 'Get thee hence. I want not thy riches because I need them not. A comfortable home in which to labor and to play, with trees and grass and flowers and skies and stars; a small garden; a few fruit trees; some fowls, a cow, some bees; and three big dogs to keep the salesmen out—and I at least have time for love, for children and for the work I like to do. More the world can give to no man, and more no man can give to the world.'"

REVIEW OF *MASSACRE*, BY ROBERT GESSNER (N.P., 1931)

When Robert Gessner first began visiting Indian reservations several years ago, he tells us, it was with the intention of studying Amerind folklore; but very soon he came to realize that something of rather greater human importance than interesting legends very much needed telling—the tragic story of the modern Indian suffering at the hands of his conquerors. Accordingly he gave up the folklore idea and devoted all his time to a survey of the conditions existing now on various reservations. In *Massacre* he sets forth the results of his inquiry. It is substantially an old story for those who have ever been well acquainted with reservation life—a story of the white man's chronic addiction to lying and shenanigan.

Helen Hunt Jackson's "century of dishonor" has become a century and a half now, and in 50 more years it will be two centuries of the same, if civilization should continue to develop along racketeering lines.[15]

It might be that Mr. Gessner is guilty of an occasional overemphasis in matters of detail, and perhaps at times he over-writes; but the irreducible minimum of truth in his book is sufficient to overwhelm any humane reader.

There is perhaps a touch of the naïve in Mr. Gessner's evident belief that if only the truth is told something is likely to be done about it. But a social organization that starves millions of its own in the midst of plenty, is hardly likely to be greatly moved by the suffering of an "inferior" people with no appreciable political power.

A short while ago one of our most pious and highly respected political philosophers informed the world substantially that what we chiefly need is reform inside of us. Could he, perhaps, instruct not only the starving whites, but the robbed and starving Indians as to how internal reform might be pushed to such an extent as to result in filling the inner man with something more nutritive than a hot-air merchant has to sell?

MEREJKOWSKI'S THESIS

REVIEW OF *THE SECRET OF THE WEST*, BY DMITRI MEREJKOWSKI (NEW YORK: BREWER, 1931)

During October an American firm will publish a book entitled *The Secret of the West* by Dimitri Merejkowski, the Russian philosopher and novelist, author of the magnificent trilogy, *Christ and Antichrist,* and justly described as "one of the great compendious intelligences of our time." The work is said to be "staggering in its scope, its learning and its implications"—a statement that might be ignored as the babble of another blurbster were one wholly unacquainted with the quality of Merejkowski's mind.

The thesis of *The Secret of the West* is one that has become familiar of late years and is stated as follows: "He feels that all our efforts towards peace, all our business of 'stabilization' has been building on sand. The only changes which have been wrought in the western world have been external, material ones; the spirit remains the same, and we are drifting inevitably to a cataclysm which will mean nothing short of the destruction of the present world, our civilization, and indeed mankind."

We need not trouble ourselves about the total destruction of mankind. That is obviously another curious notion originating in the self-regarding urban consciousness. Outside the densely populated urban areas, that have become as social cancers in our time, there are vast stretches or sparsely peopled country that the lethal gases of the Christian powers cannot cover; and even the disease germs, that many believe will be employed as killing agencies when again the various nations shall set out "to save the world" for some exceedingly lofty and appallingly hypocritical sentiment—even the germs will perish of weariness and disgust in those vast spaces.

Whatever culminating fury the Age of the Great Folly may be preparing for itself, one need not lie awake of nights worrying about the survival of the human race and its authentic culture. Rather, if we are foolish enough to lie awake at all cogitating on racial destiny and long time, might not the least hopeful aspect of our folly in the short view be the most hopeful in the long view? For does it not begin to appear that we are desperately in need of a fresh start?

It is not the prognostication of universal social catastrophe that should make one eager to read Merejkowski's forthcoming book, *The Secret of the West*. The vital center of his thesis, obviously, is in this statement: "The only changes which have been wrought in the western world have been external, material ones; THE SPIRIT REMAINS THE SAME." The importance of the meaning of this statement in any sincere effort to make human society fit for human beings cannot be exaggerated. Such is the character of our blindness that we seek causes in objective phenomena that are only results. Accordingly we are always fussing around in a misguided effort to cure our illness by doctoring the symptoms, whereas the disease is seated in the spiritual attitudes and beliefs that are generally accepted as pragmatic truths.

Recently, as a result of four weeks spent with the old men of the Oglala Sioux, this writer was able to feel with extraordinary intensity the profound and perhaps fatal truth about our civilization in its dominant aspects. During that time he was able to lose himself in the consciousness of those essentially primitive men, and it so happened that the whole mood of the experience was determined by one of them in whom the highest spiritual conceptions of his race have flowered in beauty and wisdom.[16]

The empty country and the social vacuum made it an easy matter to forget the flood of vicious and silly books that constitute so great a portion of contemporary literature, which is nothing if not an expression of the dominant contemporary consciousness. Actually, the too familiar twentieth century world passed away like a dream, to be remembered only at intervals when one was forced to buy something from a store conducted by a very "shrewd" business man indeed, or when the old Oglala seer happened to say something like the following: "The Great Spirit made the Two-Legged to live like relatives with the Four-Legged and the Wings of the Air and all things that live and are green. But the white man has put us in a little island and in other little islands he has put the four-legged beings; and steadily the islands grow smaller; for around them surges the hungry flood of the Wasichu (white men) and it is dirty with lies and greed."

At such a time one could insist with pathetic truth that there are many, many, many good men and women among the "Wasichu." "Of course," was the reply, "but surely they, too, shall drown."

Finally the time came to emerge from that spiritually clean island that is not yet washed away. The old seer had never seen a movie, so he was taken along for a new experience. Upon reaching town, this writer, quite naturally falling back into an old civilized habit, took up the first newspaper he had seen for a month; and anybody should know what he saw. The shock was rather staggering. Then we went to the movie show, and it was all insane sex and murder and criminality, with a houseful of men and women and children lapping it up greedily. When the practically naked heroine began the usual seductive wigglings, the old "savage" began to mutter in disgust. "Schitzi," said he: "schitzi, schitzi (bad)." You see the poor old fellow had never really had any opportunity to become "broadened" in his outlook. He still had the naïve notion that somehow the function of woman is as sacred as the mystery of the giving Earth and the fructifying Rain. He should really take a course of reading in our sophisticated literature.

3
TRENDS IN CONTEMPORARY LITERATURE

SEVEN

Genuine Criticism

John Neihardt had a passion for literature and ideas, which permeated his newspaper writing. In his earliest work, a self-assured impatience for wrong-headedness often accompanied this enthusiasm. In the first piece for the *Journal*, we can hear the young Socialist who stood on street corners of Minneapolis handing out leaflets. The message is delivered in the oratorical voice of the platform in a sweeping condemnation of the old and anticipation of a new world painted in optimistic terms.

Neihardt saw a new spirit sweeping through literature in the second decade of the twentieth century that he believed would repudiate impressionism and individual caprice, signaling a return to standards and an art that celebrates the nobility of the human spirit. By the end of the decade he was not so optimistic, believing that, though change would come, its arrival would be much delayed.

Neihardt believed it is much more difficult to find genuine criticism than genuine art. Genuine criticism is no less a creative act than art, so it demands the same devotion. However, because the creative gift is more often directed toward the shaping of original materials than the art created by someone else, there is a dearth of genuine criticism. In his search for this particular form of art, Neihardt looked for a Socratic spirit of inquiry, particularly in clarifying the terms of the discussions at hand. He saw very little of that spirit when he surveyed the contemporary critical scene, but when he did find it, as in the collection of Stuart Sherman's essays, his enthusiasm colors every line of his review.

THE SOCRATIC SPIRIT

REVIEW OF *ON CONTEMPORARY LITERATURE*, BY STUART P. SHERMAN

(NEW YORK: HOLT, 1917)

During the past five years *The Journal* has, from time to time, pointed out in its book reviews the relations between the popular misapplication of the democratic idea and impressionism in art. It is one of the few newspapers of the country that have stood out against anarchic literary tendencies, and has attempted to show that the impudent repudiation of standards of judgment, which has characterized so much of our contemporary literature, was the natural outgrowth of our individualistic conception of society. Also, from time to time, *The Journal* reviewer has ventured to prophesy that the return to a sane respect for standards of judgment would come as the logical result of a change in our social conceptions.

The change we hoped for seems to have begun in the spring of 1917, and since that time a profound revolution in the popular conception of social relations has occurred. We have begun to realize the true relation of the individual to the social group, and the old individualism appears to be dying rapidly. It is too soon to expect to see the inevitable effects of this social change upon our literature; but we may begin to look for them within a few years. With respect for a central authority and the consequent subordination of the individual to the group, must come a corresponding appreciation of those wise restraints which make for form and good taste in art.

The time when any literary upstart may outrage all the finer sensibilities and become celebrated for his audacity is passing away; and we may even hope for the development of genuine criticism in America.

The volume before us, we believe, points in the direction of the coming change in our intellectual temper. In it, Professor Sherman discusses the following writers of our time: Mark Twain, H. G. Wells, Theodore Dreiser, Arnold Bennett, George Moore, Anatole France, John Synge, Alfred Austin, Henry James and George Meredith. The author explains the inclusion of the final essay on Shakespeare by stating that he finds the great Elizabethan "the most interesting and suggestive of living writers"; whose presence among the company of moderns, "helps to distinguish the values of his competitors," and whose "humanism serves as measure of the degrees of their naturalism." The inclusion of the Shakespeare essay suggests, in short, the gist of the whole book; for the author's intention is to show the necessity of having standards of judgment and the occasionally painful result of basing all judgments upon individual caprice.

Each essay in the volume is a lance broken against the armor of the modern philosopher who proclaims the relativity of knowledge. "The great revolutionary task of the 19th century," says Professor Sherman, "was to put man into nature. The great task of 20th century thinkers is to get him out again—somehow to break the spell of those magically seductive cries, follow nature, trust your instincts, back to nature. We have trusted in our instincts long enough to sound the depths of their treacherousness. We have followed nature to the last ditch and ditch water. In these days when the educator, returning from the observation of the dog kennel with a treatise on animal behavior, thinks he has a real cue to the education of children; when the criminologist with a handful of cranial measurements imagines that he has solved the problem of evil; when the clergyman discovers the ethics of the spirit by meditating on the phagocytes in the blood; when the novelist returning from the zoological gardens wishes to revise the relation of the sexes so as to satisfy the average man's natural cravings for three wives; when the statesman after due reflection of the 'survival of the fittest' feels justified in devouring his neighbors—in the presence of all these appeals to nature, we may wisely welcome any indication of a counter revolution."

It must not be inferred from the foregoing that Professor Sherman, as a literary critic, is an "old fogy." Criticism is the art of finding out what a thing is and how it is related to other things; and it is in this sense that the author discusses various phases of modern tendency as revealed in the Utopian naturalism of Wells, the barbaric naturalism of Theodore Dreiser, the realism of Bennett, the esthetic naturalism of George Moore, the skepticism of Anatole France and the humanism of George Meredith.

No American critic, with the exception of George Elmer Moore, to whom the volume is dedicated, has so successfully revealed the anarchic doctrines of our time in "the hard clear light of contempt." Yet never may one suspect the author of taking himself over seriously. His touch is always light. His weapon is the rapier, not the ax; and his attack is the more effective in that he is never far from good natured laughter.

In these essays "On Contemporary Literature," we hear the old Socratic spirit once more insisting upon universal definition; and it would be well if this generation, enamored overmuch with Protagorean sophistries, would pause a while to listen.

PROVINCIALISM

REVIEW OF *THE AMERICAN CREDO*, BY GEORGE JEAN NATHAN AND

H. L. MENCKEN (NEW YORK: KNOPF, 1920)

This volume is issued as "a contribution to the interpretation of the National Mind." It consists of 83 pages of disjointed, dogmatic statements which, according to the authors, faithfully represent the opinions of the average

American. There is a preface of 104 pages, and this makes delicious reading, for the reason that cocksure youth is always entertaining, providing one has achieved some philosophical development.

Messrs. George Jean Nathan and H. L. Mencken are brilliant young fellows who take nothing seriously but themselves, and feign to laugh even at themselves. They represent a distinct 20th century urban type; nay more, they represent a distinct New York type, which is to say, a provincial type. However ridiculous this may seem to New Yorkers, it is quite true. Your thoroughgoing New Yorker is the true provincial in the American intellectual realm, for the very obvious reason that he regards New York as the whole country. Anyone who has read a large amount of stuff emanating from that city during the past eight years will doubtless agree with us.

Neither of these youngsters has been able to get deeper than appearances. They are intellectual anarchists. Their attitudes are the result, not of independent philosophical thinking, but of the general anarchic atmosphere of their time. The great thinker, even the fairly good thinker, is sure to be well ahead of his generation. These young men are a trifle behind theirs.

We do not care to tire our readers with quotations from the preface; but here are some samples of the "American Credo." You, gentle reader, are said to believe, among other idiotic things, the following:

"That all circus people are very pure and lead domestic lives.

"That a doctor's family never gets sick.

"That seafaring men drink nothing but rum.

"That it is impossible to pronounce the word 'statistics' without stuttering."

The American Credo is not intended as a funny book. We know because the authors say so in their preface.

CONTEMPORARY LITERATURE IS NEWS (1926)

In inaugurating the new policy of the *Post-Dispatch*, whereby the books of the day will be handled daily instead of at the week-end, as heretofore, it may be well to give the reader some idea of the general point of view from which the flow of books will be regarded.

First of all, it will be assumed that literature is an organic thing; that it neither began nor ended with the new movements now flourishing. It is obviously impossible to dispense with our past, however much we may be persuaded to do so at the moment, since we are as we are because of what has been. It will be taken for granted, even at the risk of sometimes seeming reactionary (a terrifying epithet in these days of headlong "progress!") that men like us have lived on this planet quite a while, and that many great human spirits have already passed through our world, not without leaving valuable records of their passing. Ours will be considered as only one of many "modern eras," and not as the topmost height of time from which all other hills, that once seemed lofty, are to be viewed with the shrewd, disillusioned eyes of an ultimate sophistication.

However, it will be remembered that values in literature are values in living; that the great life stream of the world is constantly shifting; that old forms, once vibrant and glowing with the vital flow of things, at last become obstructions and must perish; that experimentation is necessary in a world where rigidity is another name for death. Nevertheless, there is a point at which a too self-conscious experimentation may degenerate into mere perverseness and grotesquery, and there is such a thing as posing.

In our conspicuously anarchic moment, incident to the breaking down of old social custom, and in our ill-informed popular contempt for all things that cannot qualify as obstreperously new, it is possible for fairly clever writing men, with a flair for outraging the old folks, to get away with spiritual murder—and they do. The mob spirit is abroad in our literature, and the mob is notoriously hysterical. It requires only a hustling wind of rumor from the East to start a howling vogue among the crowd throughout the land; and such vogues sweep before them not only the great mass of readers, but too many of the critics who trim their sails to catch the veering wind. It is probable that if the general reading public could know something of the genesis and meaning of such vogues, there would be a far less ready acceptance of the next clamorously celebrated wheeze.

But literature, even in its less significant sense, as merely something that is printed, bound and read, is a running commentary on the contemporary consciousness. It is news—news of how the human spirit is reacting to the social environment, to the prevalent hopes and fears, the characteristic enthusiasms, prejudices and whimsies of its moment. And just as an item of the day's news, in the ordinary sense, may be of such momentary importance as to deserve a front page story, and yet have no historical significance whatever, so, sometimes, an admittedly ephemeral book may well deserve a column.

But one need not mistake a brisk fun fight in the slums for the sixteenth decisive battle of the world; and not all adulteries result in Trojan wars and Iliads.

Last, but most important, it will not be assumed that anyone can have a corner on the truth; and, accordingly, those among our readers who may have well-considered literary opinions to express, may do so here. Such communications will be welcomed.

However we may disagree, we shall be as comrades who look upon discussion as adventure.

Luminous Sanity

REVIEW OF *ESSAYS ON LITERATURE*, BY A. CLUTTON-BROCK (NEW YORK: DUTTON, N.D.)

Here comes a quiet little book with no raucous trumpets of publicity blown before it, and as it passes by into the further silence, which is wiser than our most earnest shouting, no murmur of curiosity will sweep across the land. What the crowd wants, as a crowd, is to recognize its own [reflected] misunderstandings represented as the final truth—which is [the] explanation of demagogues and [ ] literature. But there are many individuals in the crowd who know that one who cares to understand may well watch for the quiet little books, for sometimes there is light in them.

A. Clutton-Brock, who died recently, was a British critic, one of the few critics of our time who have not become mere echo-mechanisms faithful to the loudest din. In the present volume, his wife has gathered together certain of his representative essays that have appeared in the *London Times Literary Supplement* and the *London Mercury*.

The very striking thing about the book is its luminous sanity. There is an article on "Pure Literature" that should be a revelation to many essentially sincere but helpless people who have been misled by the current conception of realism. Clutton-Brock knew that art is nothing in itself; that it is not a game to be played more or less brilliantly for pastime or even for the admiration of one's fellows; but that all the arts, including literature, are merely devices through which conceptions of value on a more comprehensive level of consciousness may be communicated. Also he knew that all values that can be known to men are values in human life. This truth is not baldly stated in the essay, but the consciousness of it will come upon the reader like moonrise.

The essay on "Art and Science" will further illuminate the contemporary scene for eager seekers after understanding. "On Some Perversities of Criticism" might well be printed in a pamphlet by some wealthy friend of mankind. Surely, if widely read and understood, it would serve to discredit some of our trumpet-voiced literary hucksters who, from strategic positions, mislead the credulous public that is worthy of better things.

In the 15 essays here collected, light is thrown in many dark corners of the literary world. Clutton-Brock's work illustrates the meaning of the true statement that only when criticism is itself an outgrowth of the art process can it be more than idle chatter.

EIGHT

Vandals in the Temple

Neihardt was at his best when interacting with an audience. He was an effective lecturer and reader of his own poetry; even into his nineties he kept audiences of college students spellbound through long recitations of epic poetry. This awareness of audience permeates his newspaper writing, and Neihardt moves in and out of conversations with a variety of participants, weaving multiple messages into his text. Besides writing for a general readership, he also addressed his peers—artists and critics, both academic and in the popular press. In reviewing books of criticism he showed an awareness of the other players in the game, linking names and movements and circles of influence.

Neihardt positioned himself in opposition to much of the criticism of the day, and his frustration with contemporary criticism is a running thread throughout the columns. He attacked superficial treatment of art, shoddy workmanship, analysis rather than synthesis, and the self-indulgence of subjectivism. Most of all, he deplored a lack of creative insight in the writing of contemporary critics. He saw most critics as unable to step outside their particular time-mood and unable to help draw relations among the chaos of sense impressions. Neihardt saw much of what passed for criticism as just one more expression of the drift of civilization. Rather than a genuine criticism that helped define and interpret, most criticism merely reinforced the dominant persuasion.

MODERN AMERICAN POETRY

REVIEW OF *THE NEW ERA IN AMERICAN POETRY*, BY LOUIS UNTERMEYER (NEW YORK: HOLT, 1919)

Mr. Untermeyer's purpose in this volume is to show that previous to the outburst of haphazard poetizing during the last seven years, America had no authentic, indigenous poetry, except Whitman's. In a general way, he gives us a summary of the leading literary movements since Whitman, and illustrates his main contention by analyzing the works of certain outstanding figures in the recent movement.

We are willing to admit that modern American poetry of the better class may be called democratic, in that it had returned to common themes, simple language and directness of statement, discarding mere verbal embroidery. But we believe that Mr. Untermeyer falls into error when he maintains that such work as that of Amy Lowell and Carl Sandburg is democratic. As a matter of fact, it is anarchic; and far from representing the democratic impulse that is sweeping across the world, it represents no more than a belated reflex of the old individualism. It strikes us as just a bit funny that Mr. Untermeyer, who considers himself a socialist, should be unable to detect in literature the influence of the laissez faire conception which he claims to abhor. To regard the vers libre of Amy Lowell as democratic is simply ridiculous. It is aristocratic in the most derogatory sense—so much so that in many cases Miss Lowell's audience cannot possibly consist of more than one who understands; and were we not extremely optimistic, we could not hope that even Miss Lowell always understands herself. She is obviously not a humanist in any sense. She is not concerned with humanity, but only with the vagaries of her own inwardness.

After having given whole chapters of considerable length to upstarts and freaks, Mr. Untermeyer proceeds to jump off some of the strongest poets now living—men and women who have taken the trouble to understand their art—with a few swift phrases that betray the author's ignorance of what those men and women have done. In several instances Mr. Untermeyer judges some of our most highly gifted poets solely by the work they did more than a decade ago.

We can imagine the mood in which sane critics of the future will read this clever but shallow work.

Mr. Untermeyer mistakes the end of his nose for a mountain.

ROSES AND DEAD COWS (1927)
During the recent dark ages, before the gleeful dawn of Freudianism came to reveal the inevitable nastiness and meanness of human motives, benighted critics actually believed that literary criticism was concerned with literary values. When they discussed a great poem, play, novel or essay, they sought to determine whether or not truth and beauty were to be found therein. They were like those foolish connoisseurs of gems who will judge a pearl by its luster and perfection of form, actually ignoring the scientific fact that

even the most exquisite pearl is the product of an indisposed oyster! This is what is now referred to in certain ultra modern circles as "the aesthetic method of criticism," the proper method being psycho-analytical.

It seems probable that the popularity of this up-to-the-minute critical method may be due to the obvious fact that it is greatly soothing to the secret pangs of mediocrity. For instance, if you have cherished a dream of doing great things and the years have dealt unkindly with your dream, you look about you to see if, after all, there may not be a joker in the alleged greatness of masters. You pounce on Swinburne, for instance, and by applying the psycho-analytical method to your study of the man's product (this has been done recently), you discover just what you have hoped to find—reprehensible "complexes," appalling but unmistakable indications of "Infantilism." It does not occur to you to conclude at once that if so much marvelous music can grow out of deplorable defects in personality, then the defects are hardly to be regarded as deplorable. In the larger view of race-enrichment, they are not defects at all, but only highly desirable variations from the norm in that particular instance. This is merely the pragmatic view, of which so much is made by the same type of person who goes in for psycho-analytical criticism. And surely "a thing is good for what it is good for."

There is no reason why those who are interested in psycho-pathology should not go in for psycho-pathological studies of famous authors; but the product should not be called literary criticism. It should be called psycho-pathology.

Frank Harris seems to have been the first writer of distinction to apply the Freudian method to the works of a master. In his *The Man Shakspeare,* published 20 years ago, he attempted to reconstruct the personality of the man from passages carefully selected from the plays.[1] It was a remarkable piece of conjuring, but the resultant picture very much resembled Frank Harris.

Some years later, Van Wyck Brooks psycho-analyzed Mark Twain's work, and the "psycho-graph" thus produced was somewhat belittling.[2] But, strange to say, upon turning to Shakspeare's plays, after viewing the Frank Harris picture, one found all the marvelous power still there; and Mark Twain's work somehow wasn't changed in the least by the revelations of Mr. Van Wyck Brooks.

It is the pearl that matters, and not the creative malady of the oyster. There is something childish about the prevalent notion that once you have analyzed the mechanism by which something came to be, you have explained the something itself. You certainly haven't.

There was once a rose bush loaded with wonderful roses, and lovers of beauty came to enjoy the color and fragrance and form of the flowers. But one among the assembled people, being a scientist, took his neat little spade and, digging at the roots of the bush, revealed a sorry fact. The bush had been planted over the carcass of a cow! And so the secret was out at last!

But there were those among the lovers of the beauty of the roses who contended that nothing had been proven save that it may be well to plant a rose bush over the carcass of a cow.

Revaluing the Classics

REVIEW OF *LITERARY BLASPHEMIES*, BY ERNEST BOYD (NEW YORK: HARPER, 1927)

In *Literary Blasphemies* Mr. Ernest Boyd has written for those who are not convinced that yes and no are the only possible answers to any question. The book is therefore addressed to a relatively small public, but its appeal will hardly stop there. Those who are addicted to swallowing half truths whole with all their flattering sauce of error will find in Mr. Boyd's penetrating and stimulating discussions of great literary reputations much more than he intended to convey. Whereas he is evidently an honest critical intelligence, daring to examine famous works of literature for himself, and quite competent to do so, the illiterate intelligentsia (and this is no longer necessarily a contradiction in terms) will hail the book with great glee as another proof of the curious notion that all the alleged greatness of the literary past is bunk.

Unfortunately no human conception is likely to be quite bunkless, and in seeking and concentrating upon the bunk spots, the cultural landscape can be made to appear like the leavings of a tornado.

Many honest and thoroughly literate people, not wholly under the hypnotic spell of literary tradition, must have wondered often if there might not be considerable exaggeration in the conventional conception of great writers. Most people will read without a thought of protest the ridiculous statement of H. G. Wells to the effect that Shakspeare turned every word to music; and, in general, even those who have actually read Shakspeare and found in his works very much that is far from great, are loath to say just that aloud, so powerful may be the despotism of an unexamined tradition.

Marvelous as Homer truly is, it is not the intrinsic merit of the *Iliad* and *Odyssey* that has convinced so many generations of Homer's greatness, for only a relative few of those who have conceded that greatness have ever read the poems. It has been the tremendous enshrining legend of greatness that has impressed. Neither was it the intrinsic merit of the *Aeneid* that gave it such enormous power throughout the Middle Ages and for centuries thereafter, for there came a time when it was not read at all for what Virgil intended it to be, but for something vastly different. The original impetus given to the poem by Augustus and his court had far more to do with the matter than had the undeniable beauty and power of the work itself.

Until very recently—and even now to a very considerable extent in pedantic circles—an intelligent person was expected to throw catfits of enthusiasm over certain classical lyrics that are really inferior to much of the magazine verse of the day.

Ernest Boyd is one who has read his classics for what they could do to him—which is a very good way to read them; and his findings have not always been in keeping with the despotic traditions surrounding those classics. Undoubtedly temperament and the influence of the modern mood have had much to with some of his adverse findings; but it can hardly be denied that he has hit upon a good deal of genuine bunk. The reputations discussed are those of Shakspeare, Milton, Swift, Byron, Dickens, Poe, Whitman, Henry James and Thomas Hardy.

This writer himself happens to agree with just about half of Boyd's criticisms. Nevertheless, it is a pleasure, and seems a duty, to recommend the volume to such readers as may already realize that there are important nuances of truth between a sweeping yes and a devastating no; that a very great writer need not be conceived as a god far above human criticism; and that, in the concluding words of Mr. Boyd, "there lives more faith in honest critical doubt than in half the academic creeds."

If Mr. Boyd's strictures on certain classics should induce a few people here and there to read those classics with sincerity, it is more than probable that the sum total of genuine admiration for them would be increased.

WHY SCREAM?
REVIEW OF *ALL ELSE IS FOLLY*, BY PEREGRINE ACLAND (NEW YORK: COWARD, 1929)
Evidently we are in for a long, dreary, autumnal downpour of war novels, thanks to the popular success of Remarque's remarkable book, and we may be sure that each and every one in turn will be the greatest this and the mostest that of all war novels that have ever been written, are now being written, or ever shall be written, so help us God![3]

Referring to the latest of these supreme masterpieces, here listed, Dr. John B. Watson, father of Behaviorism and eminent literary critic, says, or rather screams quite in the best critical manner of our superlative age: "This book stands for the greatest denouncement of the war that I have ever read!" The scientific gentleman who took the psyche out of psychology neglects to state just what, if anything, he has ever read.

Mr. Frank Harris, than whom, perhaps, there is none whomer, goes Doc one better and remarks or, rather, yells to the author: "Great work, Major, this literature; the greatest a man can do; and you do it greatly." S-t-e-a-d-y now, Frank, old horse, s-t-e-a-d-y!

Next Mr. Ford Madox Ford arises and informs the cock-eyed cosmos that "It will be little less than a scandal if this book is not read enormously widely!!"

A little while ago another extremely eminent literary gentleman informed the solar system that any human being who didn't read *All Quiet on the Western Front* would be "a traitor to the human race"!! It was an excellent lead, and now we are threatened with scandal if we don't buy in enormous quantities the latest, greatest war book of them all. Doubtless during the course of the war-book craze we'll be guilty of all sorts of misdemeanors if we don't fall for every outburst of war-book ballyhoo. Each eminent critic in turn can easily hit upon a different offense, and so each can be authoritative, forceful and highly original in turn. Note the possibilities: mayhem, arson, simony, sodomy, murder in the first degree, also in the second and third degrees, burglary, body odor, driving while intoxicated, spitting on the sidewalk, adultery, jay-walking, assault and battery, etc., etc.! What an outlook for authoritative critics!

As a matter of fact, *All Else Is Folly* is a good enough thing as writing goes; but surely nothing to burst out crying about. The author was in the war, and evidently he is an educated man. He writes good English. When he finally gets down to telling about the war, he does a good, convincing job; but he has a hard time getting down to it. It's the ladies that are to blame—three of them, two married and one regularly in the business. Not that much really happens; but for a spell, there, the suspense for a modest reviewer was something awful.

By and by the hero breaks away from the henyard and lights into the squareheads like a bear cat, finally getting severely wounded.

The book ends with the question: "Does man fight because he hasn't yet learned to love?" So long as men continue to talk that sort of sentimental twaddle about the cause of war, they will not be able to swat the real cause which has nothing to do with metaphysics.

Growing Debt

REVIEW OF *LIFE AND LETTERS OF STUART P. SHERMAN*, BY JACOB ZEITLIN AND HOMER WOODBRIDGE (HEW YORK: FARRAR, 1929)

Upon beginning business a few weeks ago, the publishing firm of Farrar & Rinehart immediately placed the discriminating reading public in its debt by issuing several books of far more than ordinary merit, and, as suggested here a week or so ago, it may even have added a classic to American literature in Lizette Woodworth Reese's *A Victorian Village.*

The public's debt to this new firm is further increased by the publication in two handsome volumes of the late Stuart Sherman's Letters, edited with a running biographical commentary by two old friends of the critic. Evidently the editors undertook the task as a labor of love and it is admirably performed.

Whatever certain critical lords of misrule and flunkies of the go-getting cliques may have been pleased to say about Stuart Sherman in his years of freedom, it remains obviously true that his was one of the finest critical intelligences that America has produced in our day. How much more might be said of him is a matter for the future to decide—perhaps a remote future, for it is not inconceivable that already we have entered upon a period in which criticism and interest therein shall cease, leaving the field wholly to literary salesmen. Sherman's was a richly literate, warmly human and eminently sane personality, and here we may follow the development of that personality from early boyhood. This is a privilege for which to be grateful.

The book ends in tragedy; but as to just what was the nature of that tragedy there is a difference of opinion. Many readers will regard the critic's death at the age of 45 as the tragic thing, while others, no less sincere in their admiration of the man and his work, may look upon his going to New York and what happened to him there as a cause for deeper sorrow. "To the public at large," say the editors, "Stuart Sherman is known as an active critic who during the greater part of his writing career defended conservative standards in literature and manners alongside of Mr. Paul Elmer More and Prof. Irving Babbitt, and in opposition to the hosts led by Mr. Mencken, and then, in his later years, with a surprising and somewhat disconcerting suddenness, deserted his friends and gave much comfort to his former antagonists without actually entering into an alliance with them." The editors deny the charge and maintain that the Letters will serve to show how "the latest manifestations of Sherman's mind and character were discernible from the beginning."

This will be questioned by many readers of the *Letters,* who may ask why the change was so abrupt and why it coincided with the removal from Urbana to New York.

Even though the well-known charge should be true, it could not destroy the fact that a fine critical intelligence was involved and one to which America is indebted; nor could it be held justly against the character of the man. Rather, it would be only another saddening example of what "success" may do to a fine, free spirit, and of the tremendous difficulty of being an "outsider" in New York and getting anywhere. Nor should it be assumed that a man with such a mind need have been conscious of any mean truckling.

The happy sense of triumph in being called from the despised Middle West to a high critical position in New York would be likely to soften any but a granite heart. Sherman had developed as an individual far from the powerful literary cliques and he had been nourished by the best that men have thought and felt and done throughout the ages. His isolation from the loud moment had made it possible for him to feel the wisdom of Time, and it was as though he were viewing the contemporary scene from the vantage point of posterity. He had been free of group thinking in Urbana, and while there he was that very rare thing, an autonomous individual. But in New York group opinion dominates. There is nothing harder for a social-minded human being to resist than the opinion of his group, yet it is clear enough that all the curious literary imbecilities of our day have been incubated within groups. A sane man will come to accept as a member of a group what he could not possibly countenance as an individual.

An Honest Book

REVIEW OF *OUR SINGING STRENGTH*, BY ALFRED KREYMBORG (NEW YORK: COWARD, 1929)

In preparing this outline of American poetry from 1620 to the present moment, Alfred Kreymborg has done a remarkable thing. It is not his admirably compendious presentation of a very large body of material that most impresses this writer, though considerably more than a capacity for industry was required. Nor is it that his judgments generally are such as may reasonably be expected to stand the test of time. Perhaps that would be too much to expect from anyone in our age of whirling confusion; but most certainly it is too much to expect of anyone whose consciousness has developed at the center of the contemporary whirl.

What most distinguishes the book in the view of this writer is the unmistakable revelation of a personality that, while unconsciously and of necessity accepting in general a transient reference scheme as though it were universal and permanent, still retains its integrity and is able, within the limitations of that reference scheme, to render independent judgments, not only honestly and fearlessly, but, what is more, with genuine kindliness. This fact, naturally, is most noticeable in that portion of the work which deals with Mr. Kreymborg's contemporaries; for the prevailing temper of the time has pretty well determined what is to be said about the poetry of the past. For instance, what shall be said, substantially, of Longfellow on the one hand and Whitman on the other is a foregone conclusion, thanks to the overwhelming time-mood, and no up-to-the-minute critic need be troubled on that score. Also in dealing with certain contemporaries whose reputations, for one reason or another, have reached the intimidating stage in which unconsidered repetition is accepted as the critic's inescapable duty, Kreymborg's critical apparatus functions with automatic precision. But one feels that the faithfulness is genuine; and if, in these instances, he were not thoroughly under the influence of the prevailing group psychosis and the overwhelming prejudice of his time and place, he would speak out with perfect candor—and kindliness. In other words, his judgments must be accepted as honest, however they may have been determined.

This very remarkable quality in Kreymborg can hardly be appreciated fully by anyone who is not somewhat familiar with the literary game as it is played in New York. Over and over, Kreymborg has rendered judgments here in his discussions of contemporary poets that certainly are not calculated to advance his own personal interests, and while, even though the fact were not known in advance, it would be obvious that he is a New Yorker, whirling with the others and convinced that the whirl is cosmic and enduring, yet it is not possible to determine to what clique, if any, he owes allegiance.

Not only does he sometimes damn with very faint praise certain poets who stand well with influential groups, but, what is perhaps even more courageous, he ventures to speak rather well of some who are rank outsiders. If he should seem to show a bit more facility in escaping through the bars of powerful group opinion when he is concerned with poets from the provinces (which, from the Gotham point of vantage, may be said to include even Boston) the depth of honest conviction is not [to] be questioned. If, here and there, it should appear to some that he may have passed judgment upon a poet with whose work he is only slightly acquainted, it may be taken for granted that he has done so out of honest conviction induced by his environment.

The book deserves to go down to posterity as an exhibit of our nation's literary temper in a time when by far the least American spot in America still had the power to tell the rest of America what was American in literature and what was not. Along with many shrewd observations, and the candor and kindliness of the whole, much that cannot but amuse a less confused age will be found. For instance, the assumption that a poet who employs the language of cultivated men may be set aside as "rhetorical" and unimportant. But what amusement the book may occasion can hardly be at Kreymborg's expense. Rather it will be at the curious notions that dominated an age when provincialism was not a matter of geographical remoteness from centers of culture, but rather of an intellectual short-circuit, an isolation of the loud moment from all the rest of time.

A NEW FAD? (1930)

When Irving Babbitt's *Masters of Modern French Criticism* appeared 18 years ago, the anarchic tendency in American literature, which is often regarded as exclusively a post-war phenomenon, was already pronounced.[4] Its most conspicuous early manifestation was the "free verse" craze; but the "naturalistic" bias was growing among fictionists, and sordidness and nastiness were coming into fashion. Everybody who reads knows into what all but incredible absurdities this tendency has betrayed our writers and our reading public since then.

Had Irving Babbitt's *Masters of Modern French Criticism* been understood and accepted by the dominant literary men and women of the day, American criticism could not have been the comic thing that it has become, and a great many celebrated rotters of the writing world could not have achieved the overwhelming notoriety that they have enjoyed and now enjoy. For in that book Irving Babbitt worked out and illustrated a certain fundamental principle in direct opposition to what was then beginning in American literature. What he was getting at seems not to have been understood by reviewers in general; nor was this strange, for most critics are controlled unconsciously by the time-mood prevailing among their associates, and Babbitt's book was decidedly not in keeping with the time-mood then in process of development. This writer read as many articles on the book as he could find, and in most cases, if not all, the work was mistaken for a biographical study of French critics, whereas Babbitt was illustrating the anarchic effect of the democratic idea as misinterpreted and misapplied in the realm of the higher values.

Surely, as these 18 tragi-comic years have proved beyond a doubt, we needed cultural leadership then [if] ever; and curiously enough, now that we have grown a bit weary of our clowning and our pantagruelizing, it seems that we may be turning for leadership to the very man who, 18 years ago, strove to point out to us the folly we were then espousing; for Irving Babbitt and Paul Elmer More are the recognized leaders of the "New Humanism" that promises to become fashionable.

Alas, fashionable is almost certainly the right word; for can anyone who has any notion what humanism means to men like Babbitt and More, believe that it is possible to become a humanist by deciding to do so? Humanism may be stated as a doctrine, but it is vital only as a deep-seated attitude toward mankind and human life in general. It is a feeling for values, an attitude that can result only from long habitual association with the finest spirits that have been in this world—and accordingly, nothing could be funnier than a popular fad for humanism.

But even so, the new "movement" may have its uses. If it can serve no better purpose than to outmode the writings of roughnecks, rotters and degenerate sophisticates, it would be an excellent thing, even though laughter should be the end of it. It may do more; for scattered all over the country, there are thousands of intelligent people who are capable of reading and enjoying better things than they have been led to accept as important during the past decade and more.

The most comprehensive and authoritative work on the New Humanism thus far published is *Humanism and America*, edited by Norman Foerster and published by Farrar and Rinehart.

AN ATHLETIC MIND IN ACTION

REVIEW OF *THE NEW AMERICAN LITERATURE*, BY FRED L. PATTEE (NEW YORK: CENTURY, 1930)

In his *History of American Literature Since 1870*, which was published 15 years ago, Prof. Pattee dealt with the period of the Civil War decade to the early '90s.[5] The present volume is a continuation of the former, covering the last 40 years of literary activity in America. Prof. Pattee's own estimate of his work, so far as literary evaluations are concerned, is undoubtedly just and should be taken into consideration by anyone who may read the volume: "My study of the period so near us," he writes, "with, in most cases, practically no perspective, cannot hope to arrive at final values, but that such a preliminary survey is needed I am fully convinced. Someone must do the pioneer work with a new period, mapping—crudely it may be, yet the best he can with materials at hand—the new trails. Someone must do it. Let others in later years with more perspective and fuller materials correct my outlines."

The state of anarchy which now exists through the whole range of human values renders hopeless any attempt to appraise our doings in a way that anyone is logically bound to respect. As a generation we are absolutely up in the air. There can be no acceptable judgment without some sort of standard to judge by, and having repudiated all former standards, we have not yet formulated any new ones. The interest which attaches to Prof. Pattee's work is simply that which is afforded by the spectacle of an athletic mind in action. A comparable physical spectacle would be that of a well-developed wrestler struggling in quicksand.

A contemporary judgment rendered by some rank outsider with "a sense of all time and all men" might be acceptable to our posterity, but for all his apparent independence, Prof. Pattee is profoundly influenced by the prevailing mood. His independence operates definitely within the limits of that mood, and were it not so, he could not hope to be heard by our generation. In this he is at times like a physician who might discuss in a masterly way the relative importance of the various symptoms of an epidemic disease, being himself infected and rather under the impression that some brand-new phase of health may be involved. What really matters is the disease, and the disease is social; its literary symptoms are neither more nor less important than its appalling criminal symptoms, and there are many highly accredited contemporary writers who should be discussed along with Scarface Al. In a time like ours literary criticism, to have any vital meaning, must begin and end with radical social criticism.

NINE

Only Symptomatic

Neihardt believed one of the major tasks of the critic is to steer the reading public on a search for gems buried in the abundance of books produced each year. In looking at the quality of contemporary literature, Neihardt neither took the position of the academic who believed there was nothing worthwhile to be found nor of the shrill advertisers in the popular press who treated every new book as a ready-made classic. Neihardt believed that the truth fell somewhere between those two extremes and suggested ways for his audience to read selectively.

Neihardt examined several contemporary trends in his columns: a realism that was more a cataloguing of unrelated detail than true literature; the disparagement of rural settings and themes; an anarchic mood in the cultural realm; a materialistic culture that had put aside spiritual values; a dominating mob-spirit; even the exuberant pre-crash passion for playing the stock market. He also pointed the way to works that resisted prevailing trends. His goal was not to assign values of "good" or "bad" to these trends, for, caught up in the moment as we are, it is impossible to make such value judgments. Neihardt suggested that the goal is to understand, and we gain understanding by looking at contemporary life in a larger context.

One trend that gets a good deal of Neihardt's attention, particularly in the *Journal,* is the increasing role of women in art. Neihardt spoke out against the feminist movement, and he deplored what he saw as a feminization in the cultural realm, believing that the bulk of creative masculine forces had been "diverted into channels leading toward mastery of the physical world."[6] Powers of analysis and a preoccupation with the narrow and personal were the province of women, he argued, and an increase in the writing of women had produced an abundance of lyrical poetry and novels of manners, but a scarcity of poetry of the demiurgic kind, a "poetry in the large sense of creative structure" which he associated with masculine gifts. Though he praised the art of both men and women in his columns, he did not find the increasing role of women in the arts a favorable circumstance, calling preoccupation with the fragmentary "inconsequential diddling."[7]

Neihardt's personal relationships contradicted his public pronouncements. In a 1913 letter to Sara Teasdale, Neihardt praised her art and indicated a desire to learn "a good woman's outlook upon the great passion. I used to see so differently; but now that I have a wee daughter, I begin to understand." In the letter he sent greetings from his wife, "a sculptor of really remarkable ability," who studied with Rodin, and whose art Neihardt respected and supported.[8] However, thirteen years later, in spite of a partial disclaimer that the *full force* of his remarks not fall on Sara Teasdale (emphasis added), he used the appearance of her most recent book of poetry as the impetus for an essay on the feminization of literature, capping his musings with the statement that "If artists be not seers they might better be hemstitching handkerchiefs or embroidering doilies."[9]

THE NEW READING PUBLIC (1926)

There was a time, not very long ago, when the writing and reading of what we loosely term literature could hardly be regarded as one of the major activities of our country. Middle-aged people who were intellectually alive in the early '90s, can remember when a few conservative publishing houses issued all the books, when the number of authors was still comfortably small, and when it was still taken for granted that there were dependable standards by which literature could be judged.

As for the expansion of the reading public since those days, it is interesting to note how many of even middle-aged readers reveal a literary experience reaching back no farther than 1912; and the average reach decreases in inverse proportion to the number of readers considered.

It is probably true that the literary sympathies of the vast majority of present day readers in America extend no farther than the great war; and it must be that every day large numbers of the younger generation are discovering literature in the latest best seller, without suspecting that they have come suddenly upon a very ancient living thing whose real value to men is somehow in its organic continuity.

How can we explain the astonishing expansion of the reading public since the early '90s? What bearing has the cause of that expansion upon the dominant literary tastes of the moment in which we live and which looms disproportionately large to most of us? Can we hope to find our way through the wilderness of contemporary literature unless we find some means of orientation other than our personal likes and dislikes? And, as a matter of fact, are not most of us quite lost in the wilderness? Does it not seem sometimes that even many of our official guides, whom we dignify with the name of critic, are unable to see the forest for the trees? Every season brings forth a crop of alleged masterpieces, and the critics shout about them like lusty auctioneers; but, strangely enough, these masterpieces are generally quite dead by the time the next crop matures, when the shouting begins all over again.

There are those academic people who, noting this fact and offended by the character of much of our successful literature, leap to the conclusion that contemporary writing is pretty much a false alarm, and that genuine literature is "the surviving product of dead authors—the longer dead the better." Nevertheless, this is a very great age in literature, in spite of all the hysterical shouting and violent dust-throwing of the day. Masterpieces do sometimes appear, both with and without hoarse acclaim, and the number of books each year that deserve the attention and esteem of intelligent people is surprisingly large. Many excellent things are continually being snowed under by the blizzard of books; and one must be a stout optimist to believe that there will some day be a resurrection spring for many of them. In most cases, only the germ ideas that gave them value will grow to other forms in books more fortunate.

Even if this were not a great age of literature, to turn away from it would be intellectual suicide. Though I shall try to show in other issues of this department why it is impossible for men to read effectively, or even to live well, who limit their consciousness to the breathing moment, as so many are now trying to do, yet that moment is the precious link between what we have been and what we shall become. Literary values are values in living or they are not values at all. Contemporary literature, however poor it may seem, at least reveals the attitudes that determine our acts as a people; and to be ignorant of contemporary literature is to lack the comprehensive material for creative criticism of human affairs. But certainly to have no other standard of judgment than the prevailing fashion is the same as attempting to employ a lever without a fulcrum; and this is being done by thousands upon thousands of readers. It is being done by many of our critics who seem to have no other standard than the going whim.

In the unstrenuous '90s this was still an agricultural nation; the rural population was still greater than the urban, and there was no such complex system of rapid communication as we take for granted now. We can see now that the Spanish War was a major symptom of the great change then preparing in our country. Gloomy radicals of the time became greatly excited, shouting that the nation was being launched upon a career of imperialism. We were passing, as a result of natural growth, from an agricultural to an industrial regime. We were entering the machine age, that is to say, a market-seeking age.

Machines are profitable only for quantity production. The larger the quantity the cheaper the product, and the cheaper the product the greater the chances for success in a competitive market. The important bearing of this fact upon the vexed question of international relations does not concern us here; but there is a bearing upon the state of contemporary literature that does concern us.

Quantity production involves quantity consumption, and therefore a flourishing industrial system in a competitive world must not only supply existing demands, it must create new demands increasingly, or collapse. As a result of this fact, it sometimes seems, as Watts-Dunton once remarked, that modern civilization is little more than a scheme for creating new desires that men may toil to satisfy them. And if this be true, even though in the myopic view of the moment it should seem a colossal fatuity, who is wise enough to say that the result must be more bad than good? Our world is cruising in strange new seas on a marvelous voyage of discovery, and he is a poor sailor who will not enter heartily into the adventure. But it is none the less an important part of the adventure to keep an eye on some star that does not rise and set; to watch, in so far as one may, the curious aberrations of the compass, and to note the crank kick of the wheel to the winds and currents that drive us.

The need for greater and greater consumption to meet the necessarily increasing production of our competitive machine age accounts for practically all of the astonishing developments of our time that people commonly discuss. The modern system of transportation and communication is an outgrowth of that need; for it was necessary to reach the greatest possible number with the seed of new desires and the goods with which the new desires might be met.

More than half our population is urban now, and brooks of people are steadily flowing into the cities where the call of the machines grows louder every year with increasing production of things that no man wanted thirty years ago. Advertising is an enormous business of fundamental importance in the prevailing scheme of life. Put out all the electric signs, discontinue advertising in every form for a year, and the ensuing panic would be such as to delight the gloomiest prophet of social woe; for it is by the constant and steadily increasing stimulation of desire that our present social structure is maintained.

The rapid expansion of the reading public in America within recent years may be shown to coincide with our industrial expansion. It was not primarily a matter of increasing popular culture, though culture of a sort is necessarily a by-product widely shared. It was not primarily a matter of increasing per capita wealth and the ability to buy books. It was due primarily to the fact that the necessary tactics of a competitive machine age were applied to the problem of production and consumption in all fields, including that of reading matter. Formerly a few conservative publishers issued such books as the relatively small and relatively cultured reading public would buy in keeping with what were then regarded as fairly respectable literary standards. Relatively few went into the writing game, because it was not so easy to qualify for what was then generally considered literary success; and the financial outlook was not so dazzling as now. Most authors then looked upon literature as an art; but now, for the majority of writers, literature is frankly a branch of industry subject to the same necessities that control other industries. Consumption of literary products has been increased by the same methods that a manufacturer employs in creating demand for any of the many products that are not absolutely essential to life—by the systematic stimulation of desire where none formerly existed.

Once a relatively small reading public went to the publishers for its books. Now many publishers, under the pressure of intense competition, have sought the crowd, creating a new and much larger reading public. By systematic, modern methods they have acquainted large sections of the masses with the seductive delights of vicarious living through printed tales. Naturally the commodity offered must be well calculated to satisfy such desires as it is possible to create in the many at this comparatively early stage of human evolution. And this accounts for what appears to be, but is not, the low standard of literature in our go-getting, market-making age.

It is not an uncommon thing to hear it said that since the crowd could not rise to genuine literature, literature has obligingly descended to the level of the crowd. But that is not what has happened. What the pessimist sees most in watching the flood of books is something that resembles literature only by virtue of the fact that it is printed and bound. The greater bulk of the stream consists of a new commodity, warranted to soothe the dull pains of boredom, and designed to meet the demand of a recently created reading public.

Shall one who loves literature deplore this? Not if he can see beyond the end of his nose. "Things are good for what they are good for," and along with the negligible and pernicious brands of the new commodity there is much that has its legitimate human uses. As a people we are becoming something and it does not yet appear what we shall be. If the application of modern commercial principles to the vending of books should serve for the moment only to familiarize the many with the physical act of reading, it would be justified in the long view, and it is doing vastly more. It is only through the process of reading that men can hope to come in contact with the larger environment that alone can humanize.

Just what the larger environment is, and how it may be utilized, not only in the judging of books, but in the far more important business of living well, are matters that will be discussed in these columns later on.

THE PERSONAL NOTE WEARS OUT

REVIEW OF *DARK OF THE MOON*, BY SARA TEASDALE (NEW YORK: MACMILLAN, 1926)

In his first book, published 36 years ago, Havelock Ellis described the "new spirit" of the world as "a quickening of the pulse of life," due to the triumphs of modern science, the rise of women and the democratic idea.[10] For the democratic idea we may as well substitute individualism, for that is what democracy really is in practice.

No one can say just what the effect of those three forces may be in the future. Social prophets disagree, according to their temperaments and the state of their livers, no doubt, some seeing ruin ahead and some seeing visions of infinite progress. We of this generation need not worry, for when those three forces shall have done their best or worst in society, we shall not be here.

But it is interesting to note some of the momentary effects of those forces, and our contemporary literature is full of them.

Granting all the benefits that modern science has heaped upon us, it is nevertheless true that the scientific spirit has tended to destroy the old sustaining hope that was central in the religion of revelation, and has served to focus the minds of millions upon material conceptions and the uninspired moment. This may be good or bad, in the long run; but it has happened so. Our literature of the moment abundantly reflects this influence.

The individualistic idea tends to darken in the general mind any vision of human salvation from the brute as a social ascent, and, through need and greed, it greatly increases the natural tendency of men to think in terms of their own petty selves.

Women and Literature

The rise of women and the enforced preoccupation of men with an intensely practical materialism, has left both the making and reading of literature very largely to the feminine-minded of both sexes. Publishers will tell you that a really whopping literary success must appeal to the women.

May not this latter fact explain the scarcity in America, where the feminine spirit is most powerful, of literary works that deserve to be called demiurgic, and also the modest success of such works when they do appear—generally in translation?

However all this may be, one must grant that, in the realm of poetry, at least, it is the fragmentary, the odd, the pettily personal, the myopic thing that has scored the most conspicuous successes of late years since the many discovered the muse. Say the word poetry, and most people, including the critics, think of brief lyrics. Poetry in the large sense of creative structure is all but lost to the literary consciousness of our generation. Poets, once regarded as makers of spacious and luminous worlds, wherein men might live at will in keeping with an expanded and glorified understanding, are now expected to do, at most, the little, the odd, the whimsical, the dinkily "esthetic" thing. And too often they merely whine about human destiny, meaning their own personal destiny.

Art is in a bad way when it is preoccupied with fragments and with the narrow personal view. If art be not revelation of a wider reality than that known or suspected by the average uninspired citizen, then it is simply inconsequential diddling, however prettily it may be wrought. If artists be not seers, they might better be hemstitching handkerchiefs or embroidering doilies.

Sara Teasdale Sings Sweetly

It is not intended that the full force of the foregoing remarks should fall upon Sara Teasdale, though they were occasioned by a reading of her latest (or is it her last?) little book. She is a singer with a very sweet, maidenly voice of very slight range. It is good to hear a maiden singing of her true love even though she be limited to three of four clear notes; but there is no good reason why musical critics should mistake her for a prima donna; and that has been done. There was something fresh and birdlike about Miss Teasdale's early expression of virgin yearnings. But time has passed; she is now a middle-aged wife. The world darkens around her, and if her understanding of life has grown since her springtime, there is nothing in her lyrics to indicate the fact. She seems to have learned only that she is no longer young, and that it seems a great pity. The intensely personal note that, in her maidenhood, was as sweet to hear as a robin's is not adequate to express the deeper music of the aging summer. Age is a curse indeed, if it fails to bring with it an understanding of the sublime fact that the personal view is untenable. Sara Teasdale has not succeeded in losing herself in her art. She is still central in her little cosmos, like a maiden waiting for a lover; and the mating time is over. Dark of the Moon, from the technical standpoint, is an exquisite thing, but it is without vision. Over and over and over she tells us that autumn is coming, that the snow will blow over her, that she will get old, that she will die, that life has disappointed her, that she is waiting for nothing at all, that she will have to make her life of what she can remember, for summer will never come to her again.

No Cosmic Vision

It does not seem to occur to her, that the human race is still going strong and is likely to be on this planet for ages and ages—and that it does not matter at all what happens to one of us. She seems never to have thrilled at the glorious thought of being lost in the great process. Though she has often sung sweetly of nature, she seems never to have achieved a cosmic vision to live by. The love that she has celebrated so prettily remains a personal love; it has not been sublimated and universalized.

> So this was all there was to the great play
> She came so far to act in, this was all—
> Except the short last scene and the slow fall
> Of the final curtain, that might catch halfway,
> As final curtains do, and leave the grey,
> Lorn end of things too long exposed. The hall
> Clapped faintly, and she took her curtain call,
> Knowing how little she had left to say.

This finely wrought passage may contain the truth about Sara Teasdale, though one hopes not. It may be that she will never sing again, as she assures us in another cleanly chiselled lyric; and indeed, if there be nothing to sing about in this vast, impersonal cosmos, why sing even by way of announcing that one intends to quit?

But may it not well be that Sara Teasdale is now only beginning to discover how barren life is from the personal viewpoint; and may not the following wise and beautiful lines foretell the development of a deeper note?

Midsummer night without a moon, but the stars
In a serene bright multitude were there,
Even the shyest ones, even the faint motes shining
Low in the north, under the Little Bear.
When I have said, "This tragic farce I play in
Has neither dignity, delight nor end,"
The holy night draws all its stars around me,
I am ashamed, I have betrayed my Friend.

THE TRUTH ABOUT SMALL TOWNS

REVIEW OF *HOME TOWN SKETCHES*, BY EMILE PAILLOU (BOSTON: STRATFORD, 1926)

The steadily increasing flow of our rural population toward the cities has resulted in some curious literary phenomena that cannot be judged correctly by the majority of readers so long as the urban attitude continues to dominate the social mood of our time. One of the most conspicuous of these phenomena is what we know as "small town" literature. Ever since Gopher Prairie was laid out in the County of Nowhere and the State of Urban Myopia, it has been an easy matter for "clever" writers to attain some degree of "literary success" by playing up the small town of the Middle West in accordance with the fashionable pattern.[11] There is a curious notion abroad to the effect that just the fact of living in a city somehow renders one superior to people living in rural surroundings. The notion is one of the pitiful illusions of mob psychology. It is precisely the lower mentality that feels itself endowed with a greater importance when merged with the many; it is the rare intelligence that knows itself weakened and demeaned thereby. Small-town literature appeals to the urban mob mind. Its enjoyment is a form of urban narcissism. The truth about human nature does not change at the city limits, and the "small-town mind," which can mean nothing but the provincial mind, is to be found in both New York and Kokomo. As for the good and bad, the foolish and the wise, the mean and the generous, these are everywhere. The small town of recent American literature is a myth.

There have been a few true pictures of the Middle Western small town, but not one of them has achieved vogue, for obvious reasons. Easily the most remarkable of these has been written by a resident of St. Louis, Dr. Emile R. Paillou. *Home Town Sketches* seems almost too good to be true. It is composed of over 200 brief but surprisingly vivid pen portraits of outstanding village characters known to the author during his youth in Boonville, Mo. A generation has passed since Dr. Paillou left his old home town, and at that distance in time even the ordinary man is likely to see things "steadily and whole" and in their larger relations. Dr. Paillou's equipment is by no means ordinary. Everywhere in his wholly unpretentious work the genuine artist is revealed. He writes with love but not in blindness; and while the book has the superficial appearance of being fragmentary, little by little the reader realizes that a whole living community is being created before his eyes.

Wit and humor abound throughout the book. Profound human kindliness sweetens every page, yet there is never a touch of sentimentalism, no "slopping over" anywhere.

Mere facts may be ascertained and accurately recorded without love; but the larger truth about human beings is never to be apprehended by the loveless. In that direction lies the secret of Dr. Paillou's conspicuous success.

Genuine Realism

REVIEW OF *GOD GOT ONE VOTE*, BY FREDERICK HAZLITT BRENNAN
(NEW YORK: SIMON, 1927)

It is generally supposed that the present vogue for what we call realism in fiction is due to excessive enlightenment and a consequent "disillusionment." We are supposed to have become so thoroughly sophisticated by virtue of what we call modern progress that we can no longer be taken in by any highfalutin notions about human nature. Our temper is "scientific," whether or not we know anything about science; and most of us know little. The scientific spirit is in the air, and it does not occur to many of us that the general direction of contemporary science is determined, not by any intrinsic necessity in science as a method, but by the needs and desires of an age that is overwhelmingly commercial; that science, in an age not characterized by rapid commercial expansion, could easily take a very different direction in keeping with other dominant world interests, and that it would still be science.

As it is now, the scientific attitude reaches the millions in the form of a vague but nevertheless powerful materialistic persuasion—an unconsidered notion to the effect that sooner or later everything can be explained in terms of material mechanisms. In the realm of psychology this persuasion has resulted in an attempt to explain human personality wholly by muscular reactions to stimuli. The same fashion in thought has invaded even the realms of esthetics and ethics; but it is most noticeable and most effective in what passes for significant contemporary fiction.

Realism is the big word among our professional sophisticates; and the sort of realism they affect is a fragmentary factuality arrived at by analysis of pure sense perceptions. Since there is considerable difference between a human being and a hog, and since the essential difference is obviously not such as to be apprehended by any such method, it is not strange that typical modern "realism" should emphasize those aspects of the human animal which most nearly approximate hoggishness.

One of the most hopeful signs of the times is to be found in the increasing number of books that emphasize the necessity for a broadening of the term reality to include other values than those of the senses—the creative values, by virtue of which alone we are human. To relate values in a comprehensive synthesis is the prime business of the artist. Our vogue-ridden "realists" are not artists; they are, at best, scientists, and that in the narrowest possible sense of science. Analysis of pure sense data may achieve a more or less important collection of facts; but the truth about anything is synthetic.

In view of the prevalent narrow conception of realism, it is a notable achievement to have produced a novel of American life from the not very flattering angle of American politics in a broadly realistic manner, as Frederick Hazlitt Brennan has done in *God Got One Vote*. The tale begins back in the '90s when William Jennings Bryan was lifting the crown of thorns from the brow of labor, and ends in 1926.[12] It is a rich period for the novelist—the period in which the last frontier disappeared and in which the United States developed, with the inevitable aberrations of rapid change, from the status of a rather isolated agricultural nation to that of the greatest industrial power in the world.

The chief character is Patrick Van Hoos, an ex-hodcarrier, who, beginning as a ward heeler in a Middle Western city that will be identified with St. Louis, grows in wealth and power and becomes the political boss of the state, the maker of mayors and governors and senators. From the narrower viewpoint, the story is that of Patrick's rise in a rough-and-tumble democratic society; but when one closes the book, it is realized that a far more important story has been told than that of one man, his family, his friends, his enemies, his schemings, his triumphs and his failures. It is the story of a whole society that has somehow crept in through the pores of the personal record as one may say.

It is a big story, told in a big way with nothing of the distortion that readers have come to expect from novels of the sort. If the average "realistic" writer had undertaken to tell the same tale of Patrick's rise, Patrick, who trained with crooks and conscienceless schemers, would scarcely have been made likable. He would have been conventionalized into an abstract type such as never won love or loyalty. But in following the checkered career of Pat, as here set forth in the round, one remembers what Charles Lamb once said: "I can't hate a man I know." It is because the reader is made to know Pat Van Hoos as a complete human being that something like affection for him creeps in as the record grows. It is so with most of the characters of the book in proportion as they loom large or small in the tale; and yet not even the hard-boiled realist in the narrower sense of the moment could call the story sentimental.

In the telling of a tale that involves all the hotly argued public questions of over a generation, the author has managed to remain wholly objective—a rare feat as fiction goes just now. Nowhere does he enter the story with a thesis to defend or any ax of prejudice to grind. As the artist should, he contents himself with the construction of a representative world in which his characters live by the light that such as they would have in life; and none is wholly good or wholly bad, but all are intelligibly human.

Nevertheless, for those who care to find it, there is plenty of significant social criticism in the story—the sort of criticism that is not fault-finding or theory, but a sympathetic presentation of life in its significant relations. To present such a picture in such a way is equivalent to seeing as from a height of years, free from the distorting fogs of the moment. It is to see like a genuine realist.

God Got One Vote, is Mr. Brennan's first book. Whether or not it succeeds in a popular way—which is not at all unlikely—there is every reason to believe that Mr. Brennan will go far as a writer.

The Literary Bull Market (1928)

It is probable that occasional readers of this column may have been taking a more or less lively interest in the stock market during the great boom days that either are or are not drawing to a close. It has been a thrilling spectacle to see the blithe lambs gamboling with the bulls, while the frustrate bears looked on with the slaver of starvation dripping from their jaws. Also, it has been more than a trifle amusing to see the little boys all over the land playing at the big boys' game and running away with it in so high-handed a manner for awhile.

That was naughty of the little boys, one clearly understands. They should not have gotten the dangerous idea into their heads that one may achieve the sanctity of wealth in any other way than by humble industry and thrift. They should toil and skimp and save, as Mr. Rockefeller did.

And yet one can understand their grievous moral lapse. No doubt these little boys have been looking about them and wondering a good deal in their childish way. Perhaps in their ignorance it has even appeared to them that somehow to acquire is more noble than to produce, or at least a great deal more effective, though the opposite is still taught in certain quarters.

To cleanse one's hands of labor forever—how alluring in our blindness is that hope!

But it is not the moral aspect of the matter that need interest us here. What may well interest us is the lamentable confusion of values that has characterized the popular boom in securities. It has required no economic expert to note from day to day how stocks of relatively little or moderate value have soared to ridiculous price heights, while sound values were consistently overlooked.

In the conspicuous case of Bancitaly, rated as sound at its proper moderate valuation, the price was boosted to a point where its yield was barely one per cent, while strong securities, offering as much as seven times that yield, were listed at one-tenth the price—price here being the index of crowd appraisal.

This curious phenomenon is to be explained by the fact that while the vast buying crowd, actuated by a quite intelligible desire for gain, was composed of intelligent individuals, the bidding was not the expression of individual intelligence but of crowd contagion. Not an individual examination of values, but wild, crowd-sweeping rumor did the trick. "Everybody" was buying Bancitaly, it seemed; and it is the principal characteristic of crowds to act on the strange notion that if "everybody's doing it," it must be right. So powerful was this persuasion, as always in crowds, that even the voices of the experts were unheard and the repeated warnings of Bancitaly officials were without effect. A million intelligent men and women, fused into a mass and surrendering their individualities in the process, may easily become one huge fool.

Most readers will have foreseen the analogy that these remarks are intended to emphasize. There are other fields of value besides the economic; and in every field it will be found that the same truth holds. Whenever the crowd mentality gains control in any realm of values, the result is a ridiculous and a dangerous confusion.

For some years now we have been witnessing what may well be described as a popular bull market in literature; and to anyone with anything like a fair knowledge of literary values, the result has been astounding, to put it mildly. Now and then, as sometimes happens, even in a wild bull market, we have seen genuine literature bid high; but in every case of the sort it was to be noted that the crowd caught on, not through sound knowledge of the value involved, but because of a persistent crowd-sweeping rumor—generally contrived by deliberate publicity methods. "Everybody" was buying it!

Far more often we have seen the relatively, or quite, valueless book outrageously boomed, while other works of great beauty and power and universal meaning were "selling" at almost nothing at all. Not the rich and enduring dividend yield in understanding and human sympathy, but the artificially contrived goose-gabble of the many rules the market. And the saddest thing about the spectacle is that so many of the people who make up this crowd are capable of far better judgments as individual men and women.

It is easy enough to understand that if a man buys a stock, that yields nothing, at a ridiculously inflated appraisal, he is likely to suffer for his folly. Literary values are life values, or they are nothing. And what can we say for those who, surrendering to crowd contagion, bid up the false?

The Wisdom of Machines (1929)

Padraic Colum's alleged play entitled *Balloon* which was noted in this column yesterday, furnishes another striking example of a characteristic trend in modern literature and modern life.[13] That trend is concerned with the repudiation of form, of creative pattern, of vital meaning. Just as the organic social view of individual conduct in the realm of morals is considered passe by the intelligentsia and their dupes, so do our distinctly "modern" writers flout the old-fashioned idea that a piece of literature must be the organic product of a process of selection, rejection and integration to the end that a livable meaning, not to be found anywhere in the original unorganized data, may emerge.

Walter Lippmann's *A Preface to Morals* presents an illuminating discussion of the causes and consequences of this anarchic trend in the moral realm; and anyone who is familiar with the distinctly modernistic literature of the past decade should have no difficulty in naming many works in all fields of writing that illustrate the trend.[14] They range from the insane incoherence of Gertrude Stein and E. E. Cummings to the "stream of consciousness" type of fiction that is like nothing so much as a fever dream, and to those ponderous "realistic" novels that consist merely of a collection of unorganized data (preferably discreditable) of human life and conduct, with no attempt at interpretation of any sort.

It is readily granted that revolt against obsolete dogma, no longer supported by the sanction of human knowledge, may be justified; but to discard an obsolete pattern of life is not the same, surely, as trying to live with no pattern whatever. And the same is true in the matter of making literature, which, after all the twaddle has been twaddled, is interpretation of life.

In the anarchic mood incident to the discarding of dogmatic life-patterns that no longer serve, the typical "modern" man, in both living and literature, has leaped to the curious conclusion that there is something hopelessly wrong about the very idea of organic form, of creative pattern, of emergent meaning. He has not realized the basic fact in all human experience that all the meanings we have, ever have had or ever shall have, must be created by the human consciousness itself. Obviously, nothing can have meaning for us until we have interpreted it to ourselves. Meanings are mental patterns formed out of the apparently chaotic data of our experience by a process of selection, rejection and integration; and it is wholly by virtue of such mental patterns that we can live at all, not to mention living humanely.

This anarchic state of affairs is often attributed glibly to the fact that we are living in "the machine age"; and if one knows what one means, the explanation is correct. But it is not the machine, as such, that must be blamed. It is rather the inability of men, thus far, to use the power of machines with wisdom equal to that wisdom which is inherent in the very structure of machines.

If anyone wishes to see an overwhelmingly convincing objective representation of perfect sanity, of what organic form and creative pattern signify, of what intelligent selection, rejection and integration mean, let him contemplate a well-turned gasoline motor in action. As a matter of fact, our machines are infinitely wiser than our characteristically "modern" literature and our characteristically "modern" notion of life; and there is more downright intelligence under the greasy cap of many a mechanic than in all the heads of all our excessively "civilized" sophisticates.

Let us see what a typically "modern" "realistic" novelist might learn by studying the engine of the automobile that he drives every day. He will tell you that his novels are formless for the very good reason that human life is so, and that to represent it otherwise than as chaotic would be to lie about it. It is true, as anyone above the mentality of an idiot must often have observed with misgivings, that the facts of life, when viewed by an uncreative intelligence, are apparently a chaos. But with exactly the same justification it might be pointed out that an engine is a misrepresentation of the facts of matter and potential energy because the materials of which it was created by the process of selection, rejection and integration were originally in a chaotic state and widely scattered. It was by the application of a dynamic pattern to the chaos of material that the engine came into being; and the resultant flow of power under control is an "emergent value" exactly as the creative meaning of a great work of literature is, or the sanity and virtue of a well-lived life.

To organize the chaotic is not to falsify. On the contrary, it is the only method by which any livable human truth can be realized.

Some day our "modern" writers may become truly modern enough to catch up with the intelligence of our creative mechanics.

AN EXCHANGE OF ROLES (1929)

Among the many confusions of value that characterize the world-thought of our time, one of the most curious, and perhaps in significance the fundamental one, is the fact that the major trend in alleged poetry has ceased to be essentially poetic while science (generally supposed to be the direct opposite) has become decidedly so.

In considering poetry in this connection we should think of it not as a literary form to be contrasted with prose, but as that element in all genuine literature which distinguishes it from journalism in the strict sense. "Poetic" originally signified creative, and does yet for those who have achieved any understanding of the subject. Genuine literature is poetic in that it creates human values out of the chaotic data of the brute senses; and such creation can take place only in a higher, or perhaps one should say a more comprehensive state of consciousness than that which is sufficient for animal living.

In its Victorian period science was frankly "materialistic," and it worked upon the very useful assumption that everything might be explained in terms of matter moving, if the inquiry were only pushed far enough. "Matter" was then conceived naively as being just what the senses represented it to be—a solid substance which was the only "reality." The resultant world-view, if accepted, naturally played havoc with "spiritual" and "poetic" conceptions which, according to the scientific persuasion of the time, could have no "reality" since they could not be explained in terms of "matter," which was composed of hard little "billiard balls" called atoms.

In the intellectual realm, science, as then understood, triumphed because of its obviously marvelous practical success in mechanical invention. Literature, in keeping with the resultant world-view tended more and more to be "scientific"—the one thing no art can be and remain an art; that is to say, writers became "realistic," collecting and classifying sense data just as science was doing, and this with less and less human interpretation. This tendency is at present the most conspicuous one in our literature, which emphasizes the naïve sense view of human relations as the only view consistent with "reality." The result is to be noted in the cynicism and bestiality of so much writing that wins applause.

There is comedy in the situation, although our "advanced" literary people seem not to have suspected it as yet. The comedy consists in the fact that while literature was becoming "scientific," that is to say "materialistic" in the naïve sense, science was discarding the naïve sense view of the world and rediscovering the ancient awe that is vital in all poetic vision.

Not only our "sophisticated" novelists, but even, to a great extent, our poets so called, that is, those who practice verse writing, have more and more fallen into the way of celebrating the exclusive sense view of the world. Thus the original roles of Science and Literature have actually been exchanged. There is more revelation, in the strict poetic sense, more beauty and wonder and rhythmic pattern in the in the scientific structures of Einstein and Minkowski, Rutherford, Bohr and Planck than in all the thousands of volumes of "advanced literature" written in our generation.

Anyone who may doubt that any such exchange of roles has taken place should spend a few days reading A. S. Eddington's *The Nature of the Physical World,* which was noted once before in this column.[15] It offers a comprehensive discussion of the modern scientific world-view, and it inspires the hope that sooner or later our writers who believe themselves to be "realists' may tumble to the fact that they are hopelessly "Victorian" (a scornful epithet with them) in their notion of what is "scientific" and what is "real."

REALISM

REVIEW OF *AS THE EARTH TURNS,* BY GLADYS HASTY CARROL (NEW YORK: MACMILLAN, 1933)

Reference has been made in this column to a type of rural fiction which became fashionable some years back; a type in which the sophisticated urban consciousness complacently flattered itself by showing up the alleged meanness of life when spent in close contact with the one mother of us all.

Such fiction was, and still is, no doubt, highly commended by representative critics as "realistic," a term which in our addled time has come to signify the exact opposite of human reality; for the realistic view, in the curious present meaning of the expression, results from a limitation of the field of regard to mere sense perception and analysis thereof. But the reality that men can know and must live by is of a quality beyond mere sense perception; and, far from being revealed by analysis, human reality vanishes in the process; for it can exist only as a synthetic complexity of relations with all the resulting overtones of human experience which give life all the meaning that it has.

The difference between the false realism of current fashion and genuine realism is precisely the difference between a naïve scientific materialism (no longer held by scientists) and the poetic, that is to say, the synthetic, creative way of viewing the world (now scarcely the fashion with poets). It is the difference between analysis and synthesis, between factual science and art, between the seeking of reality in its disjointed parts and the seeking of reality where alone it may be found—in the living whole.

(Incidentally, it is of curious interest to note that while science has been rising toward the level of art in the higher sense, art has been falling toward the level of science in its lower and now discarded sense of naïve materialism).

The foregoing remarks have seemed essential to the consideration of one of the finest examples of genuine realism this reviewer has encountered in years. *As the Earth Turns* is the simple story of a farming family in Maine through the four seasons of a single year. In the usual sense of the word, it is hardly to be called a story, for there is no artificial plot; no problem is presented in the early chapters that is destined to be solved in the last; no one, after reading the book, could communicate his enthusiasm for it to another by telling "what happened." Any single event in the narrative might easily be regarded in itself as trivial. There is no artful building toward dramatic moments; there are no intense scenes to be cited as indications of the author's power. There is only the steady flow of life, and it is the growing sense of the mystery, the sad beauty and the greatness thereof, that make the book enthralling.

It is a routine life that old Mark Shaw, the father, lives, and the routine is that of day and night, the coming and the going of the seasons, the flowering and the fruiting and the resting of the earth that it may flower and fruit again. Ignorant in a worldly sense, he is unconsciously and profoundly wise in his perfect adaptation to the grand rhythms of life. There have been novels in which such characters were presented as symbolical figures; but Mark remains merely a man whom one might have as a neighbor and whom it would be good indeed to know.

Sons and daughters of differing temperaments have sprung up about him, and they must dream their dreams and go their ways. There are marriages and partings, births and deaths in his little world, but Mark does not thereby lose his imposing integrity as a character and become a pathetic figure as he ages; for his life has never been short-circuited within the self, as most lives are. There is nothing he can lose, for his is the continuous impersonal victory of complete surrender to the life force which he serves, although he is hardly more conscious of serving than is an apple tree.

But great as old Mark Shaw, the father, is, there is something in the character of Jen, the one home-keeping daughter, that may well seem greater to a man, although it is doubtless only the feminine aspect of the same unconscious wisdom that is Mark's. Surely the urban-minded "realist" could have made a sorry mess of Jen's apparently dull round of endless household duties. It would have been necessary only to play up all the baking, cooking, scrubbing, dish-washing and never-ending little services to others that constitute the outer appearance of Jen's life; but the living truth about her life would have been lost.

Curiously enough, it is in terms of just such details of an apparently sordid routine existence that the author presents the convincing and over-whelmingly glorious character of plain Jen Shaw. And, in achieving such a character, without the slightest resort to sentimental appeal, the author has performed what may be called the miracle of art. Jen is in possession of a great vital secret, as is her father; although neither is aware of ever having learned it or even of knowing it. It is the secret that many seers have attempted to reveal in such words as these: "If I lose myself, I find myself" but to know the words is not equivalent to knowing the secret as plain Jen knows it without knowing that she knows. Although she, too, is presented as a living woman and not as a symbolic figure, hers is the genius of the eternal woman, the mighty giver and conserver.

There is greatness in this book, for it reveals the enduring truth about the essential relations of men and women to the earth and to each other.

The resultant mood, when the book is closed, and the brooding over it begins, is that of a great poem. And, in saying as much, the reviewer has not forgotten that he has characterized the novel as a fine example of genuine realism. For poetry is a means of perceiving the larger patterns that are human truth and that endure for all the flux of things.

GREAT SKILL FOR WHAT?

REVIEW OF *ONLY THE FEAR*, BY LENORE G. MARSHALL (NEW YORK: MACMILLAN, 1935)

There can be no doubt about it—the majority of the best novels of the day are being written by women. Social philosophers might explain this quite obvious fact in a manner too easily misinterpreted as uncomplimentary to the ladies; but the wise women—and, though largely inarticulate, they abound as always—would be far from offended by the explanation; for they know a thing or two, in their patient way, of greater fundamental importance than anybody's literary masterpieces.

The social philosopher, then, would point out the fact that in our intensely materialistic, go-getting era, now apparently arrived at an impasse, the creative masculine forces, in the main, have been diverted into channels leading toward mastery of the physical world.

It is not too much to say that the realm of higher culture has become overwhelmingly a feminine province in our time. If one were to go into a thousand towns, he would find, in practically every instance, the immaterial values of the creative arts represented, if at all, by some women's organization. And this may be taken in general as a compliment to the ladies, however much the facts of leisure and of the dilettante spirit may have to do with the case.

In the normal, unconscious form of its greatest power, the social philosopher might suggest further, the genius of woman is instinctively self-forgetting. Through her children, she gives herself, spiritually and physically, to the continuing race. But in the realm of intellectual integrations, she is notoriously likely (far more so than man) to be intensely personal and to see the fragmentary as larger than the whole. No doubt the philosopher could find the compensation of a protective maternal value here.

This predilection for the personal and fragmentary vision is glaringly conspicuous in our contemporary fiction and poetry; and the overwhelmingly dominant interest in the literature of our time is clearly determined by the fundamental biological function of woman. Writers, publishers, moving picture producers prove conclusively in a practical way the point of these remarks.

The feminization of culture in our time has been so overwhelming as to result in the general unconsidered persuasion that woman, now "emancipated," has at last become as man—a curious left-handed compliment, indeed, and one that might well bring the knowing smile of a deep unuttered wisdom to many a well-loved face! Yet even our biologists, psychologists and educators have obliged the time-mood with quasi-scientific rationalizations of this persuasion.

But there is nothing historically new in all this. It has happened before in times of social disintegration; and in the past it has been a symptom, not of a developing cultural springtime, but of a cultural autumn. The great creative cultural eras have been masculine in temper.

When, out of the anarchy of our day, shall spring the integrating power of a new social conception, the vital meaning of what is here suggested is certain to be clarified.

Although occasioned by the reading of the brilliant novel here listed, these remarks apply to literally truck-loads of fiction that come to reviewers. Now and then some woman, unaffected by the moment and wise with the fundamental instinctive secret of her sex, writes a novel like those of Gladys Hasty Caroll or Pearl Buck or Alice Tisdale Hobart and a few others. Now and then, even less often, some male novelist presents life in its larger, impersonal relations that endure. But it is the intensely personal, fragmentary seeing, the cleverly brilliant, at best, but essentially shallow fiction, with an infinitely wearying emphasis upon the merely erotic aspect of sex, that predominates.

Only the Fear, Lenore Marshall's first book, is technically a masterpiece. It might be contended with good reason that she writes with greater skill, in certain respects, than any of the woman novelists above mentioned. She can flash a vivid picture with surprisingly few words, and her insights are astonishingly canny. But when this tale of an idle wife's erotic titillations was finished, one reviewer felt that he had wasted his time; for it didn't seem to matter much save, perhaps, as a clinical examination of a morbid mind. Maybe that is enough, and maybe the admirable skill employed somehow justifies the effort.

But how this fuddled world does need the large, clear, integrated seeing of the sane!

4
OF MAKING MANY BOOKS

TEN

The Glow of the Moment

Neihardt loved a good book, and he delighted in sharing his discoveries with his readers. He was well qualified to suggest a feast of reading, for the number of books that passed through his hands numbered in the thousands (his personal library contained over five thousand volumes; in his work as reviewer he examined more than twenty-five hundred books). He considered his responsibilities to go beyond a display of titles, however, and in his columns he attempted to let his readers know what they might expect to find between the covers of a book. Sometimes he is in line with contemporary critical opinion, as when he praises the work of Dorothy Parker or young F. Scott Fitzgerald; sometimes he is out of step, as when he champions some obscure title, lauds a work that has been overwhelmingly panned, or challenges the reputation of even the most respected of his contemporaries.

Not all of the books that Neihardt recommended were selected because they qualify as enduring literature: Cyclone Denton's sincere reminiscences can be appreciated by lovers of the American West; Kahlil Gibran's writing contains food for the spirit; Erich Maria Remarque's *All Quiet on the Western Front* is eloquent in its evocation of suffering.

According to Neihardt, criticism is not a vehicle for the venting of personal likes or dislikes; rather, it is a place for examining a piece of writing in light of one's critical standards. The effort a writer puts into a work is deserving of careful consideration and respect, and the work examined is deserving of judgment on its own terms, not in how it stacks up against the latest "clamorously celebrated wheeze."[1]

Fitzgerald Again

REVIEW OF *FLAPPERS AND PHILOSOPHERS*, BY F. SCOTT FITZGERALD (NEW
YORK: SCRIBNER'S, 1920)

When *This Side of Paradise* appeared a few months ago, it scored an
immediate success, both with the discerning critics and with the crowd.[2]
The enthusiasm that it aroused among the cognoscenti would seem to
indicate that its author is a genius; for Mr. Fitzgerald is still in the early
20s, and the normal man in the 20s is certainly not conspicuous for that
understanding of the complex motives of men and women, without which
a distinguished work of fiction cannot be produced. On the other hand, the
popular success may be explained by the youthful outlook of the author;
for the crowd never grows up. If Mr. Fitzgerald continues to develop,
he will necessarily outgrow the crowd, appealing more and more to the
select minority whose judgment is likely to be prophetic of the attitude of
posterity.

However, there comes a time in the life of every developing man of
unusual powers when he must choose between the higher and the lower
values. It is the old story of Satan and the high mountain and the kingdoms
of the earth. The situation calls for both wisdom and heroism. With
magazine editors bidding for his work, Mr. Fitzgerald is already standing
on the mountain. What will he say to his companion?

This young author's second volume, *Flappers and Philosophers,* has all the
uncanny wisdom and the exuberant vitality of the first book. It contains
eight short stories collected from various magazines. The first, "An Offshore
Pirate," is a comic opera without the score. Probably every spoiled "flapper"
has dreamed luxuriously of love on a tropical island, and here is that dream
made into a tale by a young philosopher. "Dalyrimple Goes Wrong" is
essentially a laughing criticism of prevailing social ideals, and has a light
touch of cynicism that is healthy, and shows how well the author can see the
obvious—generally the last thing seen by the average person. It sets forth
the experiences of a war hero who, after being for several months the darling
of his home town, is at length forced to go to work at uninteresting wages.
As a result of some whimsical and lucrative adventures in burglary, he gets
a glimpse of what seems to him to be the efficient philosophy of life, and
at length, thanks to the new stimulus, becomes state senator. "The Four
Fists" should be read by every man with a touch of the cad in him—that
is to say every man. The hero of this wise and diverting yarn goes through
four distinct stages of development, each culminating in a sharp blow from
the fist of some outraged fellow mortal. As a result of this strenuous course
in the art of living, the hero finally comes to appreciate the other fellow's

viewpoint. This, we take it, is Mr. Fitzgerald's contribution to the theory of higher education.

Those who remember the early years of Robert W. Chambers' career are likely to note some similarity in Mr. Fitzgerald's start. Chambers surrendered to the lower values—and certainly he has his reward.

AN EXCELLENT BIOGRAPHY

REVIEW OF *GEORGE ELIOT AND HER TIMES*, BY ELIZABETH HALDANE (NEW YORK: APPLETON, 1927)

It is quite probable that if the name of George Eliot were pronounced to 10,000 people of average intelligence, with the understanding that each was to set down his first response thereto, in 9000 cases the first flash of thought would include a more or less vague sense of something "shady" about the lady's morals. It would be mingled with a compensating sense of greatness, in most cases unrelated to any very definite knowledge of the lady's achievements; but the moral shadow would be there, in most instances, however vaguely felt. Such is the curious thing called fame, against which so many philosophers have spoken eloquently—in the hope of attaining it.

Perhaps some will take up this study of a great woman with the unconfessed but nevertheless active hope of finding something entertainingly scandalous therein. And the hope seems not unreasonable, considering the prevalence of Freudian "criticism." No doubt, by means of an adroit isolation of certain facts in George Eliot's life and a clever misinterpretation of passages selected from her works, something juicy could be invented. But Elizabeth Haldane was evidently concerned with George Eliot and what she did, not with any desire to impress the reader with her own superior brilliance. The result will prove a sad disappointment for the sensationalists.

What we have here is a full length portrait, evidently drawn with scientific accuracy against the background of a period vividly realized. There are no temperamental highlights and shadows cast by the biographer's personality. Hers are the clarity of detail and the firmness of line that characterize a Holbein drawing; and the book is left with the feeling that one has seen George Eliot very much as she was in life.

But it is not to be inferred that the work is merely factual and scholarly, and therefore dull. The stuff with which Miss Haldane has worked is in itself fascinating and it is evident that she has brooded long and lovingly over it, seeking out those subtle relationships which alone gave life and meaning to facts.

The study begins with an examination of the social situation of the novelist's time and a comparison of our own persuasions with those then in vogue. In the examination of her subject's childhood and young womanhood, the biographer reads no prophetic meanings into trivial details, as is so often done. There are vivid chapters on early literary associations and efforts, when the future novelist had no thought of ever writing fiction, but regarded herself as a critic and translator. A chapter is given to the discussion of each of the novels and one to the poetry.

As to George Eliot's private life, it appears that if there was ever a woman who lived consistent on the highest moral plane and was piously wedded, it was she. Far from being a shady affair, her life with George Lewes seems to have been one of the most conspicuous examples of a perfect union on record. It was through no fault of theirs that a sane law governing divorce should have been tardily enacted; and it is significant that, as soon as the new law went into effect, the marriage that had then been a beautiful fact for some years, was duly solemnized in the most conventional manner. The idea of "free love" never was involved in the relationship, as no doubt many still suppose. As a matter of fact, George Eliot's attitude toward sex relationships would now be considered exceedingly straight-laced.

As to religious views, George Eliot, deemed unorthodox in her time and occasionally described as an "atheist," would now seem no more terrible than a Modernist of the milder type. She believed in Science, but was aware that what is deepest in human experience is not to be explained by the scientific method. She was unquestionably sincere, as her life proved, when she spoke of "one comprehensive Church whose fellowship consists in the desire to purify and ennoble human life, and where the best members of all narrower Churches may call themselves brother and sister in spite of differences." It was the Church in which she worshiped both by words that live and deeds that are good to remember.

An Old-Timer Remembers
REVIEW OF *A TWO-GUN CYCLONE*, BY B. E. (CYCLONE) DENTON
(DALLAS: DENTON, 1927)

When one who has lived in the golden age of he-men find himself an old-timer of seventy in a modern city with only a pick and shovel wherewith to meet the wolves of need, it is no wonder that he should remember the glory that was his youth and the grandeur that was a world unspoiled. B. E. Denton of Dallas is in that predicament. He is only B. E. Denton now, but once he was "Cyclone" Denton in the good old days before they fenced in "God's own country" and began to plow it up.

Denton was born down on Hog Creek in Texas, "and proud of it," says he. His father before him was an old-timer in that country. It was shortly after the close of the Civil War that the boy set out on "Old Hoss Topsy" and began those rovings which were to lead him all over the Old West in pursuit of something that, he tells us, was never to be found by the longest journey and is still a tantalizing mystery to him. He has trailed long-horns out of the Staked Plains up into the valleys of the Powder and the Big Horn. He has killed thousands of bison and fought Indians and roped wild stallions. He has mixed with bad men and hobnobbed with the famous characters of the West. He saw the fading out of the old frontier and participated in the Oklahoma rush. The years have passed like a Kansas twister, as it seems to him now, and the world is changed beyond all recognition. There is no longer any chance for a first class two-gun man to make his way with honor. "Teague," his old pal, has been dead these many years, and "Old Hoss Topsy" perished in the last great stampede for homesteads.

He who once moved blithely through a heroic world, bearing the proud name of "Cyclone," now wields a pick and shovel.

So there is nothing to do but remember, and in this book the old-timer "remembers out loud." Grammar never bothered him much and neither did spelling; but the story he tells is good to hear, nevertheless.

"Old Hoss Topsy" is really the chief character, and he seems to have been a stout-hearted hero indeed. He was little more than a colt when his young master began to rove. He was 20 years old when he was killed, and he had borne his master through many tight places from the Brazos to the Yellowstone and from Kentucky to Santa Fe.

First it was "Teague," the beloved comrade, who died with his boots on, and then it was "Topsy" that got rubbed out; and after that the evil days set in for good.

There isn't much "literary" quality in "Cyclone" Denton's reminiscences, but the narrative should hold any reader who is genuinely interested in the Old West. Let us hope that 10,000 copies of the book may sell. Then the pick and shovel may be given a long rest.

Hurrah for Dorothy

REVIEW OF *SUNSET GUN*, BY DOROTHY PARKER (NEW YORK: BONI, 1928)

Somewhere beneath the most audacious flippancies of Dorothy Parker there is an extremely sensitive and serious person—one who has felt too deeply for comfort the ironies of life. She has all the equipment necessary for an exquisite lyrical poet, as she very often proves, sometimes, by flashes, even in her most abandoned satirical moods. Her characteristic product seems to be the result of a conflict between a deep love for spiritual values and a disillusioned sense of their practical futility in a world conspicuously given over, for the moment at least, to blatant animalism. One often feels in reading her verses that she was about to weep when she remembered what sort of world she was in, and so shifted suddenly to hilarious laughter. Perhaps we should have had a feminine counterpart of A. E. Housman but for the accidents of time and place. She [seems] Housman's spiritual sister, [ill] at ease in a shallowly cynical, wisecracking generation. . . .

A Book by a Seer

REVIEW OF *JESUS, THE SON OF MAN*, BY KAHLIL GIBRAN (NEW YORK: KNOPF, 1928)

It is probable that anyone who has sincerely appreciated Kahlil Gibran's work, both in writing and in drawing, will be inclined to suspect that his is one of the finest spirits now among us. In all of his six books, including one devoted entirely to drawings, there is to be felt a strange white light of vision that transfigures common things. This statement sounds like twaddle, no doubt; but something very definite is meant. Often in reading Gibran, or in poring over his drawings, there come moments when the hard and life-denying surfaces of things seem to thin and flow like gauzy veils, revealing unsuspected verities beyond. And this, too, may sound like twaddle; but give yourself whole-heartedly to Gibran for awhile, and see.

Jesus has been having quite a literary vogue of late, but it is not in the spirit of the vogue that Gibran writes of Him. Surely no other now writing in America is better gifted in all ways to realize the deeper meaning of the Christ story than is Kahlil Gibran, the Syrian.

The scheme itself of *Jesus the Son of Man* is illuminating, even though not a word of the text be read. It is based upon a fact that is the source of all our human confusions—the fact that all light from without breaks upon the understanding of each one of us as through a refracting medium, and the color the light we see is determined largely by the angle of refraction that is ours. Here Jesus is beheld, not as some absolute Understanding might comprehend Him, but in many ways as many men and women of widely varying temperament and experience could have judged Him. Seventy-nine such fragmentary and distorted views are here set forth. It is as though all had looked at white sunlight, each seeing no more than some variation of the seven split-up rays. Each of the 79 speaks, certain that he or she is revealing Jesus as He was, and what each reveals is self.

Strange discords and stranger music break from the text as the voices of the witnesses change, and there are many outbursts of the true lyric fury such as few poets in any generation ever achieve.

As in the former books of Gibran, the text is supplemented with drawings. They are not illustrations of the text, but rather illuminations of the informing mood.

The Heart of Hun

REVIEW OF *ALL QUIET ON THE WESTERN FRONT*, BY ERICH MARIA REMARQUE (BOSTON: LITTLE, 1929)

Many reviewers who, in keeping with the habit of a publicity-driven people, have been proclaiming book after book as positively the this-est and the that-est and the other-est, must feel considerably embarrassed when they come upon a work like *All Quiet on the Western Front*. Not because it, at last, is really and truly the this-est or the that-est or the anything-else-est. Contrary to a going notion, things don't have to "beat" other things in order to be of great value in themselves. The chronic screamers and shouters among the critical gentry should be embarrassed before such a book, because its peculiar merits deserve some emphasis, and they have long since exhausted their stock of emphatic language. All they can do under the circumstances is to strive to emit a more strident howl than heretofore, and that being impossible, they are likely to achieve a hysterical falsetto. This note is to be detected in much of the comment. "Greatest," "supreme" are among the epithets that are being hard worked, and one authority remarks: "I regard any mature reader who has a chance to read this book and does not, and who, having read it, does not pass it on among a dozen others, as a traitor to humanity!" That's telling 'em!

But what a pity it seems that it is no longer possible to achieve emphasis by descending in the scale of noise! It is probably true that *All Quiet on the Western Front* would not, in that case, deserve the profound and reverent silence appropriate to enduring masterpieces of the human spirit, but it would deserve a rather low-toned and well-modulated voice; for it is undoubtedly a very fine thing of its kind, conceived in suffering and written with the simple eloquence of a deep sincerity that cannot possibly be faked.

The book has been advertised as a novel, wholly without reason, unless the fact that the author calls himself Paul Baumer in the narrative and gives fictitious names to his buddies would justify the description. There is no plot of any sort. That is what makes the war experiences of the author and his comrades so overpowering. So far as they are able to understand, the whole bloody, muddy, filthy, lousy, cruel business is as patternless as a nightmare and utterly without meaning. Somewhere or other at the center of the human social scheme there's simply nobody home, and these youngsters, who are flung into the hell of acute social insanity before they have whiskers enough for a razor, come to know as much. "We are forlorn like children, and experienced like old men. We are crude and sorrowful and superficial— I believe we are lost." That's the tragic point in the book; not the mere suffering and dying of men, but the suffering and dying for no human purpose.

Yet there is no railing at the scheme. There is only the dogged prosecution of the incomprehensible business in hand, the heroic struggle with weariness and hunger and terror and hopelessness.

The book stands out among war books not because it presents more of the brutalities of war and so is more shocking, more sensational than the others. The distinguishing difference is not at all quantitative; it is the quality of the spirit that suffered and remembers here that makes the book notable. There is nowhere any obvious attempt at eloquence, and yet out of the quality of the spirit that recalls its suffering there emerges a peculiarly impressive eloquence.

For example, note the fine passage in which the terrified child of Earth cries out to the mother of all men. There's no affectation in it. And the passage in which Detering, the simple-hearted farmer lad, listens to the screaming of a troop of shell-torn horses. "It's unendurable. It is the moaning of the world, it is the martyred creation, wild with anguish filled with terror and groaning."

Over and over throughout the book this distinguishing spiritual quality emerges—in the description of the night in a shell-hole under fire and the stabbing of the Frenchman; in the appalling narrative of the night in the graveyard under shell-fire; in the description of the raw recruits with "their pale turnip faces, their pitiful clenched hands, who are so terrified that they dare not cry out loudly, but with battered chests and torn bellies and arms and legs only whimper for their mothers."

It's a book worth reading, and if only yelling can sell it in great quantities, then more power to the sorely strained throats of the yelling fraternity. It has recreated for one reader, at times, something of the mood that is in Aeschylus and Sophocles; and perhaps, after all, to say as much ever so quietly is a kind of yelling.

The author, Erich Maria Remarque, is a German citizen of French descent. He is now 31 years old, having entered the war at the age of 18, on the German side, of course. In the original German the book is entitled, *Im Westen Nichts Neues,* evidently an ironical use of a common expression in the official communiqués of the time. A bit more irony might have been injected into the title for us over here had the English translation been called "The Heart of a Hun."

An Oklahoma Epic

REVIEW OF *THE RANGE CATTLE INDUSTRY*, BY EDWARD EVERETT DALE
(NORMAN: UNIVERSITY OF OKLAHOMA PRESS, 1930)

Each new volume that comes from the University of Oklahoma Press tends to deepen the impression that nowhere in the country is a genuine American culture more conspicuously in flower than at Norman, OK. Were it not for the fear of appearing to exaggerate, thus dulling the fine edge of a heartening truth, one might well venture to use the superlative in this connection. Centering about the University and its Press there is a very considerable group of gifted and accomplished men and women over there who are working creatively with a fine spirit of youthful enthusiasm that is not to be felt in any of the older centers. A goodly percentage of these workers came from Eastern universities, but if they were ever infected with the disease of degenerate European sophistication that now passes for cultural health in fashionable literary circles, the clean winds of the spacious country of their adoption have purified them. They love their new home, its people and its heroic traditions, and they are building nobly out of the rich stuff of their environment. Those who are not yet aware of what is being done at Norman would do well to write the University Press for information.

Dr. Edward Everett Dale, head of the history department at the university, is one of the more conspicuous members of the Norman group. He was born in Texas 51 years ago, and in addition to having lived the life of a pioneer on the vast plains, he is a graduate of Harvard and has done much important research work for the Bureau of Agricultural Economics. In Norman he is sometimes affectionately called "the cowboy professor"— but no cheapening sensationalism is to be read into the description. For some years during his young manhood—to be explicit, as far back as 1896— he was a cowboy, and happily he has retained the character of the old-time plainsman while pursuing scholarly interests. It is this rare combination of scholarship and practical knowledge of the cattle industry that has made possible the present fine study of a subject not hitherto treated in a comprehensive manner.

Although the work is evidently based upon years of research, the result is by no means a dull book even from the average intelligent reader's point of view. It is a great story that Dr. Dale has undertaken to tell, and even though much of it is of necessity told in terms of statistics, the resultant mood is that of high adventure. Beginning with the close of the Civil War, the author follows, year by year, the expansion of the cattle business northward in the wake of the vanishing bison herds and traces the history of the great cattle trails and turbulent "cow towns" that sprang up along the westering railroads, throve mightily for a few years and died into dull respectability.

Like all the books of the University of Oklahoma Press, this one is handsomely made.

REVIEW OF *SACAJAWEA*, BY GRACE RAYMOND HEBARD (GLENDALE CA: CLARKE, 1933)
For nearly a century after Lewis and Clark returned to St. Louis, Sacajawea, the Shoshone Indian woman who served as guide and interpreter of the expedition, was little more than a name, even to students of Western history. She was that "one of the wives of Charboneau" who was "delivered of a fine boy" while the party was with the Mandans, and who "also accompanied us with her young child." References to "the Indian woman" or to "Bird Woman" (which was not her name) or to "Charboneau's squaw" are scattered throughout the several journals of the expedition, and it is made clear that she won a peculiar respect from the party of white men, as well as their gratitude for valuable service rendered.

The St. Louis Exposition of 1904 aroused a new interest in the Shoshone woman, beginning with the search for a suitable model for the statue of Sacajawea to be erected at the gates of the exposition grounds. Nevertheless, to the vast majority of us who have thought of her at all since then, she has remained the Indian mother, forever young in a preserving atmosphere of romantic sentiment.

But Sacajawea did not cease to live after the brief moment of her youthful glory. There were 80 years of life still left to her after that day among the Mandans when she first broke into history by being "delivered of a fine son." Surely, considering the character she revealed during the few years when the spotlight of history fell upon her, what happened to her during those eight decades of obscurity ought to be of genuine human interest. Readers of Dr. Hebard's study will agree that it is so indeed.

Dr. Grace Raymond Hebard, who is professor of political economy at the University of Wyoming, has for a generation pursued her researches in Western history with the patient devotion of love, and all students in that field are deeply indebted to her. Her history of the Bozeman Trail and the Red Cloud War (written in collaboration with Brininstool) is likely to prove the last word on the subject, and she has made other important contributions, notably her study of Washakie, the great Shoshone chief.[3]

One who had spent much time on the period of Red Cloud was astonished at the wealth of original material in her *Bozeman Trail;* but her *Sacajawea* seems even more astonishing. To follow the experiences of an Indian woman through nearly 80 years of obscurity would appear impossible; but Dr. Hebard has succeeded to a very remarkable degree, and it is hardly likely that anything of importance can ever be added to her record. She tells us that her researches into the life of Sacajawea have extended through 30 years, and some of her most interesting material was discovered abroad.

And what a story it is, even in the carefully documented matter-of-factness of the record as the author presents it! And how much more may the sympathetic reader feel between the patiently assembled facts! For Sacajawea was the heroine of Odyssean wanderings and vicissitudes, courageous and respected to the last.

Windstorms of the Spirit

REVIEW OF *AN UPTON SINCLAIR ANTHOLOGY*, COMPILED BY I. O. EVANS

(NEW YORK: FARRAR, 1934)

Several years ago, many admirers of Upton Sinclair, in practically all the nations of the Western world, joined in a movement to obtain the Nobel Prize for him. Doubtless, had that very remarkable effort succeeded, Sinclair could and would have made excellent social use of the cash involved, devoting it to propaganda against the social order that made possible the giving of the prize.

But it is difficult for at least one of his old and still faithful admirers, who felt somewhat abashed by the movement, to see how, in reality, anything more than cash was involved; and Sinclair is notoriously no mercenary man. For a quarter of a century and more, he has not lacked recognition, and he is more widely read in numerous translations abroad than at home.

Nothing could have been added to his significance by awarding a large money prize to him; and surely the notion that the award of the largest money prize to a man somehow increases his stature, or that it "honors" him more than does the sincere appreciation of any unknown reader anywhere, is a bit naïve. Greatness is qualitative wholly, and is unmeasurable by any quantitative means. The spiritual stature of Ivan Bunin was unaffected by the Nobel Prize award, as was the significance of Thomas Hardy by the failure to receive it.[4]

That there is real greatness in Upton Sinclair, after making generous allowance for all adverse criticism, ought to be apparent to any fair-minded reader after spending several hours with the anthology here listed. Even those who, for one reason or another, have developed a strong prejudice against the man and his work, are likely to experience a revelation in the reading of this book, even, perhaps, without ceasing to dislike that upon which the prejudice is based. For when the book is closed at last and the brooding over it begins, surely it is a rarely bright and valiant spirit that emerges, one endowed with tremendous energies that for more than a generation have been devoted to furthering human welfare.

The volume is divided into two sections, the first being devoted to such extracts from the author's various works as seemed to the editor fairly representative of Sinclair as a literary artist. The second section represents the Socialist philosopher and reformer. There was no intention of presenting "the best" extracts, and anyone fairly familiar with the author's voluminous writings—comprising nearly 50 books and four or five times as many pamphlets and articles—will doubt that a half-dozen other Sinclair anthologies of equal merit could easily be compiled.

It is probable that most readers of Upton Sinclair seldom, if ever, think of him as a poet; but, after musing over this volume awhile, it should become clear that poetic vision, in the true sense that is but little understood for all the talk about poetry, forms the burning central core of all his interests. To those familiar only with such works as *The Profits of Religion, The Brass Check, The Goose Step*, etc., he may well seem an industrious collector of facts, the uninspired and often provoking literalist.[5] But back of all his books is the true Dionysian fury of the poet with his driving dream of human welfare. . . .

In other times, and under the influence of other interests, Sinclair, as a result of such experience, occasionally repeated throughout his life, might have become known as "a God-intoxicated man," a seer of the "other world." But, by virtue of temperament and early encounters with social injustice and deprivation, the focus of that light within him burns white upon the world of men about him.

There are various ways of fulfilling the poet's destiny. It may be done, and has been, in the form of saintly living; in the building of beautiful and harmonious patterns in words or sounds; in martyrdoms for great, enduring principles; or in any of the many modes there are of throwing oneself away for something felt as being far greater than oneself.

Upton Sinclair's old friend, George Sterling, fulfilled his destiny by singing greatly the strange vision that was his—of interstellar spaces and the littleness of man.[6] Sinclair has striven to build his poem, not with singing words, although his words can sing gloriously upon occasion; but in the very stuff of everyday reality that men must live with. He has created works of art, but not "for art's sake"; always as propaganda for a better human world—for man's sake.

Sinclair has often been accused of lacking a proper sense of humor, and in the pursuit of new ideas, as, for instance, health fads, he has sometimes seemed to deserve the accusation. Even in the prosecution of his social aims, perhaps, his sense of humor seems often less than perfect. But the power of the man grows characteristically out of the utter loss of self in that which appears to him important. As in his initial experience of illumination, he is swept along by a "windstorm of the spirit."

It is the self-conscious man who is careful never to misplace his sense of humor. Greatness is not afraid of ridicule, for the self is lost in moments of greatness. Nevertheless, there is plenty of humor in this anthology, when the "windstorms of the spirit" have blown by and left the mood of calm reflection.

Few writers of the day can have covered so wide a range of ideas as one finds here; and they are all interrelated, forming a consistent, comprehensive philosophy of man's relation to man and his possible relation to the universe. A list of headings will serve to indicate the book's wide scope: Art, Love, Science, Industry, Wild Nature, Religion, History, Toil, The Outcast, Revolt, Martyrdom, Christ and the Church, Country, Humor, The Poet, Socialism, and The New Day.

It seems scarcely likely that any book of the year can greatly surpass this one, either as a source of intellectual stimulus, or of pure delight on the higher levels of human interest.

WELLS AT 67

REVIEW OF *EXPERIMENT IN AUTOBIOGRAPHY*, BY H. G. WELLS (NEW YORK: MACMILLAN, 1934)

Having attained the age of 67, and having said more in print than all but very few indeed of his contemporaries, H. G. Wells finds himself "in a phase of fatigue and of that discouragement which is a concomitant of fatigue." He wants "peace of mind" that he may say yet a great deal more in print and presumably of a different quality. For, in looking back over his voluminous writings, he confesses: "It scarcely needs criticism to bring home to me that much of my work has been slovenly, haggard and irritated, most of it hurried and inadequately revised, and some of it white and pasty in its texture as a starch-fed nun. I am tormented," he continues, "by a desire for achievement that overruns my capacity and by a practical incapacity to bring about for myself the conditions under which fine achievement is possible."

Yet here we have another book of 700 closely printed pages, and one which, by the author's confession, was written with the old headlong haste that he rightly deplores.

"The habit," he remarks, "is ingrained. I had meant to loiter over this autobiography for years—and perhaps not publish it in the end. I sketched an opening for it two years ago. And here it is being pressed to a finish."

Well?

There is good reason for admiring, in many respects, this geyser of human energy that has been prodigiously in action for the better part of a generation; but the following suggestions seem pertinent. First, if a man should note any slowing down at the age of 67, the fact is hardly remarkable enough to justify discussing it with the world at large. Second, if, after a generation of constant outpourings, a writer feels sincerely convinced that his work has been in a large measure "slovenly," "haggard," "irritated," "inadequately revised," not to mention "white and pasty," he might just as well call it a day and let his ego have a well-deserved rest; for the desired miracle is simply not going to happen. Any man's essential quality dominates his activities in the heyday of his powers.

The obvious fact is that H. G. Wells has done enough for a half-dozen men of extraordinary gifts, and certainly he will die no debtor to the world, regardless of posterity's estimate of him, if posterity remembers him at all. His contribution to the ferment of ideas in his day has been very notable, even if nothing but his *Outline of History* were considered—and how much more there has been![7] For this reason, it is not improbable that some of his admirers here and there will read certain portions of this new volume with impatience, to put it mildly.

Mr. Wells explains that, because of this fatigue which he has noticed and his alleged belief that his work has been as described, he has undertaken to tell the story of his life in the hope of thus clarifying his mental atmosphere, presumably in the hope of getting a fresh start at the age of 67. But if this were the real reason for writing the book, would the end be furthered by publication?

Mr. Wells' voluminous discussion of himself is prefaced by what purports to be a frank consideration of the quality of his brain and body. "The brain upon which my experiences have been written," he observes, "is not a particularly good one. If there were brain shows, as there are cat and dog shows, I doubt if it would get even a third-class prize. Upon quite a number of points it would be marked below the average, and I believe that its defects are mainly innate. It was not a good brain to begin with."

As for his physical handicaps, among other things he remarks: "My head is small—I can cheer up nearly every one of my friends by just changing hats; the borrowed brim comes down upon my ears and spreads them wide—my heart has an irregular beat and I suspect that my carotid arteries do not branch so freely and generously into my grey matter as they might do. I do not know whether it would be of any service after I am dead to prepare sections of my brain to ascertain that." And so forth.

If this be wholly candid, should he not be astonished and delighted with the work he has managed to do, rather than discouraged? What in the name of horse sense has one a right to expect from a third-class brain? And if a third-class brain has failed to get first-class results, the phenomenon is hardly to be regarded as world news.

The suspicion that Mr. Wells may know, quite as well as do his readers, that his "brain" is not so poor as he says, obtrudes at various points in the book. For a man who sincerely believes his brain to be "third-class" is not likely to tackle such intellectual jobs as Mr. Wells habitually tackles. Toward the end of the volume he seems to have forgotten about his alleged cerebral inferiority when he remarks: "The particular brain whose ups and downs and beatings about in the world you have been following in this autobiography, has arrived at the establishment of the Socialist world-state as its directive purpose and has made that its religion and end." What a purpose for a consciously third-class mind!

But aside from the faint flavor of fatuity that obtrudes and the regrettable rationalization of the desire to talk at great length about no less a man than H. G. Wells, his work and his dreams, the book is decidedly worth reading, as the man's other books have been, and for the same reason—that it is the outpouring of a restlessly questing, far from ungullible, but always brilliant, mentality.

In other words, when that geyser spouts, the result is, at least, an exciting spectacle, and often very much more.

It would be useless to attempt anything like a "review" of such a book. As for the contents in general, it is enough to say that, beginning with his earliest memories of a rather wretched childhood, Wells undoubtedly strives to "tell all," and quite as undoubtedly he gets a big kick out of his exhibition. There are moments in the book when, not without nostalgic yearnings, one remembers that there used to be a virtue called reticence. The approach is, of course, at all times highly scientific, and the somewhat belated materialist is always in evidence, as for instance, in the case of the "brain" examination.

Throughout the book, as throughout the whole personality, there is a conspicuous lack of awareness of the imponderable, which is the vital stuff in the pattern of human reality. The lack is to be noted often in his books. It was revealed in his absurd comments on Greek poetry in the later editions of the *Outline*. It is apparent in his peculiarly loveless discussion of his mother and father and of his childhood memories in the present volume.

And that he is proud of the lack, not knowing it for a lack, is very clearly indicated. When he expresses his scorn for the "esthetic valuation of literature," he unwittingly exposes what is perhaps the chief infirmity of his brilliant mind. Thus he rationalizes the lack into a virtue: "I write as I walk, because I want to get somewhere, and I write as straight as I can, because that is the way to get there."

To get where, and why the rush? It is neither by going nor by hurrying that the vital spiritual understanding may be overtaken in a universe that even the physicists have come to conceive as somehow qualitative. This brilliant, powerful, courageous twentieth century mind, with its eager reachings into the future, has nineteenth century furnishings.

ELEVEN

Impeccably Unremarkable

Neihardt wrote some of his most entertaining prose as invective against the vapid, the sentimental, the insincere. He was never unkind in reviewing a work he felt was produced by genuine effort, but when he was up against what he believed to be pretentious posturing or a lack of integrity, the attack could be deadly. He had this to say about a recently published book by Edmund Wilson: "There is nothing at all wrong with the book, except, perhaps, that it might well be entirely rewritten on a very different theme by some other author with a better understanding."[8]

For those books that represented genuine effort but just didn't quite measure up to his critical standards, Neihardt was generally kind, sometimes pointing out how the work could be improved, sometimes damning with faint praise, sometimes expressing confusion or frustration at not being able to "get at the fine feast"—for example, when reading the poetry of Ezra Pound. We need never guess, however, where Neihardt stands regarding a book discussed in his column.

Any evaluation is subject to error and misinterpretation, but Neihardt worked to tie his criticisms to standards rooted in a shared tradition to mitigate the arbitrariness of personal opinion. His negative assessments of writers like Ernest Hemingway, Robert Frost, E. E. Cummings, Gertrude Stein, and James Joyce were often at odds with those of his contemporaries. Though occasionally his explanations are less than satisfactory—for example, when he dismisses several chapters of a book devoted to "upstarts and freaks"—more often his discussion details his objections based on clear critical standards.[9]

A New England Poet

REVIEW OF *MOUNTAIN INTERVAL*, BY ROBERT FROST (NEW YORK: HOLT, 1916)
Among those who pass for critics in this standardless age, and especially in
this most uncritical nation, there has been a well nigh universal outcry of
approval for the young New England poet, Robert Frost. His two previous
volumes, *North of Boston* and *A Boy's Will,* were hailed as great poetry.[10]
Now comes a third volume, and doubtless the same critics will greet it with
the same superlatives.

If, by any chance, there are yet standards by which poetry may be judged,
Mountain Interval certainly contains little that deserves praise.

Poetry works its magic chiefly through an appeal to individual and
racial memory. The major poet appeals to both; the minor poet entirely, or
almost entirely, to the former. Mr. Frost gives no evidence of being aware
that anything at all happened before the 20th century. Even with such a
limitation a poet may deserve immortality. There are "great minor poets,"
and the works of such constitute a priceless heritage in themselves. But
Mr. Frost is by no means master of his limited realm, as the great minor
poets have been. He has not served his apprenticeship, and in all but a few
instances, his technique is wretchedly poor. Having already won the ear
of the uncritical modern public (which is not worth a poet's winning), it
is hardly likely that he will ever subject himself to that rigid self-criticism
which makes the master. Much of his work is merely bad prose arranged in
lines. He seems ignorant of the subtleties of the poet's craft; or perhaps he is
only careless, for in one sonnet he has written surprisingly well. It is a pity
that he should have been so widely acclaimed in his immaturity; for now
he is likely to go on giving the uncritical mob what it thinks it wants—and
that, for an artist, is fatal. Now and then one comes upon a line that reveals
an astonishing faculty for observation, and there are flashes of exquisite
beauty at intervals. He might become a notable poet if he could discipline
himself. To prove this to those who understand poetry, we need quote only
the sonnet entitled, "Range Finding." We have too much respect for the
personality that could produce so fine a thing to present any of the many
examples of slipshod workmanship that we could easily find. Here is the
sonnet:

> The battle rent a cobweb diamond-strung
> And cut a flower beside a ground bird's nest
> Before it strained a single human breast.
> The stricken flower bent double and so hung.
> And still the bird revisited her young.

A butterfly its fall had dispossessed
A moment sought in air his flower of rest,
Then lightly stooped to it and fluttering clung.
On the bare upland pasture there had spread
O'ernight 'twixt mullein stalks a wheel of thread
And straining cables wet with silver dew.
A sudden passing bullet shook it dry.
The indwelling spider ran to greet the fly,
But finding nothing, sullenly withdrew.

Book of Great Significance

REVIEW OF *IS FIVE*, BY E. E. CUMMINGS (NEW YORK: BONI, 1926)

Recently there appeared in these columns an article on E. E. Cummings'
latest volume of alleged poetry entitled *Is Five*. Doubtless some who read
that article concluded that the book in question was not to be taken
seriously. From the standpoint of literary values, we may assume safely
that the book is indeed of no value, if we agree to regard literature as
a means of communication between human beings. Surely literature is
that fundamentally. The mere communication of some idea by means of
language obviously does not constitute literature, but quite as obviously
there can be no literature without communication.

No one can say that Mr. Cummings had nothing in mind when he
composed his alleged poem; one can say only that he did not communicate
what he had in mind, if anything. His incoherence is evidently intentional,
since he has achieved it, not only in substance (which might be simply
a matter for pity and an alienist), but in the quite obviously laborious
distortion of the very mechanics of language and topography.

No one can say with certainty that Mr. Cummings had not sublime
thoughts when he wrote his utterly unintelligible passages, but it is a
suspicious circumstance that whenever, for a brief moment, he allows
himself to lapse into intelligibility, the idea expressed is always of an
extremely low order, ranging from childish nastiness to idiotic silliness.

In every brief moment of intelligibility one notes that it is the lower
nerve centers that are functioning utterly without control. If, by piecing
together those moments of relative lucidity, the reader is able to arrive at a
vague approximation of the author's general attitude, the meaning of that
attitude can be expressed fairly by the formula, "To hell with everything."

Nevertheless, those readers are mistaken who have assumed that the
book in question is of no importance. It is beyond question one of the
most significant publications of this generation and this is written with no

ironical intent. All intelligent people who sincerely desire to understand our time should borrow the book from the library and try to read it. It cannot be read, but it can be examined.

No doubt, after a few minutes of effort to read the alleged poetry of Mr. Cummings, some will decide that the man is insane. But he is not insane. The matter would be simpler if he were, for then there would be only Mr. Cummings to forget. But if there were no Mr. Cummings, the social fact, of which his alleged poetry merely is symptomatic, would continue to be a fact.

War a Danger Signal

In the volume entitled *Is Five* we have merely a typographical and pseudo-literary picture of the moral and cultural anarchy into which, as a society, we have fallen. That is why the book is important. It reduces to absurdity a general anti-social mood that affects, and more or less controls, all of us under many disguises that impose upon us as sacred "liberty."

What Mr. Cummings has done in the realm of verse writing, the population in general has been, and still is, doing in ways less obviously absurd, but no less essentially so.

In Mr. Cummings' book, it will be noted that not only is communication of ideas generally lacking, but that there is observable a conscious effort to be unintelligible. Communication between individuals is the sine qua non of society. There can be no society without communication and to break off communication deliberately is to espouse absolute anarchy; yet we are gregarious beings, utterly dependent upon each other. We could not exist long without some degree of social organization.

We are living in a great individualistic age, and the benefits of individualism, as a stimulant to initiative, have been tremendous. But individualism is centrifugal and, if unchecked, must result in atomization and ruin. Danger signs began to appear some years ago. The war was one of those signs, demonstrating what may happen to peoples when nations, as units, become absolutely individualistic.

Social Body Wrong

Several years before that war, an exhibition of cubist and futurist painting was held in various large cities of the country. Many of us went to satisfy our curiosity and some of us remained to laugh. But it was no laughing matter, for out of those grotesque daubs already leered the hideous spirit of disorganization that was even then driving us on to an unthinkable catastrophe.

The arts (including literature) are social phenomena, and their character is determined by the prevailing mood of the time. The arts are social barometers; or it may be better to say, weather vanes, indicating the direction and velocity of the social trend.

A time in which it is possible for men, presumably educated and otherwise apparently intelligent, to discuss the alleged poetry of Mr. Cummings, not only without hilarity but with actual respect, is a time in which a danger point has been reached in the outward swing toward anarchy.

It is not Mr. Cummings who is mentally unbalanced. He is no doubt a clever and likable chap with much vanity and a strong opportunist bent. He wishes to "succeed" in a generation cut loose from cultural standards and mad for novelty—the more outrageously novel, the better. He writes what he writes because society will let him do it.

It is the social body that is not quite right in the head.

REVIEW OF *THE COLLECTED POEMS OF EZRA POUND* (NEW YORK: BONI, 1926)
Back in 1912, Harriet Monroe, then just launching her now famous poetry magazine, introduced Ezra Pound to that very small portion of the American public that is interested in experimental verse.[11] Miss Monroe's enthusiasm amused those who could not determine what Mr. Pound was trying to communicate. Some were of the opinion that if Mr. Pound's product was poetry, then there had certainly never been any poetry until he arrived. Others saw or professed to find profound significance in his product. No less a man than Ford Madox Ford has stated that Mr. Pound is "the greatest living poet" though he has not revealed the means by which such a judgment may be rendered with confidence.

Here we have 230 generous pages of Mr. Pound's work done into a beautiful book that is good to hold in the hand. One who has spent a great share of his life with the mighty poets of the world feels, in contemplating this volume, much as a hungry child might feel in looking through the plate glass window of a delicatessen shop. The display looks like a fine feast, and it may be so; but how to get at it?

It may be that Mr. Pound is right and all the great poets of the past have been wrong. That would be an encouraging indication of progress indeed. But it seems only fair that we, who hunger greatly for diving poesy, should not be let into the necessary secret of appreciation.

REVIEW OF *WILD HONEY*, BY FREDERICK NIVEN (NEW YORK: DODD, 1927)
Once upon a time there was a soaring tree aloof in violet air upon the shoulder of a lonely mountain, let us say; and, being tall, it caught the

music of the master winds when lesser trees were silent; and in the hushed nights with its head among the stars it was a holy thing to see. It is cut down now, and part of it is the paper upon which these mild and inconsequential adventures have been recorded by human labor that might have been used in the potato patches of the country.

CERVANTES READ BACKWARDS
REVIEW OF *THE LIFE OF DON QUIXOTE AND SANCHO ACCORDING TO MIGUEL DE CERVANTES SAAVEDRA EXPOUNDED WITH COMMENT BY MIGUEL DE UNAMUNO* (NEW YORK: KNOPF, 1927)

If the foregoing rather long-winded title is read carefully—and that is a good deal to expect when nearly everyone must chase his own shadow unceasingly—it will be noted that the volume does not present the text of Cervantes' masterpiece. Unamuno, the world-famous novelist, playwright and philosopher, does not here assume the modest role of the mere annotator. He is an expositor; and it is the time-honored function of expositors to read into any chosen text that which the author never suspected might be there.

There was a once a certain Nazarene who would be greatly surprised to learn that he had the prime qualifications of a modern business man (*vide* Bruce Barton);[12] and Cervantes would be no less surprised to learn that a modern philosopher of his own country has actually made a plea for Quixotism as the crying need of the modern world. In each case, the amazing interpretation is achieved by the very simple process of reading the meaning backwards.

Unamuno's exposition of Quixotism originally appeared 22 years ago when Spain was undergoing the social throes incidental to rapid industrial expansion. Eight years later he issued an enlarged and revised edition, which is now offered over here for the first time.

Like many others in our time, Unamuno deplores the mechanization of life and the regimentation of humanity that are seen to result, at least for the present, from machine industrialism.

Like many others, he has felt the need for an idealistic conception of life to set against the narrower view that now controls the world. His comment on the episode of the windmills, which Sancho saw for what they were while the Don believed them to be giants, is characteristic:

The knight was right: fear, and fear alone, made Sancho and makes all of us poor mortals see windmills in the monstrous giants that sow evil through the world. Those mills ground flour for bread, and men confirmed in blindness ate of the bread. Today, they do not seem to be windmills, but locomotives, dynamos, turbines, steamships, automobiles, telegraphy with and without wires, bombs, instruments of ovariotomy; but they conspire to the same damage. Fear, san-chopanchesque fear, alone inspires the cult and worship of steam and electricity, makes us fall on our knees and cry mercy before the monstrous giants of mechanics and chemistry. And at last, at the base of some colossal factory of an elixir of long life, the human race, exhausted by weariness and surfeit, will give up the ghost. But the battered Don Quixote will live, because he sought health within himself, and dared to charge at windmills.

By a curious twist of thinking it is possible to read a ghost of noble meaning into the above; but upon closer examination it will be noted that the meaning doesn't "track" somehow, and that it is created by reversing the true Cervantean idea. Had Sancho deemed the windmills to be giants and had the Don known them to be only windmills, the point that Unamuno had in mind would have been somewhat more defensible. But it is the very essence of Quixotism to ignore the obvious, for which reason Unamuno has grasped the matter by the wrong handle and so played directly into the hands of his antagonist, the hard-headed, blind, commonsensical literalist, who, in the fullness of time, may come to be seen as the true Quixotist!

Unamuno professes to believe that what we need in the modern world is a host of Don Quixotes, devotees of the inner life. It is true enough that "without the inner life the outer is without significance," and it is quite true that the inner life, lacking the outer, is insane. Either extreme is insane, and at this point the true Cervantean meaning appears.

Unamuno insists upon the need for a new Cervantes, and no doubt the time will come when once more the Cervantean laughter will play with full force upon another outlived conception of human society. Already, here and there, the Cervantean chuckle may be heard in spite of the roar of the machines, but the whole-hearted, devastating laughter is not yet. When a new Cervantes appears, the central figure can be no other than a caricature of the "go-getter," now honored by the world even as the Bayards of feudal society were honored in their day—and with reason in each case.

Before a new Cervantes can appear, it must have become apparent to all men, perhaps through the teaching of catastrophe, that there was a fatal joker in the old view of life.

Don Quixote was not a prophecy; it was a belated criticism. Or, to indulge in a bit of grandiloquence, as is usual in discussions of masterpieces, may we not say that *Don Quixote* was the echo of the laughter of the gods heard after the comedy had been played out?

Knowledge and Opinion

REVIEW OF *THE OUTLINE OF MAN'S KNOWLEDGE*, BY CLEMENT WOOD
(NEW YORK: COPELAND, 1927)

When Mr. Clement Wood was persuaded to join the presumably affluent company of outliners, he found that every important field of human knowledge had already been outlined by some gigantic intellect. He therefore decided quite sensibly, that there was nothing left for him to do but to outline the outlines—an undertaking obviously requiring the most gigantic intellect of all. The result is *The Outline of Man's Knowledge*—a single volume of only 614 pages.

Resting after his labors, Mr. Wood has looked upon his work and, in a sabbatical mood, has found it good. After pointing out the great advantage to the average man of a speaking acquaintance with universal knowledge, Mr. Wood asks: "Where can this essential knowledge be found—in such a presentation that it is compellingly interesting, as well as accurate?" Answer: Here only. Mr. Wood further says that outlines of everything "are available on every hand; usually in several expensive volumes, and occasionally told dully and with inaccuracies and omissions." The natural inference is to the effect that Mr. Wood is not, even occasionally, dull; that he is always accurate and never omits anything of importance. Again he says: "What saves time, saves life; this book does that." And what will not a man give for life? Surely $5 is not excessive.

An outline of human knowledge in a single volume of less than 700 pages can scarcely be condemned with fairness if important omissions should be apparent. Even an occasional inaccuracy and some dullness could be forgiven. What one may fairly criticize at the outset, perhaps, is a somewhat obvious complacency. Universal knowledge is a big order, seeming to involve, in addition to humility, the fundamental question: What is knowledge and what is not knowledge?

The reviewer does not insist upon a comprehensive answer to that question, since no one can be supposed to have such an answer. But surely the humble reader, who craves instruction, has a right to be told when the author of an outline of universal human knowledge is presenting established fact, when he is presenting his own peculiar view of a matter, when he is following the fashion of his generation, and when he is stating a theory that happens to be useful in the present stage of human thought.

Such distinctions are seldom made by Mr. Wood. Being himself wholly convinced as to the truth of a given social or scientific theory, too often he states his own beliefs, not as beliefs, but as facts. To state a theory as a theory is to convey knowledge of the existence of that theory; and yet the theory itself can scarcely be called knowledge, since it is not to be assumed that even our excessive modernity has attained the absolute.

The matter of stating personal opinion as fact, even though that opinion be in keeping with some prevalent intellectual fashion of the moment, is even more reprehensible than the statement of theory as fact. Throughout the volume it is apparent that Mr. Wood has settled many doubtful matters in his own mind. This is the more surprising in that everywhere he affects the ultra-scientific attitude.

A few illustrations may be given.

"In the beginning, science tells us, was energy." This is a legitimate statement of theory as theory, but Mr. Wood proceeds to accept it as fact, admitting only that man does not know how "energy transformed itself into its twofold forms of energy and matter." Neither does any man know that "in the beginning was energy." . . .

In speaking of prehistoric man's normal habitat, Mr. Wood tells us that man "did not haunt primarily salt or fresh water districts. Man's inborn inability to swim establishes this last fact conclusively." But does not a hog or a horse swim naturally for the same reason that a piece of wood does? Is not this so-called "inborn inability to swim" a matter of specific gravity and displacement?

In speaking of the Greeks, Mr. Wood states, dogmatically as usual, that they were, not that they are thought to have been, "closely allied to the Teutons." Is this actual knowledge?

The Homeric epics, we are told, not as theory, but as fact, "grew not the product of one man, but of generations of singers." This may be quite true, but is it not still in question? If not, who settled the much argued question and when?

Julius Caesar is characterized as "an effeminate sensualist." That he was a sensualist may be stated as knowledge, but to describe him as effeminate is ridiculous in view of his achievements as recited by Mr. Wood.

In discussing Scandinavian Literature, Mr. Wood refers to "Knut Hamsun, whose *Hunger* and *Growth of the Soil* are epic studies of peasant life."[13] But *Hunger* is decidedly not a study, epic or otherwise, of peasant life, as anyone who has read the book should know. Verner von Heidenstam is mentioned, in passing, merely as a lyric poet, as though he were not the author of *The Charles Men* and *The Tree of the Folkungs,* neither of which (and this may be significant) has achieved vogue in America.[14]

As an appraisal of Virgil's *Aeneid,* we find the following: "The manuscript has been preserved for us, among whom it occupies an unloved place in high school courses in elementary Latin." The fact that the *Aeneid* is unloved by high school classes seems hardly to alter the fact as to the power and beauty of the first half of the poem, or as to the enormous influence the poem has exercised in human history. One fears that Mr. Wood himself knows it only as a high-school text, and one fancies that it did not strike him as excessively "elementary."

At the end of the dissertation on English Literature, we are told that "The five best books of modern English poetry are" so and so. This is opinion, not knowledge, and there are a great many people who will not regard the opinion as especially intelligent.

How is the following justified in an outline of universal human knowledge? "Amy Lowell, hailed by many as an outstanding poet, is slowly subsiding, since her death, to the lesser position of a celebrity rather than a poet. Her critical studies are marred by slips in grammar and a general impassivity to beauty, etc." This may be true, but is it knowledge?

"Greatest among short story writers of today," Mr. Wood asserts, "is Ring Lardner." Does he know this, and if so, how does he know it?

"Only the poetry of the recent past," we are informed, "possesses vital significance for the present." Considering that great poetry is great because it deals in a universal way with fundamental human nature, this seems odd. It seems especially odd when we read in another place that Mr. Wood himself once played in the *Antigone* of Sophocles "both in Greek and in English, and found the audience responsive alike to both renditions." Shall we not classify the *Antigone* as poetry?

In general it may be said truthfully that Mr. Wood's *Outline* reveals a partisan mind, greatly under the influence of the intellectual fashions of the day.

THE BENEFIT OF THE DOUBT

REVIEW OF *THE STORY OF THE AMERICAN INDIAN*, BY PAUL RADIN (NEW YORK: BONI, 1927)

A little over a year ago Dr. Paul Radin published *Crashing Thunder: The Autobiography of an American Indian.*[15] It was offered to the public as a revelation of the typical Indian consciousness, and in a preface the author explained that he greatly regretted the necessity of destroying the popular romantic notion of the Indian. The book was almost universally hailed as being exactly what the editor claimed for it. Critics who never knew an Indian in their lives announced with enthusiasm that here, at last, the typical Indian consciousness was revealed.

Crashing Thunder, by his own confession, was a "no-good" Indian, a thief, a sot and a lecher, absolutely without moral sensibilities. This was quite in keeping with the "naturalistic" mania of the moment, the fundamental idea of which seems to be that the truth must be sordid and nasty. Having lived in close contact with Crashing Thunder's people, the Winnebagoes, and their neighbors, the Omahas, for many years, this writer had the following to say at the time:

> Those who have enjoyed intimate acquaintance with Indians will recognize Crashing Thunder's type early in the book. He is to be found around all reservations, and he represents all Indians only as any bum may represent all white men. Twenty-five or 30 years ago there were many old men on the Winnebago and Omaha reservations in Nebraska, whose reminiscences, if obtained, would have revealed the true Indian consciousness. Many of those old Indians were strictly honest, and truly pious in the fine old Vergilian sense of love for their land and people and profound reverence for the Great Mystery that is central in all religion. Such men were still true to the tribal conception of ethics—a very high conception—and had refused to adopt the white man's vices as they had refused to accept his civilization. They were not 'romantic' beings. They were intensely human and, if one really knew them, very lovable. Certainly they commanded one's respect.[16]

It is said that Dr. Paul Radin is a distinguished ethnologist. This may be true; but, judging by the Crashing Thunder performance, he would be a much better authority on Indians if he had a better understanding of them as human beings.

How authoritative Dr. Radin's *Story of the American Indian* may be in the strictly scientific sense, this writer does not know; but the suspicion naturally aroused by the former book is hard to allay. The *Story* is certainly told in a smooth and interesting manner, and if true it is important. There are times when even a layman feels that Dr. Radin may be rather an ingenious inventor. "In covering so vast a field," he tells us, "I have naturally had to rely on a large number of writers and my indebtedness to them is great." It is seldom indeed that he mentions one of these writers.

In general the book in concerned with the northward spread of Mayan culture and its diffusion and alterations in North America. We are told that

Mayan culture entered the Mississippi Valley from the vicinity of Vera Cruz by sea, and that the Mound Builders were descendants of invading peoples from Mexico and Central America.

In the final chapter of the book, Dr. Radin deals briefly with the Messiah Craze of the Indians which culminated in the slaughter at Wounded Knee in December, 1890. He does not mention his source for this chapter, but obviously it was Mooney.[17] Had he read his Mooney more carefully, he could have learned that it was not the prophet Smohalla who brought on the great Messiah Craze. It was Wovoka, otherwise known as Jack Wilson. Smohalla, a Columbia River prophet, is discussed early in Mooney's book, and Dr. Radin seems not to have read over to where Wovoka appears. "In no case, needles to say," remarks Dr. Radin, "has accuracy ever been sacrificed."

However, Dr. Radin did read at least some of Mooney's description of the affair at Wounded Knee, since he quotes verbatim therefrom—without quotation marks and without giving credit.

It is only fair to give an author the benefit of the doubt, and it is good to assume that Dr. Radin read all of his other sources much more carefully than he read Mooney.

MOB FLATTERY
REVIEW OF *THE WAYS OF BEHAVIORISM*, BY JOHN B. WATSON (NEW YORK: HARPER, 1928)

At last the oracle has spoken in no ambiguous terms and now it is possible for every free-and-equal man, woman and child to grasp as a scientific fact that a human being is at best merely 30 feet of "guts"; that such terms as "mind," "consciousness," "soul," "spirit" can have no meanings whatever; that the supreme manifestations of human nature in the lives of seers and saints have been and could be no more than the results of "gut squirmings" due to purely mechanical stimuli of physical environment.

This glorious news has been abroad for some years, but not until now has it been made so unmistakably clear, and by no other than the inventor himself.

If any sensitive reader should object to the use of the term "guts" in this connection, it should be understood that Dr. Watson himself insists upon using the term. So often was the term encountered in reading *The Ways of Behaviorism* that the present writer finally turned to the index, curious to see if it might appear there. It does, with various references; and quite properly so, for the doctor not only admits but frequently shouts that his is purely a "gut" psychology. It is true that the term is broadened to include heart, lungs, liver, kidneys and glands as well as the alimentary canal. The doctor admits that he could have used the term "viscera," but that, he intimates, would have been a highbrow word, not at all in keeping with the absolute equalitarianism of his gutology. Dr. Watson is exceedingly "democratic," as the nature in his ingenious theory demands. All human beings, according to the eminent doctor, are born with absolutely equal potentialities, the only difference between any dolt and a Charles P. Steinmetz or a Shakespeare being a matter of purely mechanical stimuli from the physical environment—or, as the charmingly free-spoken doctor would say, how were the "guts" made to "squirm" by environmental ticklings?

Having thus established universal human equality, he would be inconsistent if he were not just as common as an old shoe in teaching us all about ourselves: He must use expressions that are easily within our common grasp and presumably characteristic of our everyday utterance. Children, to the democratic doctor, are just plain "kids"; viscera is "guts." Thus he avoids abashing us with his accidental advantage in wisdom. He would not be so wise, you understand, but for the sort of accidental tickling his "guts" received in infancy and adolescence. He realizes this keenly, and so why should he be cocky and use terms that would embarrass the rest of us who were not so advantageously tickled?

Doctor Watson is a regular fellow and uses plain, homely commonsense in attacking all problems, though he does not, unfortunately, take the trouble to show just how commonsense can be universally valid in this very mysterious universe. He is far more "scientific" than the greatest scientists of our time; for men like Eddington, Haldane, Thompson, Einstein have gone rather beyond the commonsense stage of Science, and the time seems overlate for basing a new system of psychology on the old, narrow, materialistic dogma of the mid-nineteenth century.

In following the doctor's explanation as to how human temperament, character and special abilities of all sorts are produced by visceral "squirmings" due to environmental stimuli, one wonders what would happen if a pig were raised in the parlor of a highly cultured family. Surely the same "gut" equipment would be there, as any butcher knows. Might not the full grown hog develop into an Aeschylus or a Beethoven or a Buddha? No doubt Dr. Watson would smile in a superior way at this point and remark that a pig is not human. But if it's all a matter of properly tickled viscera, why couldn't a hog be made excessively human by wise and persistent tickling?

Such a doctrine is made possible only by the vigorous suppression of a great deal of important data. For instance, what could Dr. Watson do with the fact of telepathy or the highly suggestive if not conclusive findings of psychical research? He must take for granted that all this and much more is necessarily pure "bunk," to use another of his favorite, regular-fellow expressions presumably agreeable to the ears of disadvantageously tickled folk among the laity.

If Dr. Watson should ever catch up with Science as it is understood by the greatest scientists of our time, he would be far less "scientific." In the meanwhile his doctrine should flourish, being admirably adapted to mob-flattery. Far from having made an original contribution, he has merely formulated a going mass persuasion into the semblance of a scientific theory. Behaviorism is an expression of the mood of the time—a mood that has grown out of a popular misinterpretation of the democratic idea.

REVIEW OF *GREEN HILLS OF AFRICA*, BY ERNEST HEMINGWAY (NEW YORK: SCRIBNER'S, 1935)

"In this book," so the publisher avers, "Ernest Hemingway has recorded the events of an exciting hunting expedition in Africa so skillfully as to infuse into it those qualities of imagination, perception and suspense which one usually finds only in a masterpiece of fiction." When a highly respected old publishing firm speaks thus about a book, it ought to be a whale!

Mr. Hemingway himself holds the work in high esteem, for he confides: "The writer has attempted to write an absolutely true book to see whether the shape of a country and the pattern of a month's action can, if truly presented, compete with a work of the imagination." When a world-renowned author speaks thus of his book, it ought to be at least two whales!

After reading the book with a breathless expectancy, wondering when those "qualities of imagination, perception and suspense" would begin to eventuate, two things seemed perfectly clear, to-wit: that Hemingway is doubtless a jolly hunting companion; that he had a right good time shooting kudus and rhinos by day, and perhaps an even better time getting tight in the evenings—not to mention frequent draughts of the Oh-be-joyful during working hours. One gets the impression that fire water was plentiful in that outfit. Not that one begrudges the abundance. This is no temperance lecture. It's a hunting expedition of another sort—hunting for that promised literary treat.

Still, it cannot be questioned that the book is exceedingly "virile" and "frank." You've got to give it to Hemingway—he can "cuss," as he frequently proves in the present opus. It is not inconceivable that he knows as much naughty language as any of our other modern masters, which is saying a great deal, as some of them know very little else.

He can write smashingly virile sentences when he lets loose, as for instance: "I know just what kind of a–s I am and I know what I can do well." Only, being a powerful writer, he says it right out loud.

Did you ever sit perfectly sober and listen to an illuminated gentleman garrulously enjoying his personal liberty?

Did Mr. Hemingway write much of his book in the evenings?

5
This Mysterious Universe

TWELVE

Et Tu, Scientia?

Neihardt was in no sense anti-technology. He recognized the remarkable material benefits to society from that realm but recognized also that the rapid strides made had invested technological progress with almost deistic regard. A widespread cultural belief that science could solve all human problems sanctioned a reliance on sense data as the primary means of knowing, pushing aside spiritual and other ways of interpreting the world. Neihardt was frustrated by this one-sided perspective:

> For some years, in fact since 1912, I have been reading scientific works as they floated in the stream of books, and I have noted the astonishing growth of the mechanistic view and the corresponding increase of pessimism and flippancy and cynicism. . . . They name and classify and think they have eliminated mystery, and they have merely ignored mystery. The mellower scientists know this well; and I know their views. But the world does not know, and Science is regarded as supreme in our world. Why can't they see that their method gets no farther than that by which a curious man in a sand waste might plot the characteristic sand formations, forgetting the fact of the wind always blowing across the waste?
>
> It's the fashion of the moment and it's no more. In their rebound from superstition they have fallen into a different phase of superstition.[1]

Neihardt believed that such a perspective severely limits our ability to respond to our world. The evidence of the senses is not objective, as science claims, for it is consciousness that must order and interpret the data those senses provide: "[T]he thing examined [is] itself the examiner—a state of affairs with which one could scarcely associate the word objective."[2] Generation after generation, what science "objectively" discovers is exactly that which reinforces the dominant scheme.

Neihardt saw in Eastern philosophy an opposite emphasis on subjective states of knowing based on the assumption that the evidence of our senses is illusion, and, therefore, all response to that data is unreliable. Neihardt believed this perspective to be inadequate as well. He granted that our world may be illusion, but we must live in it as if it were real, "for one must wrestle with matter, not as it may be, but as it seems—and it is sometimes a stubborn stuff."[3]

Though a layman, Neihardt showed a learned interest in the fields of physics and mathematics. He was familiar with other works of the authors presented here, and he displayed knowledge of the larger discussions of which these books were a part. He showed his impatience with books defending a limited perspective and was particularly offended by petty "angels on the head of a pin" arguments in a world where the most serious problem facing humanity, namely, "how to keep the human race from starving or worrying itself to death in a world of abundance," remained unaddressed.[4]

SOCRATIC QUESTION
REVIEW OF *THE BREATH OF LIFE*, BY JOHN BURROUGHS (NEW YORK: HOUGHTON, 1915)

Nearly everyone with whom one talks nowadays seems to be obsessed with the idea that the affairs of this world are advancing toward a yet distant perfection on a steadily rising curve. In all realms of thought this obsession seems to be dominant. Sociologists are ready to prove that the perfect state is being slowly approached through democracy; scientists are willing to demonstrate to their own satisfaction in what way their specialty is wiping out religion; pacifists can show how wars are going to become impossible—and so on.

However idealistic all this may seem, it is, nevertheless, an outgrowth of modern materialism. The mass, having discovered evolution, has proceeded to make it ridiculous by misapplying it—the usual procedure of the mass with an idea. Scientific materialism necessarily grew out of the evolutionary theory [ ].

[For more than] fifty years a preoccupation with the things of the material world has characterized our civilization. Owing to this preoccupation we have advanced rapidly in things mechanistic, and our mechanical triumphs have aided in the vast illusion of progress toward ultimate perfection.

But we forget that life, in the last analysis, is not to be judged by material, but by spiritual triumphs. The Greeks of the fifth century B. C. had no "modern conveniences," and yet they reached a higher level of life than we can now boast.

One needs but to scan history with care to see that we do not advance on a steady up-curve, leading to ultimate perfection. Beyond a certain height civilization does not go, and that height has already been reached more than once and will be reached again and again, no doubt. A diagram of the course of civilization would not be a straight line, nor even a continuous upward curve. It would be a continuous horizontal series of loops, varying in size, each loop representing the rise and fall of a civilization.

These prefatory remarks seem necessary in approaching the volume under consideration, which deals with the prevailing scientific view of lifeprocesses, and in doing so, touches upon the fundamental concept of religion.

For many years, as has been noted, materialism has been gaining ground, and religion (we do not mean merely dogma) has seemed to be losing. Those for whom evolution is an obsession have accordingly leaped at the conclusion that man's religious sense is becoming obsolete, after the manner of [the] vermiform appendix and in keeping with the same law. But these headlong people forget to consider the easily demonstrable fact that man's attitude toward religion is subject to the same rhythmic rising and falling that characterizes the whole history of civilizations. Dogmas, growing out of the abiding religious sense of man, appear, develop to maturity, and pass away; and with each passing of a dogma, men become for a moment of history, cynical and materialistic. But it is only the arbitrary form that dies; the spirit, which is the endless religious yearning, persists, to build yet other bodies of dogma. And in this connection let it be emphasized, with history as a witness, that the race has never reached its supreme expression in any but a religious age; and by this we mean an age intensely conscious of the awe and mystery of man's relation to the cosmos.

Once more we appear to be on the rising side of the endless spiral in the matter of religious consciousness; and *The Breath of Life* by John Burroughs voices in modern terms the world old questions wherewith the resurgent spirit of man challenges the audacious materialist in all ages. Mr. Burroughs ventures upon no hard and fast statements regarding the mystery of life; he is concerned wholly with questioning those scientists who have attempted to explain everything in terms of chemistry and physics. His purpose is not to discredit science; he is himself a scientist and glories in the revelations of science. He merely points out the limitations of science. It is the old controversy between the dualist and the monist, though the author prefers

to use the terms "vitalist" and "mechanist"; and the question fundamental
in the whole book may be summed up as follows: "Without holding to
any belief in the supernatural, and while adhering to the idea that there has
been, and can be, no break in the causal sequence in this world, may one still
hold to some form of vitalism, and see in life something more than applied
physics and chemistry?" In other words, without being superstitious, is it
not possible to regard matter as acted upon by some vital principle which
is not to be explained as a result of the interaction of physical properties?

Mr. Burroughs strives to show that the scientific explanations of life-
phenomena are all after the fact, and that they do not account for the
fact itself. They start with the ready-made organism and then reduce its
activities and processes to their physical equivalents. "Vitality is given," he
says, "and then the vital processes are fitted into mechanical and chemical
concepts, or into moulds derived from inert matter—not a difficult thing
to do; but no more an explanation of the mystery of vitality than a painting
or a bust of Tyndall would be an explanation of that great scientist." . . .

The field of discussion is that dim region which lies between the outposts
of science on the one hand, and fundamental religion on the other. It is
not, obviously, a discussion that can be definitely settled by experimental
science. It lies in a realm where philosophy and religion move. But it would
seem that Mr. Burroughs' Socratic questioning of the mechanistic theory of
all things might do much good in an age that has been too materialistic and
that now seems about to turn once again toward a more spiritual conception
of life.

In that direction lies all great achievement.

EINSTEIN AND THE AVERAGE MAN
REVIEW OF *RELATIVITY*, BY SIR OLIVER LODGE (NEW YORK: DORAN, 1926)

It is natural that the average busy man, perplexed with his personal affairs,
should not feel himself greatly concerned with the scientific theories of his
time. Let the physicist and the natural philosopher pry into the secrets of
the atom by way of determining, if they may, the ultimate constitution of
matter. Matter may indeed be no more, in some last analysis, than intricately
related points of stress in a universal magnetic field, whatever that means.
That does not affect one's practical affairs, it would appear, for one must
wrestle with matter, not as it may be, but as it seems—and it is sometimes a
stubborn stuff. The average man is willing to accept the hypothetical ether
as something quite as real as payday, if you insist, but he can not use it in his
business; and the question as to whether or not there are any dependable

absolutes knocking about this mysterious cosmos of ours troubles him not at all.

Nevertheless, it can be shown that there is a closer relation between the dominant intellectual theories of a time and the everyday life of men than is commonly suspected. Whether or not the theories by which men of any age attempt to explain their world to themselves grow out of the general temper of the time, or vice versa, it would be impossible to say with certainty. Perhaps the two interact. Certain it is that the things men are commonly persuaded to strive for are always strangely justified by the intellectual theories peculiar to the time; and even the most abstruse theory that is favored by the higher intellectual levels has a way of seeping down through all the social strata as a modifying influence upon the unconsidered notions by which men live, however little that influence may be suspected.

In the matter of creating cosmologies, it may well seem to one, who is not unacquainted with the history of human thought, that men may merely shape and reshape the universe in keeping with their dominant desires at the time, seeking what they wish to find and finding it; and that we are now no nearer to the solution of the ancient mystery of things than when our dreams were simpler.

A being, unacquainted with human music and the ecstacies of the dance, would be greatly embarrassed to explain the rhythmic movements of a throng seen through the windows of a soundproof ballroom. But we may be sure that he would hit upon some ingenious theory in keeping with his own prevailing notions. If he could only hear the music, it might all be simpler. To what unheard music may the atoms dance, or whatever it is that moves to make the shifting patterns of our world?

An age of materialistic persuasions in practice has a materialistic science; or turn it around, if you wish. The truth has an uncanny habit of reading well both ways.

There was a time, not so long ago, when we were still convinced that there were absolute standards for the judging of many things, from art to personal conduct. Some, no doubt, still believe so, but it seems scarcely the fashion. Some mourn this tendency as a simple manifestation of original human cussedness on the rampage; but perhaps the correct explanation is far less simple. New values can come into being only through the breaking down of old forms; and as human beings, in the process of becoming more so, we are surely far from finished in our conception of values. We can stand a great deal of experimenting yet.

But what should strike us as interesting is the fact that suddenly in the midst of our revolt against the old standards conceived as absolute, came what is widely acclaimed as the master intellectual structure of our generation—Einstein's theory of universal relativity. Whether or not it may be regarded as a colossal work of creative art expressed in mathematical symbols, or a purely scientific structure in the veritable stuff of fact, it expresses essentially, on a cosmic scale, a sublimation of the mood that characterizes our generation.

Perhaps if our generation could understand what Einstein's meaning is in all its implications, we might achieve more genuine liberty and less license. For it is the central idea in his thesis that, although there are no absolutes—standards valid throughout the universe—yet there may be truths that are unalterable within a given "reference scheme." And certainly, for the individual, human society in its broader relations is such a "reference scheme."

There have been many attempts to offer popular explanations of the Einstein theory. Einstein himself, several years ago, attempted to tell us, in a little book, just what he meant; but there must have been many readers who wished that he might kindly begin all over and explain his explanation.

That is exactly what Sir Oliver Lodge has done for him in the lean and commonsensical book here presented. Naturally there can be no simplified explanation of the theory in its complete mathematical form; but a general understanding of it, in so far as it may modify the common attitudes of men, is now at last made possible to almost anyone who may sincerely care to know.

THE MATHEMATICAL MIND

REVIEW OF *MOLE PHILOSOPHY AND OTHER ESSAYS*, BY CASSIUS J. KEYSER
(NEW YORK: DUTTON, 1927)

Dr. Cassius J. Keyser, most widely known as the author of a brilliant and provocative little book, entitled *Thinking About Thinking*, is the head of the Department of Mathematics at Columbia University.[5] He is 65 years old and his chief interest seems always to have been in mathematics.

It is probable that most people think of a mathematician as a matter-of-fact, plodding sort of fellow with little of the sap of life in him; but the truth is that in their farther reaches the mathematical mind and the poetic mind become all but indistinguishable. Of all scientific methods of seeking for an understanding of the complex relations that bind together the phenomena of our world, mathematics is by far the most daring. Truly it is the winged science, and under the guidance of its modern masters it has brought back reports of regions and relations that seem definitely beyond the reach of men's crude senses. If there be any principle of unity in the universe, the reports may be true. For instance, mathematics seems not at all embarrassed in the apparently fantastic worlds of Lobachevsky and Gauss and Einstein. It seems to know its way in a non-Euclidian world of multiple dimensions quite as unerringly as in our familiar three-way world of Euclid's mapping; and there is something about a great mathematician's structures that can not but be identified with the beauty that great art reveals.

This view of the mathematician is strangely emphasized by reading anything that Dr. Keyser writes. Far from being dehumanized by his life interest in mathematics, he has reached, by a scientific route, some far-seeing summit where he neighbors in the clear air of sanity with authentic poets and philosophers.

Mole Philosophy and Other Essays is a collection of many sketches and essays, for the most part brief, that have appeared in various periodicals, and of speeches, also brief, that have been delivered by the author on various occasions. The book is not to be ranked, as a contribution, with the author's major works, but it does serve to give an all around view of a rare and truly significant personality. It is, therefore, important. Furthermore, even the slightest sketches in the book are pleasing, and always something is said that is decidedly worth the saying.

It would be easy to fill a column with examples of insight and wisdom to be found in this book. Also many paragraphs, at once amusing and profound, might be cited. For instance, Dr. Keyser tells us of the chance he once had for the presidency of our own State university. A distinguished alumnus of the institution was delegated to approach the Doctor on the subject, and naturally certain important questions were asked. One was as follows: "Do you believe in the existence of God?" Dr. Keyser replied as follows: "If I say no, I shall mean a God that you can describe. If I say yes, I shall mean a god that I cannot describe." There the interview ended, and the Doctor was not nominated.

In the essay entitled, "The Significance of Death," delivered as an address at Columbia University 14 years ago, the author sets forth and defends the idea that death is not to be regarded as the tragedy of life, but rather as the one fact that makes life beautiful.

"Were it not for death," he writes, "if life did not end, if it were a process of infinite duration, it would be devoid of the precious things that make us yearn for perpetuation." Death, he contends, is "essential to life's beatitudes." "All these solemn beatitudes of reason and meditation derive their poignance from the transitoriness of the life that contemplates them."

It is an interesting idea persuasively presented. Doubtless if it could be accepted by all men in an unselfish spirit, it would tend to direct our efforts toward the development and preservation of race-values. We would identify ourselves with the race and all our hopes would be in an impersonal social immortality such as George Eliot conceived in "The Choir Invisible."[6]

But so long as selfish individual interests struggle for dominance in our world, so long will our conceptions of justice and right and mercy make a higher stage of development, beyond the mystery of death, seem the only possible justification of our confused lives here. Surely, many are likely to feel, if this darkened life of sense be all the life there is, it is expensive even at the cost of a single twinge of toothache, not to mention the terrible price that is paid by every generation in sorrow and suffering.

Swapping Illusions

REVIEW OF *THE FUTURE OF AN ILLUSION*, BY SIGMUND FREUD (NEW YORK: LIVERIGHT, 1928)

Doctor Freud of Vienna has written another book for "tough-minded people," that is to say, people who are willing and able to face the "bitter truth" and reshape their lives thereby. The bitter truth in this instance is concerned with the psychoanalytical discovery that all religious ideas are the bunk, being fantastic attempts on the part of poor human nature to escape the pangs of reality. This would be astonishing news to millions upon millions, were they ever to hear of it. They will not, and even if they did they would scarcely be affected, for when were we of the millions ever convinced of anything by reason?

Nevertheless, the proud parent of many complexes proves that religion is doomed for the curious reason that it has been shown to be an illusion. "As he has taught us to forsake childish things (!)," writes the publisher's blurbster, "and to become adults in our conduct (!!), so he urges us to maturity in our philosophy of the cosmos." This seems an ambitious program.

Without a doubt, *The Future of an Illusion* is a masterpiece of rationality. It may even be a profound contribution to the literature of Twentieth century science; and "Science," says Dr. Freud in conclusion, "is no illusion." So the matter seems to be settled at last. Having "forsaken childish things" and "become adults," we may now dismiss our preachers and go into the maturing business.

But here and there an occasional layman, with who knows what infantile complexes, may have a few silly questions to ask about this illusion business in general. Without questioning the obvious practical triumphs of scientific technology, and without the least intention of either defending or attacking anybody's religion, such a person might ask, for instance, how it happens that scientific theory is so admirably adapted to flatter the dominant social psychosis? Why, in a democratic, materialistic time, do the most celebrated psychologists happen to discover exactly the sort of "truth" that agrees best with the going notions of the crowd? Have not celebrated psychologists assured us that all the older, aristocratic ideas about human nature are piffle, and that we are the brute victims of gut reactions? Are not many of us glad to hear that all men are born with exactly equal potentialities and that environment explains all excellence in others who may surpass us in ability? Are we not told, what is well calculated to please many of us in our present temper, that sex is about all that really matters in determining our attitudes? Is it not strange that, with the "emancipation" (and greatly increased buying power) of woman, our scientific theorists should suddenly begin to discover extremely flattering truths about the feminine mentality? Is it possible that there may be some relation between the scientific doctrine of universal relativity and the prevailing anarchic mood of a competitive society?

Suspicious circumstances of this sort abound in our scientific theorizing and there can be no harm in asking if, by any chance, there might be such a thing as swapping illusions as the wind of world-whim veers.

Dare We Giggle Now?

REVIEW OF *OUR CHANGING HUMAN NATURE*, BY SAMUEL D. SCHMALHAUSEN
(NEW YORK: MACAULAY, 1929)

It does sometimes seem to a mere layman that this business of scientific theorizing may have reached a point where it either is or promises to become a matter for furtive giggling if not for robust laughter. If it were only a matter of providing an indoor sport for a few super-intellectuals, it would be no layman's business. But ours is an age of popularizing, and not even the illiterate have escaped the results of scientific theory; for those who do not get the results of scientific worldview through the press, get it nevertheless in the form of an unconsidered mass persuasion, and no priestly caste ever wielded greater power over the credulities of man than has been and still is wielded by the scientific caste.

The reason for this power is clear enough. Can we not see with our own eyes that science works miracles? It seems not to occur to many of us that we might well distinguish between science as a contriver of very useful mechanisms and science as a dictator of [ ]ble human conceptions. A wonderful servant may be a poor leader of men.

Without reference to either the "right" or the "wrong" of it, let's [see] what scientific theorizing has [done] to us common folk who don't know much, know that we don't and are beginning to venture upon the timid suspicion that our scientific leaders themselves may not know any more about certain things that matter tremendously to us in our difficult business of [getting] through this world decently. In the heyday of the Victorian era, science set out to prove a cocksure naïve materialism that, when carried to its logical conclusions, could not but involve the destruction of all the distinctly human values that have resulted from thousands of years of trial and error and struggle and suffering on the part of the finest spirits that have been in our world. Such values could not be accepted as scientific for the very simple reason that science was in its very nature exclusively concerned with the very narrow field of "physical phenomena," which could hardly include such values as honor, love, [beauty] pity, unselfishness, decency, all the many humane conceptions [that] are involved in the meaning of that richest of Greek words, [sophrosyne].

Little by little, what science [hadn't] proved and couldn't hope to prove came to be considered by an ever increasing proportion of the people as of little or no importance. Not that many thought about the matter; the change just took place as the result of the changing world-mood developed out of the scientific outlook. That the dominant world-mood of our day, as evidenced by our literature, our news, our plays, our movies and our characteristic conduct, is conspicuously cynical and bestial can hardly be denied by anyone who has been observing these things. The old sanctions for the higher human striving simply are not in good standing any more. Science has "disillusioned" us, and many of us are persuaded to laugh at "superstition," little realizing that our acceptance of the scientific world view can not have been with the vast majority of us anything but a superstitious acceptance—an act of blind faith based wholly upon the going say-so and the fashion of the time.

Where, then, do we laymen get this chance to laugh, or, at least, to giggle furtively? It would seem that the chance is getting to be pretty good when a great scientist like A. S. Eddington can say, as he does say in a recent book that all we (meaning scientists) know "is that something, we don't know what, is doing something!"[7] May we not laugh, if only by way of remaining fairly sane, when we consider at what a cost we have arrived at scientific "disillusionment," only to learn that our leaders have learned that they haven't learned anything to justify what they have taught us? But it's hard to laugh when one notes that they are not giving back to us any of those lost "illusions" which, somehow or other, kid yourself as you like, did succeed in producing some fine types of men and women in the past.

If it's a matter of illusion anyway, haven't we made a rather poor trade—a hopeless for a hopeful illusion?

In his truly magnificent work on *The Universe Around Us,* Sir James Jeans, one of the greatest scientists in the world, after describing a universe in which man is of no significance whatever, puts a curious question which runs substantially as follows: Has all this somehow produced us, or have we produced it as a construction in consciousness out of wholly illusory data?

And now we have an extremely scientific work by Dr. Schmalhausen, widely accredited as a powerful scientific thinker, in which he asks and answers the question: "Is civilization going insane?" "What do we mean by civilization?" he asks. "Apparently," he answers, "the conquest of matter by mind. Actually, the subjugation of mind to matter." This state of affairs he, a scientist, attributes to the scientific world view, to our industrial madness, which is scientific in origin, and to the war, which was an aggravated phase of industrial competition. The answer to his first question is an affirmative. "Instead of that integration which promises a wider and wider scope for the healing works of sanity," he says, "we discover the rapid rhythm of disintegration infecting life with tumult and chaos and conflict."

Are we laymen, who wish to live as good lives as may be, any longer under any obligation as moderately intelligent beings to credit science with the ability to guide us? Can we not do a much better job of living by being a great deal less sophisticated and listening to some of the old fogies, such as Socrates, Jesus, Confucius, and all of the great poets and humanists?

LIGHT ON THE PEAKS
REVIEW OF *THE REVOLT AGAINST DUALISM,* BY ARTHUR O. LOVEJOY (NEW YORK: NORTON, 1930)
It is doubtless assumed by most practical men whose interests are necessarily bound up with the struggle of each moment as it passes, that philosophical dissertations are scarcely to be regarded as anything more than intellectual exercises for those who like that sort of thing and have nothing more important to occupy their minds. It is also doubtless quite true that most philosophical dissertations are just that. Henshaw Ward, in a work entitled *Thobbing,* has ventured to assert that all the truth men know is that which has been gained through the eyes, all conceptions otherwise arrived at being false.[8] This is an extreme statement of that naïve form of scientific materialism which, though now definitely rejected by the real leaders of science, still influences the lower levels of scientific thought, as, for instance, in the extreme form of Behaviorism.

But while it is true that most philosophizing gets nowhere, and even though it be granted that human thought is by its very nature unable to penetrate the mystery in which we are immersed as in a sea, yet it must be remembered that there are world-fashions in thought which change from age to age and are seen, by taking a long historical view, to exercise a most profound influence upon the generally accepted view of man's relation to man and to the cosmos, which in turn determines the general direction of striving and the conduct of men.

It is a simple historical fact that the general trend of philosophical thought, on the upper levels most remote from the interests of the great mass of us, may be studied profitably as being in a general way prophetic of a new world-mood in the making, providing no great social catastrophe shall divert the prevailing stream of change.

It can be shown clearly, and it is shown in the work here noted, that the dominant world-view of the nineteenth and twentieth centuries may be traced to thought-patterns developed by Descartes, Galileo and other thinkers of the seventeenth century. The triumph of these seventeenth century thought-patterns has been overwhelming; but within a quarter of a century a profound change has come over the advanced thinking of the Western world, and within the past 10 years the philosophical revolt of the twentieth century, on the highest intellectual levels, against the seventeenth has become more and more apparent. What Prof. Lovejoy offers here is a survey of the history of thought during the past three centuries, and a discussion of present day scientific philosophy by way of making clear the nature and meaning of the profound change now taking place in the dominant thought-patterns of the Western world.

Though Prof. Lovejoy is not concerned with any idea of "better" or "worse" conceptions, it may be said that the social implication of his study is hopeful. For the "revolt" under consideration points in the direction of a far more widely extended and humanly livable realism than that which men like Henshaw Ward, John B. Watson and utterly sense-bound "practical" men in general are able to conceive. There is reason to believe that it is in truth a profound world-change that is here considered, though generations may pass before the new thought-patterns shall have influenced all social and mental levels in the form of an unconsidered mass persuasion. Such changes come first as light upon the highest peaks before the shadows in the valley are affected.

But there is always the possibility that some catastrophe inherent in our headlong blind devotion to an impossible view of the meaning of life may overtake us before the light can reach us.

A Burning Issue

REVIEW OF *THE SUPREME LAW*, BY MAURICE MAETERLINCK (NEW YORK: DUTTON, 1935)

Maurice Maeterlinck's latest work, here noted, is described as "a ringing challenge to the relativist theories of Einstein." It is also a defense of Newtonian principles, which, the author, contends, have not been "completely overturned," as is often assumed.

The row, it may be pointed out, is over that mysterious and apparently ubiquitous influence called gravitation. Newton stated the observed law that "matter attracts matter in direct ratio to mass, and inversely to the square of the distance." He regarded gravitation as a force and envisaged the problem involved as somehow mechanical. The relativist approach is not mechanical, but mathematical. The Einsteinians conceive gravitation, not as a force, but rather as a property of "curved space," thus substituting a geometrical concept for a mechanical one.

Anyone can see that this is certainly a burning issue, and that it would be just too bad to be mistaken about it! It is as though we were to think of the Almighty as a mere mechanic, whereas He may really be a very distinguished higher mathematician!

Maeterlinck, after demolishing the relativists, leaves not only them but himself pretty much up in the air. For, after seriously discussing such matters as space, time, eternity, infinity, et al., he clearly states that nobody knows anything whatever about the meaning of such names, if any. He quotes Eddington to the effect that all men really know about the universe is that "something is doing something, we know not what." And as for gravitation ("the supreme law"), he again quotes Eddington, who once remarked "in a moment of lassitude": "The whole thing is a vicious circle. The law of gravitation is a put-up job."

A layman might be forgiven for wondering why the author did not say all this in the first place.

In closing what appears finally to be an essentially naïve discussion of an essentially naïve discussion, "It is with gravitation," says the author, "as with all the great problems of the world: The more one studies them, the more do they become covered with obscurity." This, however, is not true of the one really great problem of the world just now, to-wit: How to keep the human race from starving or worrying to death in a world of abundance.

Here is some red-hot and vastly reassuring news from the scientific front: Just now, upon dropping the book "in a moment of lassitude," this writer noted that gravitation, whether a spatial curvature or a force, was doing business as usual, whether geometrically or mechanically.

Could anything be funnier, in the long view, than the spectacle of "first-class minds" seriously at work on such problems in a time like ours? There is a pressing problem of incalculable human suffering to consider, and we mere laymen are supposed not only to keep straight faces, but to be much impressed while our "great thinkers" discuss such an utterly nonsensical question, for instance, as to just what the circumference of the universe may be!

By the way, did the great thinkers of the Middle Ages ever determine exactly how many angels could stand on the point of a needle?

THIRTEEN

Exploring the Unknown

John Neihardt was comfortable ranging outside the boundaries of ordinary consciousness. He had visited mediums and engaged in psychic research. Though maintaining a healthy skepticism about psychic phenomena, he had enough experiences of his own to make him unwilling to dismiss out-of-hand the claims of others. Neihardt believed that most of us are restricted by a view of the world that limits understanding, even though, occasionally, flashes of insight break in and mystery is revealed.

Neihardt believed that most of us stumble through our lives without realizing that just beyond the edge of awareness is a world of wonder. He believed that revelations of religious mystery also take place at the edge of normal consciousness but that much of organized religion impedes rather than enhances connection to mystery.

These moments of expanded awareness intrigued Neihardt, and he welcomed books that explored the borderlands of ordinary human consciousness and considered human life as an integral part of mystery.

Scientific Pessimism

REVIEW OF *EOS, OR THE WIDER ASPECTS OF COSMOGONY*, BY J. H. JEANS (NEW YORK: DUTTON, 1929)

It was Schopenhauer—wasn't it?—who, in considering the human predicament, remarked substantially that after ages upon ages of unconscious and fortuitous evolution the universe had accidentally developed the phenomenon of consciousness to no end save that it might at last realize the utter futility of the process that had resulted in consciousness.

Surely this is a world-record in pessimistic utterances, not to be surpassed by even the most enlightened of our modern intelligentsia; and, believe them, that is saying a mouthful. What's more, Schopenhauer's notoriously troubled liver seems to have prompted him aright, if Science—that sacred cow of our age—may be accepted as an infallible judge.

Dr. J. H. Jeans, who is secretary of the Royal Society and Research Associate of Mount Wilson Observatory, is a very great astronomer, and in his popular lectures on cosmogony here presented he has nothing very encouraging to say to the human race. In the first place, according to his and his colleagues' observations, there is no evidence to support the fond belief that the universe is at all friendly to life. On the contrary, life seems to have blundered into an antagonistic cosmos, and is indeed itself an accident that doesn't matter in the least. Furthermore, the human race got here too late for the real cosmic show. "What we are witnessing is less the rising of the curtain before the play than the burning out of the candle ends on an empty stage on which the drama is already over." And it seems that we can't even get our money back from the box office—because there isn't any box office.

You see, unfortunately the universe is running down like a clock that was wound up a long while ago—how, God only knows, and He nonexistent—and there's nobody in sight to wind it up again. Even science, as yet, doesn't know how to wind it up. Matter, you see, is constantly transforming itself into radiation; and when you stop to consider that, to begin with, matter is no more than a complexity of stresses in the universal ether (which, in turn, seems to be a sort of highly attenuated nothing at all) you can readily realize that radiation is bound to end in something less than nothing whatever—a minus zero. It's going to be a complete fade-out, and then some!

It's a sorry outlook, but it seems that we need not take any immediate action in the matter. In fact, there will be ample time for the consideration of the farm problem, prohibition, universal peace, the marriage question, etc., before we even appoint a commission to look into our cosmic difficulties. As Dr. Jeans points out, though we human beings have been on the planet about 300,000 years, we are as yet only a baby just beginning to have its cross-eyed attention diverted from its bottle to the great world around its tiny cradle. "Taking a very gloomy view of the future of the human race," says Dr. Jeans, "let us suppose that it can only expect to survive for 2000 million years longer, a period about equal to the past age of the earth. Then, regarded as being destined to live for three-score years and ten, humanity, although it has been born in a house 70 years old, is itself only three days old."

Maybe there's a gleam of hope here. Since it is this three days old baby, just beginning to look away from its bottle, that is presenting us with all this weighty knowledge about the cosmos, might not a layman (though admittedly pig-headed) be justified in asking just how much value should be attached to its gurglings and cooings, especially insofar as they may have a direct bearing upon the prevailing conception of human life and consequently upon conduct?

The very idea of babyhood implies the possibility of manhood; and, assuming that the baby's consciousness may develop somewhat during the next 2000 million years, isn't it at least interesting to suspect that the present cocksure obsession with quantitative conceptions may one day prove to have been truly infantile? To what extent is this baby of the highly self-congratulatory present merely fumbling with the exciting errors of its own psychological processes?

Dr. Jeans himself, though stating many scientific conceptions as definite facts, ends upon a doubtful note. "And even the old question," he says, "obtrudes itself as to whether the infant has any means of knowing that it is not dreaming all the time. The picture it sees may be merely a creation of its own mind; the universe we study with such care may be a dream, and we brain cells in the mind of the dreamer."

If a great scientist, after all his apparent certainty, can let go talk like that, is there any good reason why we laymen should accept any scientific view of human life and the cosmos that doesn't promote a sense of human dignity and worth?

And even if it's all illusion, what's the matter with the idea of cultivating the sort of illusions that makes this adventure in consciousness seem gloriously worth while? For in a world of illusion, the dominant seeming is certainly the effective truth.

Seed and the Soil
review of *WHAT'S LIFE ALL ABOUT?* by bertha conde (new york: scribner's, 1930)

Bertha Conde, who is the author of several works of an inspirational religious character, has lectured widely in the United States, and she tells us that everywhere she is confronted with the question that serves as a title of her latest book here noted.

It would be strange if she were not so confronted, for that is the most pressing question of our time and for a very good and obvious reason. It is implicit in the whole modern attitude, even when it is not formulated in words, and the fashionable answer is a flippant cynicism, too often coupled with a frank surrender to animality. Outside sophisticated circles, the answer ranges from an appallingly feather-brained "I should worry" attitude to a state of chronic pessimism and despair, though no doubt there are large numbers of people upon whose consciousness the question seldom if ever impinges save in the form of vague and transient bewilderments.

Men have always asked that question, and they could not be human if they did not. But there have been periods in history when it was the commonly accepted belief that a sufficient answer had been found, and so long as the accepted answer seemed convincing, the inevitable woes and irritations and failures of life could be related to some comprehensive pattern that in the large seemed glorious.

Though many still cling, or partially persuade themselves to believe that they cling, to some comprehensive religious view of man and his higher destiny, it cannot be said that the temper of the modern world favors any such faith. The whole trend of characteristically "modern" ideas is dead against any such conception. The materialistic obsession of modern society is the outgrowth of triumphant physical science arbitrarily limited to the examination and relationing of sense phenomena. Its method is analytical, and in the end all analysis must, if pushed far enough, end in the disappearance of the thing under examination, since anything (whether an idea or an apparently objective entity) may have reality for the human mind only by virtue of organic relations. "Matter" has been thus analyzed out of existence in any humanly conceivable sense, and, by the same process, so have many of those conceptions concerning human worth and meaning that once sustained the hopes of men tolerably well. Is there not now a very powerful school of thought that discredits all noble human motives and ends in an uncontrolled and meaningless mechanism?

The chain of cause and effect from science to mechanical invention to machine industrialism and to the all powerful profit motive is not hard to follow, and the resulting tendency has been to discredit all ideas not supported by sense evidence and to penalize in various ways all those who refuse to surrender to the passion for getting. That way lies the brute, and we are traveling on high.

What we do not understand is that men must realize their humanly livable truth CREATIVELY: that nothing of the sort is to be sought with success outside the creative consciousness, and that if men are persuaded to accept only what their senses may report or "prove," however marvelously aided by clever mechanical contrivances, they are not going to find anything that will justify their struggles on this planet. "Truth," "meaning," "beauty," "decency," "honor" and all such humanizing conceptions are not objective and cannot be found by any manner of exterior search. They must be created out of inner experience and aspiration; and when commonly shared this is what a people's culture signifies in the only sense of the term that was ever valid.

Bertha Conde undertakes to answer the question, "What Is Life All

About?" by concentrating upon one particular phase of culture, religious faith, and one aspect of that faith, the Christian doctrine. She is at pains to meet the modern temper part of the way by relating the spiritual teaching of Jesus to recent scientific deductions, such as one encounters in the writings of thinkers like Eddington; and the relationing is effective, for in the higher reaches of our scientific leaders, who are a quarter of a century ahead of the procession at least, physics seems to have become metaphysics, and epistemology, long a scientific outcast, begins to seem of crucial importance again, as indeed it always was.

What Miss Conde has to say by way of applying the meaning of spiritual discipline to life may be accepted gratefully and without cavil. It is beautifully stated and should strengthen hearts here and there. But with genuine respect for a sublime faith, it does seem that Miss Conde may not have begun at the beginning in offering her answer to the world at large. Before such lofty conceptions can even be considered to any effect, is it not necessary to consider the social atmosphere in which so large a portion of humanity must live—an atmosphere from which such conceptions are automatically excluded—a poisonous atmosphere that is artificially produced and made overwhelmingly potent for the average man and woman by the very constitution of our mass-exploiting industrial system?

If the chain of cause and effect, previously cited, has produced our prevailing world-mood—and of that there can be no intelligent doubt—then why begin at the wrong end of the chain to consider the human problem involved? To be specific, a jobless man on any of the numerous Market Streets of the world, with a wife and children at home wondering when daddy will get some money, is not to be approached with the loftiest spiritual conceptions as a solution of his difficulties. His first and fundamental need is concerned with economic organization and with nothing else in God's world. And there is a profound sanctity in that need, if anything may still be regarded as sacred.

Good seed can flourish only in appropriate soil. There must be, first of all, the appropriate soil; and the social soil of our time is hopelessly alkaline with the driving greeds and needs of exploitation.

Something to Think About

REVIEW OF *THE STORY OF PSYCHIC SCIENCE*, BY HEREWARD CARRINGTON
(NEW YORK: WASHBURN, 1931)

One of the risks that must be incurred by anyone who may venture to speak otherwise than contemptuously of any unorthodox view of any sort is that he is likely to be branded with a name generally held to be opprobrious; and having been so named, he will be regarded, by those who need to consider his view may be most vital, as quite definitely unworthy of attention. The old saying, "Give a dog a bad name and hang him," has meaning.

The old savage notion that dominating control of a thing may be attained by the magical process of naming it is amusingly apparent even in the best intellectual circles of this "our age of enlightenment!" Can we not put even the wisest social critic under the ban of our scorn and hatred by the simple process of naming him "Bolshevik," for instance? If, by any chance, anyone should happen to see a great deal farther into the puzzle of our life than we do—and of course we know this to be quite impossible—may we not render that person innocuous to us by naming him "dreamer" or "visionary," thereafter pursuing our complacent blundering as usual?

We have, indeed, amazing faith in the power of magical words, and this as much in the matter of acceptance as of rejection. Have not our politicians commonly described as "democratic" a scheme of living that is so designed that the predatory few may exploit the many at the cost of incalculable injustice and misery, and have we not, as a crowd, hailed the magical word with great enthusiasm, our chests swelling with the glory of being free and equal?

If, for even the best of reasons based upon a knowledge of human experience through long time, one should oppose some thriving folly in a time conceived as superlatively "modern" and "progressive," can we not demolish the impertinent fellow by dubbing him "reactionary?" And yet may he not be profoundly radical in the saving sense of going to the roots of things for understanding?

Have not "modern" and "progress" become utterly unconsidered terms used magically and with no thought of their possible connotations?

As a matter of fact, our vocabulary is pretty well furnished with such magical words and phrases, the sole function of which is to fortify us in our disability or disinclination to consider vital problems in a spirit of good faith and intelligence.

Some rainy Sunday, when you have nothing else to do, amuse yourself by setting down as many of such going words and phrases as you can, and note by what a high verbal wall we are commonly cut off from even a sincere desire to understand!

And what may be the application of these oblique remarks to the volume above listed? Simply this: To confess that one really takes at all seriously the subject discussed by Hereward Carrington is to incur the risk of being tagged with the name "spiritualist." And having been so named, it will be apparent to many—they have only to glance at the damning tag!—that the nominee is a "superstitious" fellow who is not shrewd enough to know, even without examination of the data involved, that the whole subject under discussion is to be explained by a simple assertion of mere trickery and fatuous credulity.

This writer will not "review" Hereward Carrington's *The Story of Psychic Science.* It is the sort of work that needs to be studied—conscientiously and without prejudice with a sincere desire to learn anything that may possibly be learned. A synopsis of the book would too readily serve as assurance that it is known and therefore need be considered no further.

But two or three statements may be made in the hope of arousing interest where there may have been none before. First, it may be said that the writer of these paragraphs is decidedly not a "spiritualist" and neither is Hereward Carrington. To explain the indubitable phenomena, here discussed with a caution and canniness that may prove surprising to many, by asserting a dogmatic explanation thereof would be to put oneself in quite as ridiculous a position as that of the orthodox scientists who ignore or deny the mass of phenomena without condescending to examine it in good faith—a most unscientific procedure. It is no less silly to attempt to establish a universal positive than a universal negative.

What Carrington claims for the phenomena, after more than 30 years of experimentation in the field, is that, after all possible allowances are made for fraud and error, a very great deal that is genuine remains, and that if the genuine phenomena were taken into consideration by scientists, the scheme of science as now understood and imposed upon the world, would be revolutionized.

It is certainly true that accredited science in our day arbitrarily excludes all but a set of selected data, and the necessary falseness of the resultant view, tending to limit man's consciousness to the "material" aspects and interests of life, may some day be seen as a bestializing influence. There are those who would insist that it is the commercialization of science that has determined its contemporary trends and triumphs. Perhaps a broader and more humanizing conception of science is impossible, as Carrington suggests, until a broader view can be made commercially profitable.

But the world has not always been made in the matter of "making money." Nor is it likely always to be so hereafter.

THE PRACTICALITY OF PRAYER

REVIEW OF *CAN PRAYER BE ANSWERED?* BY MARY AUSTIN (NEW YORK: FARRAR, 1934)

There was a time when the question which serves as a title for this deeply sincere and very notable little book would have been regarded as an impertinence, at the very least, by most people. But when asked, with the implication of a positive answer, by a sophisticated person of the modern world in no way identified with institutional religion, it is likely to carry with it an air of sensational novelty—especially for those who regard themselves as "enlightened" and quite abreast of the times. (The author, noted for her stories and novels of the Southwest, died at Santa Fe, NM, last Monday.)

For the modern world, in general, is about as far from the deep, impersonal, creative mood that is prayer, in Mary Austin's meaning, as a world could conceivably be, as a result of its intense preoccupation with the individualistic struggle for wealth and its truly fanatical acceptance of the leadership of a science arbitrarily limited for "practical" reasons to the narrow field of "that which can be measured."

We have been too long and too intensely occupied with the sense-surface of things; and, as a world, we have forgotten what should be obvious, that we live in mystery as fish in water; rather, that we ourselves are an integral part of the mystery; and that there is a vast field of vital phenomena which our science has ignored as non-existent, and to consider which has quite commonly been regarded as an indication of soft-headedness, if not of a "screw loose" somewhere.

Mary Austin's answer to her own question is an unequivocal Yes. "I am convinced," she says, "that I have experiential results, results that can be catalogued and identified, methods that can be named and discussed. I am aware of these experiential realities going on under the surface of what we call human nature. I have not been afraid to experiment with them, nor to make my experience known. I can take stock of these experiences and measure the degree and extent to which they can be taken into account as life appliances."

Her experimentation with prayer as a normal activating force in human affairs, she tells us, began 35 years ago; and some of her experiences in that time, as well as methods employed and her tentative conclusions, are given here.

The principal concepts upon which she builds a tentative explanation of the power exerted by prayer are not at all strange to many modern front-rank scientists, and are not rejected by them. The general idea, as Mary Austin views the matter, is that consciousness is not limited to the space within the walls of the skull, as it seems to be in ordinary states, but is somehow universal; and that the seeming isolation of the personality in the so-called objective world is an illusion. By attaining a deeper state than that in which men live the seeming humdrum life of every day, the individual consciousness "breaks through" and may become a motivating force in the extensive consciousness of which it is always, though unwittingly, a part. The above wording is necessarily crude, but may serve to suggest the author's attitude.

"The one indispensable item to the successful working out of prayer," says the author, "is that you have to believe that there is mind working within the constitution of the universe, so essentially like mind that works individually in man that the two can meet and co-operate." Perhaps she would even go so far as to suspect that the two are the same in differing states. She stresses the point that effective prayer cannot be selfish; a point which may well be concerned with the inevitable loss of the sense of self in the deeper creative states of mind.

DARING ACADEMIC DEPARTURE

REVIEW OF *EXTRA SENSORY PERCEPTION*, BY J. B. RHINE (BOSTON: HUMPHRIES, 1935)

Some years ago, in an evening's conversation with a group at one of our universities, this writer was urged by several of the company to set forth in detail a striking case of what seemed to be supersensory perception that had come under his observation.

The case involved a meticulous written description of a remote scope of country, approximately 10 by 20 miles in extent, by one who had never seen the country and had no recognized means of knowing it until eight years after the description was written. When the country was examined by several who were well acquainted with the circumstances, the bare, incontrovertible facts of the matter did seem to make a fantastic yarn, the whole landscape having been described with photographic accuracy and the peculiar topographical features correctly related.[9]

To make the factual story seem even more "spoofy," the description, which occurred in an account of happenings in that land a century before, properly placed a river channel where clearly it had formerly been.

A rather distinguished and unquestionably able science professor who was present, being asked what provision he would make in his scientific scheme for such a yarn, assuming that it was true, stoutly insisted that "coincidence" made sufficient provision. Nor was he moved by any appeal on the scientific grounds of mathematical chance.

The attitude was, of course, only logical to one who had definitely accepted a tight little scheme of things based upon the assumption that nothing is real that cannot be physically sensed, and that the limits of reality are therefore well established.

No doubt most people have had experiences of a similar general character, apparently involving perception without the aid of the senses. Many have always given an emotional and wholly uncritical acceptance to such matters; and there have been many others whose experiences of a like nature have served at length to overcome a stubborn scepticism. Psychical research societies have for many years been accumulating evidence of a most impressive nature in this unorthodox field of inquiry; but so powerful has been the materialistic superstition that, until recently, the whole subject could be ignored by orthodox science, and it has seemed scarcely respectable to confess any serious interest in it.

But the main thought-trends of the world have changed greatly in recent years, notably since the catastrophic disillusionment of 1929, and more and more one notes the willingness of scientific thinkers to consider at least the probability of supersensible reality.

Duke University is the first of our great educational institutions to give official sanction to investigation in the field of psychical research, and the volume here noted, which contains a detailed report of the experiments thus far conducted by Dr. Rhine, professor of psychology at that institution, might well come to be regarded as of prime importance in the history of human thought; for, aside from its impressive weight as evidence, it can scarcely fail to lend a much-needed air of conventional respectability to a subject that has thus far been relegated largely to the realm of superstition.

Dr. Rhine and his associates have begun their investigation of supernormal (as distinguished from "supernatural") phenomena, with telepathy, realizing that if the fact of thought-transference can be established scientifically beyond question, the wider field of inquiry into "the strange phenomena of the human mind" will be thrown open to scientific consideration, to the end that men may know more of "the place of human personality in nature and what the natural capacities are that determine that place."

For three years past, Dr. Rhine, with the collaboration of members of the faculty and many students, has been investigating the phenomenon of perception without aid of the senses under the most rigid test conditions. Nearly 100,000 tests have been made, the results carefully tabulated, and the mathematical chances for "coincidence" computed. Any open-minded person who reads the volume carefully can hardly fail to agree with the author's conclusion stated as follows: "It is independently established, on the basis of this work alone, that extrasensory perception is an actual demonstrable occurrence." Already, we are assured, the odds against chance as an explanation of results are some billions to one, and we are told that, as the experiments proceed, the figure mounts rapidly.

The results here recorded are the more impressive in that specially gifted subjects have not been chosen for the tests, and that the phenomenon, generally occurring spontaneously in subconscious states, is here shown to occur at will with many types of people in an apparently normal conscious state.

The purpose of the author and his associates far transcends mere academic curiosity. He realizes that our conception of the human being is pitifully inadequate, and that the whole matter of human relationships is concerned in such an inquiry.

"But it is a 'philosophy for use,'" he says, "that these studies are meant to serve. The need felt for more definite knowledge of our place in nature is no mere academic one. Rather it seems to me the great fundamental question lying so tragically unrecognized behind our declining religious system, our floundering ethical orders and our unguided social philosophies. This work is, then, a step, a modest advance, in the exploration of the unrecognized boundaries and reaches of the human personality, with a deep consciousness of what such steps might lead to in the way of a larger factual scheme for a better living philosophy."

FOURTEEN

The Flesh and the Spirit

In looking for viable alternatives to a Western model of thought, Neihardt turned to the writings of Eastern mystics. In his adolescence he had become interested in Vedanta philosophy and such writings as the Upanishads and Jacolliot's *The Bible in India*. In Bancroft, as a clerk for a trader on the Omaha Reservation, he built friendships among the "long hairs," the elders of the tribe, and he noted many similarities of the Omaha life philosophy to Eastern mysticism. This connection is drawn in Neihardt's short stories inspired by Omaha tales and later in *Black Elk Speaks*.

Neihardt wrote in *Poetic Values* of a visit to his home by an Eastern mystic and a lively discussion of Eastern and Western points of view that lasted long into the night, Neihardt defending (often halfheartedly) a Western perspective. Neihardt believed Eastern mysticism to be too unfamiliar a worldview to be embraced wholeheartedly by Westerners and itself too one-sided to meet the complexity of human need. He believed, however, that its emphasis on the spiritual conception of life was desperately needed by Western culture because "while science, operating on the level of the senses, can give us power over our environment, it cannot possibly give us the wisdom necessary to a humane control of that power."[10] He saw many hopeful signs in the "upper reaches" of science, physics, and mathematics that perhaps this blending of the two world views was coming to pass. He believed that the artistic realm, lagging behind by several decades, might eventually catch up as well.

Neihardt argued that no antagonism between the two views exists. He believed that "our scale of values is continuous. All our values, from 'lowest' to 'highest'—from common sense through science and on through the esthetic, the ethical, the religious values are obviously creations in consciousness from selected data of our experience."[11] He called for recognition of the value of both science and poetry, because the artificial separation of the two modes of thought and the ranking of one over the other portends disaster for our world.

O'NEILL'S NEW PLAY

REVIEW OF *MARCO MILLIONS*, BY EUGENE O'NEILL (NEW YORK: BONI, 1927)

Eugene O'Neill's new book, published today, is hardly to be called a drama in any strict sense. It is a series of vivid scenes accompanied by dialogue. From a pedantic viewpoint the play might well be described as formless; and if O'Neill were a friendless newcomer, obliged to depend for acceptance upon the judgments of the sophomoric it is easy to imagine what the sophomores would say. "This ought to be a drama. It is not a drama. Therefore it is negligible." But the O'Neill bandwagon is in full blare, and many climb on eagerly who cannot be aware of their host's profound contempt for the values they hold sacred.

O'Neill is a mystic; and the spectacle of a go-getting multitude singing his praises in unison is a trifle funny, or pathetic, according to the mental weather of the observer.

It is true that there is no dramatic culmination in the play; and the reason for this becomes clear when the author's purpose is understood. That purpose is to represent concretely and to place in bold contrast the two major views of human life that obtain on this planet—that of the hard-boiled materialist, who limits all reality to sense perception, and that of the idealist who insists upon a higher reality of the spirit, upon values not adapted to quantitative measurement. These two conceptions divide the world geographically into two hemispheres, and it would seem, in view of the turmoil in the Orient, that a testing time of both may be drawing near.

It is true that the Occident has dedicated one day in seven to the higher view, but it is doubtful if, as a society, we devote anything like one-seventh of our energies to the realization of the vaguely apprehended values so honored. Such is our scheme of life that few could do so if they would.

Marco Millions is a timely book with some timeless implications. It is a commentary on the present Chinese situation, if you do not care to venture beyond the concrete and the momentary; and it is an ironical examination of the whole structure of Western civilization, if you care to see it so.

Superficially, O'Neill tells in dialogue the story of Marco Polo's journey to the realm of Kublai Kaan, of the years he spent there in getting rich, and of his triumphant return to Venice, a man of vast complacency and solid substance. There is no dramatic culmination in this story of opposed ideals of life simply because Marco remains blissfully unaware of any other values than his own. He is "shrewd," he is "practical," and though the court of Kublai knows him for a fool, Marco never suspects. Indeed, what better proof of his towering superiority could be imagined than the pop-eyed truckling of his envious neighbors when he returns? It does not occur to him that, after all those 20 years of getting, it is only Marco who returns, as much a fool as ever and as blind.

There is much diverting unconscious humor in Marco's passionate defense of his religion (obviously only because it is his) against the seers of the court of the Great Kaan, who, far from assailing the essential truth of the belief he professes but does not understand, are merely wondering at the vast discrepancy between the man's profession and his acts. Marco would prove his belief by argument (which is easier than proof by living), and there is not a glimmer of light for him in old Chu-Yin's profound remark: "But I believe that what can be proven cannot be true."

Marco has a scheme for conquering the world—a familiar scheme, as will be noted. It involves two clever devices, one being the use of gunpowder for slaying men and destroying the works of men; the other being paper money. Marco is willing to sell his scheme to Kublai at a fair price, and his selling talk runs like this: "You conquer the world with this (patting the model of a cannon), and you pay for it with this (patting a piece of paper money). You become the bringer of peace on earth and good will to men, and it doesn't cost you a yen hardly."

Bayan, the Mongol general, thinks well of the scheme, for he is "a man of action," and he is all on fire to conquer the West, proving by his highflown, statesmanlike twaddle (which elicits prolonged applause from the multitude) that he has learned much from Marco.

"Why do you want to conquer the West?" asks the Great Kaan. "It must be a pitiful land, poor in spirit and material wealth. We have everything to lose by its greedy hypocrisy. The conqueror acquires first all the vices of the conquered. Let the West devour itself."

That O'Neill has little faith in the efficacy of his teaching in *Marco Millions* would seem to be indicated by the following which he puts into the mouth of Kublai: "What good are wise writings to fight stupidity? One must have stupid writings that men can understand. In order to live, even wisdom must be stupid."

The play ends with an epilogue in pantomime, designed to identify Marco unmistakably.

A VALUABLE INTERPRETATION
REVIEW OF *THE STORY OF ORIENTAL PHILOSOPHY*, BY L. ADAMS BECK (NEW YORK: COSMOPOLITAN, 1928)

Kipling's much quoted line about East and West being fundamentally so different the twain can never meet is beginning to seem much more doubtful now than when it was written.[12] In the first place, the scientific preoccupation of the West has resulted in various means of rapid communication tending to break down ancient barriers of misunderstanding in both hemispheres; and in the second place, Western Science, in elaborating its materialistic dogma, has arrived at a point where matter, as formerly conceived, has vanished, leaving nothing but a mystery called energy. There are passages in the teaching of Buddha (600 B.C.) that read substantially as though some advanced modern physicist had written them, the difference being not in conception, but in terms.

Those who are accounted experts on the subject tell us that the vast apparent difference between the characteristic Eastern and Western world views is the difference between the conscious states in which the Eastern and Western minds have specialized. We of the Western world, it is insisted, have assumed that there is only one sane conscious state, that in which the senses are absolute; and it is out of this state, so Oriental seers would say, that our marvelous physical science and technology have been developed. But also they would tell us, what many of us are beginning to suspect for ourselves, that while science, operating on the level of the senses, can give us power over our environment, it cannot possibly give us the wisdom necessary to a humane control of that power. Certain findings of our own psychology, convincing to some, unconvincing to others, as yet, have seemed to contradict the old materialistic assumption as to there being but one valid conscious state, the one in which the senses are regarded as absolute. Such findings, together with the vanishing of matter as a sense phenomenon, are tending to increase Western interest in Oriental thought, and the interest is likely to increase rapidly when it is understood that no contest between the two world views is involved.

We are told that the Western view is "wrong" only in being a partial view of the livable human world; that the values realized by the sense are as "real" as any other; but that the scale of human values ascends unbroken from the lowest to the highest level; that only by the realization of those values which are of the higher levels can we hope to save ourselves from ourselves. This is doctrine that we of the West have long professed to believe, stating it in another way; but in our intense preoccupation with sense values and the consequent emphasis placed upon the acquisitive instinct, we seem, as a society, to have forgotten what our professed religion once meant, though there are still many individuals who do know and prove their knowledge by their way of living.

For those to whom the foregoing remarks do not seem necessarily to be associated with the sentimental dilettantism of "goofiness," *The Story of Oriental Philosophy* may prove an interesting and valuable work. Considering the great popular success of Durant's book,[13] it was inevitable that someone would offer a work on the Philosophy of the East, and the reading public is fortunate in that the task was assumed by L. Adams Beck. Many scholars could have written interesting factual accounts of the various phases of Oriental thought. But the very subject is of such a nature that mere knowledge of it matters scarcely at all, understanding being everything; and it is evident that Mrs. Beck has undertaken to interpret the vital ideas of Oriental teachings out of her own rich inner experience with them.

Why Not Both?

REVIEW OF *MYSTICISM AND LOGIC*, BY BERTRAND RUSSELL (NEW YORK: NORTON, 1929)

In discussing the relative merits of mysticism and logic as means of arriving at a livable world-view, Bertrand Russell defines the former as being "in essence little more than a certain intensity and depth of feeling in regard to what is believed about the universe." It is certain that no mystic ever gave him that definition, and he assures the reader that he himself has enjoyed no mystical experiences. The latter statement may be questioned in view of what one reads in another essay of this collection, "A Free Man's Worship"; but this essay is mentioned apologetically by the author in his preface, where he explains that it was written some time ago and that the war seems to have changed his viewpoint—for the worse, it is to be feared.

Since there is no logic in mysticism and no mysticism in logic, it seems a futile business to compare the two with a view to choosing either to the exclusion of the other as a guide to human values. It would seem much more worth while to seek some means whereby the two can be shown as relating to a continuous scale of values.

Early in the essay Mr. Russell says of Heraclitus that in him occurred "the true union of the mystic and the man of science—the highest eminence, I think, that is possible to achieve in the world of thought." If he believed this, he might better have been concerned with such a union than with the effort to set one against the other, deciding ultimately in favor of logic. Surely logic cannot humanize nor can mysticism meet and solve the important and immediate problems of sense. There is a little book called *Poetic Values: Their Reality and Our Need of Them,* which might serve to suggest how the transition from logic to mysticism (from science to poetry) may occur, and how the values revealed by each are to be realized in an unbroken scale.

Further, if Mr. Russell believed his statement about Heraclitus, he was in poor business when he wrote his essay on "Science and Culture," which presents from another angle the same curious conception of science and the poetic, logic and mysticism, as being antagonistic to each other. Therein he undertakes to support the contention that a more livable culture can be attained through the study of science than through the study of literature. The implied antagonism and necessity of choice simply do not exist, for it is a continuous scale of humanly conceived values that is involved; and the higher rungs of a ladder are in no way opposed to the lower; rather, they justify the lower.

Mr. Russell, in choosing science rather than literature as a means of culture, explains that "in the study of literature and art our attention is perpetually riveted upon the past," whereas science is always straining toward new things and the future. But is it possible to overestimate the cultural value of human experience to human beings, and what is great literature but a means of vicarious living under the guidance of the greatest spirits that have been in our world? It is not necessarily true, as Mr. Russell supposes, that "the men of Greece and the Renaissance did better than men now." Better for what purpose? Is there an absolute "better" to be considered? Nor is it true, as he maintains, that "originality is rendered harder of attainment" by the earlier achievements in literature. Originality is not a matter of attainment, but is present wherever a human consciousness differs from that of the majority. There can be no time limit for the occurrence of such differences. Mr. Russell seems to have the same idea of creative literature as that held by a young man who asked this writer recently whether or not he "liked modern poetry." The answer was "Poetry is poetry whenever and wherever it occurs." The little volume called *Poetic Values* might make the statement clearer.

In spite of one's deep admiration for the technological achievements of science, there is something faintly amusing about the prevailing fashion for attempting to explain everything by the present limited methods of science. And is it not to be noted that such attempts generate an atmosphere of pessimism? Surely Russell's book here noted scarcely gives one any justification for remaining alive save that one just happens to have been born. Why employ a learned man to tell us what so many puzzled and struggling people already suspect when they allow themselves to think about the matter?

There is more than the logicians can admit into their pint-pot systems; there are values that do not admit of measurement and "scientific" proof. Those who question this statement may test it by becoming well acquainted with the great poetry of the world beginning with the Greeks. They may give it a preliminary test by reading Mr. Russell's essay on "A Free Man's Religion."

HUMANE PHILOSOPHY
REVIEW OF *MATTER, LIFE, AND VALUE*, BY C. E. M. JOAD (LONDON: OXFORD UNIVERSITY PRESS, 1930)

Anyone who is somewhat acquainted with trends of philosophical thought since the Victorian flowering of science knows that an outstanding tendency has been to regard the establishment of materialistic monism as not only desirable but essential to any possible understanding of our cosmos. The desire to resolve our universe, with its apparently infinite complexity, into some single substance diversified only in seeming by varying conditions that delude the crude senses, is a very ancient desire; but in our time it has been greatly emphasized. It may well be due to no more than the nature of the troubled human mind itself, its inherent necessity for logical simplification.

In keeping with the extremes of human temperament, perhaps, we have the idealistic monist who sees the universe as mind or spirit only, and the materialistic monist, who sees nothing but matter, all phenomena that apparently are not material, being merely manifestations of a material mechanism in action. The former view, by its very nature, obviously cannot be popularly accepted in the Western World—not while its present and characteristic temper persists, at least. The latter view has proved to be enormously persuasive as a result of the technological triumphs of physical science, its sponsor, and because it is such as to seem self-evident on the level of mental development in which the senses are supreme.

As a theory, materialistic monism has been extremely fruitful in applied science—a fact which does not prove it true; but of late years, when the leading scientists of the world had gotten away from the old naïve materialism, as evidenced notably by the writings of Eddington, it has reached the realm of psychology in the form of Behaviorism, which reduces all mental and spiritual phenomena to "gut reactions," to quote a favorite expression of its chief exponent.[14] Also its influence in social theory, in ethics and in all the arts has been distressingly obvious. When a given theory, however practically fruitful in certain ways, is reduced to apparent absurdity by a too wide application of it, the reaction against it is certain to have been under way for some time; for a powerful social tendency of any sort is always belated in reaching the realm of higher human values. In fact, it never arrives there until it is already greatly modified or rejected in the lower realm of its origin.

For some years, but increasingly, it seems, within the past two or three, works opposed to materialistic monism have been appearing. It is not that the pluralistic conception of the universe has lacked champions, but that there was no definite trend of leading thought in that direction, as seems now to be the case.

Not long ago it was far from uncommon to read or hear some statement to the effect that there seemed to be "an unfortunate dualism" involved in this or that philosophical concept, as though monism were established beyond question. But here in a masterful work, *Matter, Life, and Value,* C. E. M. Joad, one of the leading thinkers of the world, boldly espouses dualism; seeing no reason "why the universe should necessarily be of such a kind as to appear simple to human intelligence." He would be willing to go any length beyond dualism, were the data for a complex pluralism available; but he limits his inquiry to matter and life, which he believes to be independent of each other save as the latter acts upon the former. He does not presume even to guess what life is, but he studies it by its effects, as other forces (all ultimately mysterious) are studied. For that matter, neither does he know what matter is—and who does? He accepts it as a commonly experienced reality.

The purpose of the work is to show how evolution may be a process whereby matter, acted upon by life, achieves awareness which tends to rise to higher and higher levels, with the result that a realm of pure values is achieved—values that are neither of matter in itself nor of the life force that acts upon it, but are "emergents" of the organizing consciousness. These justify the whole process.

Thus he undertakes to relate the world of matter and the world of immaterial value in an unbroken sequence of rising levels of awareness— from lifeless matter to ethics and to the mystical understanding of essential religion, poetry and all the arts in their highest forms. In this process he finds purpose, not in the sense of an end predetermined outside the process, but as a self-direction on the part of the developing awareness toward an enlarged understanding of value.

It is a beautiful logical structure that Joad builds out of the raw material of science and human experience generally, and any questing mind should find the book a joy. There are those who might ask what practical value such books may have. Such questioners are likely to be those who believe "truth" to be not only an absolute cosmic thing, but a humanly discoverable one, not yet suspecting that man evolves the patterns by which he lives, changing them as they cease to serve his needs and desires. In response to the objection that might be raised to such a view, it may be said that a thought pattern may be better or worse as judged by its influence upon men's attitudes toward each other, upon the direction of their striving and upon the conduct of their lives.

If for no other reason, Joad's *Matter, Life, and Value* is extremely important as emphasizing the fact that a strong contrary wind has begun to blow in the realm of human attitudes, now, and for long, under the control of a naïve materialism that has found no place for humanizing values in its hopelessly limited scheme.

No philosophical theory that any human mind can construct with logic is going to be "eternally true" or valid throughout the cosmos. But certainly a theory that tends to debase man's conception of himself cannot flourish forever. And for that reason, Joad's book is valuable. Others have elaborated somewhat similar or related ideas, to less effect, within the past year—enough to show that the new wind is indeed a wind of tendency, and that it is rising. Whether or not the more humane view of human life that is involved will grow strong enough to influence men in the mass before the prevailing world-view has wrought catastrophe is a matter for prophets to decide—or, better, for men to experience.

THE MESSAGE OF THE DUST

REVIEW OF *DESERTS ON THE MARCH*, BY PAUL B. SEARS (NORMAN: UNIVERSITY OF OKLAHOMA PRESS; NEW YORK: SIMON, 1936)

In their so-called "practical" moods, men commonly speak of "Nature" as something to be "conquered" by human ingenuity. In their moments of what passes for poetic sentiment, "Nature" is something to be celebrated with dithyrambics of admiration. In either case there is primary assumption that man is something other than Nature—an outsider, appraising now with the predatory, now with the esthetic, eye.

This sense of separation is so common that one of the most widely known and best-liked poems of our day expresses it in no doubtful language. "Poems are made by fools like me," so run the celebrated lines, "But only God can make a tree."[15] As though the maker of verses were himself not quite as much a part of Nature—and of "God's" creation—as the tree, whether the fruit of either's spirit be sweet or sour, a wholesome food or poisonous to men.

According to the cult of "Nature lovers," one goes to the woods and fields and brooks to find the object of one's devotion. Birds are of "Nature," and therefore to be loved, at least in sentimental moments of relaxation. But one's human neighbor in the city?

It is exactly this, man's tragically mistaken sense of separateness, not only from Nature as he conceives it, but even from his fellow men, that constitutes the dynamic theme of *Deserts on the March*.

Mr. Sears tells us that when he began to write his book, "dust storms, obscuring the sun for days at a time, were raging." Being a scientist, an expert in the field of soil conservation, the immediate physical causes of the appalling phenomenon were well known to him, as to many others; and were he concerned only with the factual and immediate, this would be largely a repetitive treatise.

But there is seership in this book, which serves admirably to illustrate, as few books do, how the scientific mode of knowing may change without the slightest shock of contradiction and with great increase of light, into that higher mode of knowing without which the lower may be—indeed has often been—a curse to men: poetic revelation of abiding truth.

Over a wide range of time and space, as far back as the flourishing season of the now long dead cities of the Sumerian desert, through the heyday and the downfall of Mayan civilization, to our own headlong, self-inspired conquest of a continent, the author seeks the vital data for the elaboration of his theme.

Even the most uncompromising literalist will find no dearth of interest in the strictly scientific aspects of the discussion; and there is much curious information as to the paradoxical methods whereby natural checks and balances are achieved and the long rhythms and returns of the vast natural process are maintained and assured.

Insofar as the story is that of human history, it is one of recurring tragedy for man, who never "conquers" Nature as he strives to do, deeming himself somehow apart from it; but succeeds, at last, only in "building desolate places" where he can no longer live.[16] "Man, Maker of Wilderness" could well have been the title of the book, as of the opening chapter; wilderness not only in what he conceives as "Nature," but also, and for the same reason, within the no less natural realm of human society.

And so we come to the following consideration of our own dust storms of today:

The really practical thing is not the immediately practical. To regard the dust plague as misfortune due to the wrong kind of plow, or a

chance drouth, or even to concede that it is due to an unhappy shift
from pasture to wheat, is to miss the point. Unless the dust is seen
as a symptom and a symbol, instead of a direct problem in itself, the
misery which it has caused is of no avail. It is precisely this clever,
efficient and speedy solving of immediate problems, without regard
to their general setting, which has brought us where we are. We have
stretched to its limits the merely opportune. Let us not forget that the
last bumper crop of wheat from the dry farming country lay beside
the railroad tracks in vast heaps for months while people willing to
work for food were not getting the chance to do it, and were hungry.
If tomorrow some ingenious fellow were to insure that the soil of
the dry West would never again be lifted into the air, it would be no
solution to the real problem which lies back of the dust storms of this
year of grace, 1935.

No work of ignorance or malice is this, but the inevitable result
of a system which has ever encouraged immediate efficiency without
regard to ultimate consequences.

Mile-high, these gloomy curtains of dust are the proper backdrops
for the tragedy that is on the boards. The lustful march of the white
race across the virgin continent, strewn with ruined forests, polluted
streams, gullied fields, stained by the breaking of treaties and titanic
greed, can no longer be disguised behind the camouflage which we
call civilization.

Thus emerges the vital teaching of a wise and beautifully written book.
Only as men conceive themselves and their fellows as integral in the vast
natural process; only as they may subordinate their personal desires to the
large impersonal relations of Nature, including their fellow men, may they
hope to achieve the triumph they have sought so long in vain.

6
POETIC VALUES

FIFTEEN

Hill of Vision

Neihardt periodically stepped back from the discussion of a current book to reiterate his poetics. He elaborated on details, clarified terms, and applied principles to specific books in a reminder to his readers of the role of art and the artist. In an essay examining the role of the woman artist, Neihardt focused on three questions to determine whether or not a work should be considered poetry: Is the work characterized by an architectural quality? Is it concerned with the creation of a self-completing whole? Is it marked by demiurgic power rather than accumulation of detail?

Neihardt conferred much honor on the poet, a word he used interchangeably with "artist," drawing on the meaning of "poetic" in the original Greek sense as "maker." He also charged the artist with heavy responsibilities—one gifted with the powers of heightened awareness and interpretation must use those gifts wisely. Hence his argument with those who use their gifts for personal gratification rather than the human good and for the sordid and nasty rather than the noble endeavors of humanity.

BUILDING OF A MASTERPIECE
REVIEW OF *THE HEART OF EMERSON'S JOURNALS* (NEW YORK: HOUGHTON, 1926)

Any thoughtful reader of Emerson must have noted what his critics long ago took pains to point out, that he had not what may be termed the architectural sense. That is to say, his power in any single piece of writing did not depend upon the cumulative effect of closely related details in a structure. It is undoubtedly true that in the greatest works of literary art there is an indefinable power that grows out of the mood of the whole, that is not to be accounted for by addition, but that suggests, rather, a geometrical progression. The idea may be illustrated by any impressive piece of architecture—for instance, the new Liberty Memorial. There is not, so far as this writer has been able to see, any single detail in that structure that is in itself especially beautiful. Scan it from top to bottom and from end to end until your eyes are weary, and if you are the sort of person who habitually sees parts and never the whole, you will capture little beauty. But if, suddenly, you should be able to see the whole as by a vivid flash of lightning, you might be deeply moved.

A work of art, in any medium, is first and last a structure. Obvious as this fact certainly should be, it is nevertheless generally overlooked in our generation; and as a result there is very little really significant criticism of poetry. As to the other arts, this writer cannot say; but it is safe to assume that the same tendency is found there. All genuine art must be poetic in the original Greek sense of the word, the sense of being architectonic.

Emerson was decidedly not an artist in this strict sense—the only sense that conveys any definite meaning. He was a seer. With him the momentary flash of vision was everything. Few men have seen more or seen more vividly than he. But the world revealed to him was as a world revealed by lightning—flash by flash. There was not the steady synthesizing glow by which lesser men than he have captured revealing beauty in the complicated net of relations that make a structure. He himself, at 45 years of age, unconsciously stated his own limitation in the following sentence: "Every poem must be made of lines that are poems." That is precisely like saying that every piece of architecture should be made up of details completely beautiful within themselves.

Emerson Almost Pure Genius

Nevertheless it is a fact that any distinguishing excellence in a great personality is closely related to some notable limitation. If genius be, as F. W. H. Myers once remarked in substance, a predisposition to subliminal uprushes of a revealing nature, then Emerson was almost pure genius. He saw flashes and set down as glowing fragments what he saw. It has been remarked that his essays may be read backwards, paragraph by paragraph, as well as forwards, and with equal profit. The obvious exaggeration serves to emphasize a truth. If anyone desires to know Emerson, it is necessary to build up his personality out of luminous fragments, and that is why the volume here listed is truly a golden book.

Twelve years ago the last of the ten volume edition of Emerson's diaries was published; but it was not to be expected that very many of even the most devoted readers of Emerson would ever struggle through so vast a work, for

all its priceless worth.[1] Thanks to Bliss Perry, the treasure that was hidden
from the many is here made readily accessible in a single glowing volume.

Fifty-five years of the great seer's life are represented here, beginning
with 1820, when he was 17 years old. The commonest man, in certain
important respects, lives in a unique world; and here is revealed in his own
language month by month, the developing world of Emerson, from the
days when there was not a little of the selfconscious prig in his thinking, to
his wise and almost passionless autumn in the solitude of 75. Here are to
be found many entries that later became famous as parts of the essays and
addresses; for it was the lifelong habit of Emerson to record in his diary,
which he called his "savings bank," his flashes of insight along with the most
commonplace happenings. Those who have constructed for themselves a
vague Emerson out of casual impressions received from his well known
works and from commonly accepted conceptions of the man, are likely
to be shocked or agreeably surprised more than once in reading this "the
heart" of his journals. But the total result of such shocks of surprise must
be accounted as gain, for thereby the genius is seen as human.

Interesting Self-Criticism

The earlier portion of the book is full of interesting self-criticism that may
or may not have been wholly justified; but, at the least, it reveals a profound
essential honesty. Often he deplores, in various ways, his "humiliating sense
of dependence and inferiority, which, like the goading, soul-sickening sense
of extreme poverty, palsies effort." "I find myself often idle, vagrant and
hollow," he writes at seventeen. And he adds that if he does not discipline
himself he is doomed to suffer "from remorse and a sense of inferiority
hereafter." Over and over this note is struck. He seems, in his youth, to
have been goaded by a rather overgrown ego. He feels it incumbent on him
to become great, and is made extremely self-conscious as a result. Days of
faith in his powers alternate with days of self-depreciation. He seems, in
those early years, always to have been pulling up his ego to see if it was
growing properly. And too often, as he thought, it wasn't. "I have not the
kind affections of a pigeon," he tells himself at eighteen. "Ungenerous and
selfish, cautious and cold, I yet wish to be romantic, have not sufficient
feeling to speak a natural welcome to a friend."—"There is not one being
to whom I am attached with warm and entire devotion."

In the next entry he unconsciously explains what had seemed to him
a serious defect. "I dedicate my book to the Spirit of America." It is
the overgrown ego speaking—a powerful ego, not as yet guided to wise

and beautiful ends by the flashes of vision that were to come. Genius is individualistic in impulse, and probably never was it more so than in Emerson. Contrary to a very common sentimental notion, genius is always intensely aware of itself. Are not the early questionings of Emerson merely manifestations of an intense egotism momentarily appalled by the task of self-justification?

Lack of Blood Warmth

There undoubtedly is a conspicuous lack of human blood-warmth in Emerson's work. Is not this explained by such as the following? "There is no greater lie than a voluptuous book like Boccacio. For it represents the pleasures of appetite, which only at rare intervals, a few times in a life time, are intense."

This could be written by him at the lusty age of 31! Only at rare intervals, a few times in a life time! And note his curious remark about marriage made at the age of 46 when he had been twice married: "Love is temporary and ends with marriage." The fact that he continues in praise of marriage as a wholly spiritual union only emphasizes the point here suggested. Doubtless the mesdames Emerson sometimes wondered.

In following the development of the man and the genius it is interesting to note how humor creeps into the entries with increasing years. The early portions not only lack humor expressed, but show in various ways that the sense of humor was then extremely weak.

Emerson at 24 notes and justifies the fact. "Why has my motley diary no jokes? Because it is a soliloquy and every man is grave alone." But that is hardly true. It is only as self-regard is lost that humor grows.

Emerson a Regular Fellow

It will be a matter of gratification to many, as this writer confesses it is to him, to know that Emerson could be a "regular fellow" on occasion. Once it is recorded that he actually "cussed." This astonishing occurrence took place during the month of July, 1851, when the seer was 48 years old. He was thinking about the Fugitive Slave law, and, red hot for once, he wrote scorchingly in his diary: "This filthy enactment was made in the nineteenth century by people who could read and write. I will not obey it, by God!" Bravissimo, Ralph! We all get you there!

This intensely interesting volume may be read with joy for its intimate personality alone; but its significance reaches far beyond the satisfaction of curiosity as to what manner of man the sage of Concord was in private. There are very few pages that are not illuminated by some flash of vision.

The numerous frank comments on his great contemporaries whom he knew intimately are of great value. Channing, Hawthorne, Thoreau, Alcott, Margaret Fuller, Carlyle, Tennyson and many others come alive in his vivid phrases. Occasional remarks on religion, science, art, literary criticism and social questions reveal his spirit as a mountain catching light that would not fall upon the valleys of the world until another generation had come and gone.

Emerson was not a creative artist . . . if the strict sense of the term be accepted. But he was nevertheless a great creative artist, and the stuff of which his masterpiece was wrought was the stuff of his own life. His masterpiece was Emerson; and here we have in detail, year by year, the manner of its making.

LITERATURE (1927)

Literature, if the term be allowed a definite meaning, is art. Art is the representation of vision transcending the ordinary animal consciousness of the world. Essential art and essential religion differ not at all in kind, but only in degree. What then shall we say of our "realists," our cynical reporters of life, "who stick to the facts," as they and their claquers boast? Shall we not say that they are blind men presuming to show the way to the blind, and that their so-called facts are no more than formalized misunderstanding?

Literature is seer-stuff, or it is nothing. And so it is usually nothing.

This is set down for the pleasure of those who already know.

A LESSON FROM ORIENTAL SONG

REVIEW OF *LOTUS AND CHRYSANTHEMUM*, EDITED BY JOSEPH LEWIS FRENCH (NEW YORK: BONI, 1927)

This valuable anthology which was designed to be "A fairly representative compendium of the whole body of Chinese and Japanese poetry" is issued in a numbered edition of 1000 copies. Both in format and content it is a desirable item and is not likely to remain long on the market. The relatively few readers who have been persuaded to regard poetry from the viewpoint of the Imagists and other modern schools that specialize in fragmentary, visual impressions, will be enthusiastic over this collection. Others may find much in minor detail that seems exquisitely poetic, without being greatly impressed by any single composition viewed as an organic whole.

This difference in attitudes seems to be explained by the fact, as we are informed, that there is no word for poetry in Chinese. In order to appreciate the meaning of this statement, it is necessary to consider the original connotation of the word. The Greek verb "poieo" from which the term poetry is derived, signifies an act of creation, construction. In our Occidental sense, poetry is not primarily a matter of singing, nor is it merely a matter of seeing or feeling and expressing esthetically what is seen and felt. The poetic process is fundamentally a process of combining, or "making" an architectural whole in keeping with some synthesizing vision of the significant relations between apparent fragments of experience.

If the reader of these remarks is at all interested in poetry, he should go back over the preceding paragraph, for it contains the one idea that can explain all the windy controversies between contending schools in our time, in so far as they apply to fundamental conception and not to mere versification. There never should have been any quarrel as to the latter, for poetry is something quite independent of verse mechanisms. It is wholly a matter of conception.

The fact that much of the product of Amy Lowell and H. D. would not sound strange in an anthology of Chinese verse has a very definite meaning. What is to be noted in Mr. French's collection of Oriental verse is the fragmentary, impressionistic nature of that which is communicated to the reader; and by far the greater portion of the data concerned is visual. It is as though the songster were merely a painter in the Oriental manner, who, lacking the materials of the painter, was forced to use words instead, and strove to compensate with musical sound for the lack of color.

The point is that these Oriental singers evidently had no intention of making poetry in our Western sense. Poetry in our sense is essentially dynamic, creative, a building of fragments into a new and living whole. These Oriental singers sang the fragment.

The difference involved is as great as that between the passive Oriental temperament and the active Occidental. It is the difference between the characteristically feminine and masculine attitudes. Poetry in the Occident is a distinctly masculine art; and it is hardly a matter of coincidence that Imagism should have achieved vogue in a time when a general feminization of literature is to be noted.

THE BITTERNESS OF TRUTH (1928)

For most of us "the world is so full of a number of things," as R. L. S. observed, that it is no wonder so many of us are persuaded to regard fact as being the same thing as truth.[2] Facts crowd us all and they have a brutal way about them. Most of us are always jumping sidewise in our efforts to dodge or overtake them, and all lives are, in some measure, the result of compromise with, or surrender to, these tyrants of sense.

So bitter seems this truth to a certain human temperament, that vast sections of the human race long ago decided to deny the whole objective world of what we call fact, seeking truth in subjective states alone. That, virtually, is what Oriental philosophy does; and it would require a very wise man to prove just yet that the Oriental view is foolish.

We Occidentals are of a different temper; so different that we have gone to the opposite extreme; and too much can kill as well as too little.

All of us in the western world are born into a scientific atmosphere, and our thinking is conditioned by that fact, whether we know anything about science or not. It's "in the air." It is the business of science to deal with facts, and he would be a sorry philosopher, in our eyes at least, who could not admire the efficiency with which science has been, and still is, attending to its business.

But some people do not realize that, while it is the business of science to discover, name and classify facts, it is the business of art to do something very different; and, of course, literature is a form of art. Art in its largest sense is applied philosophy working in the concrete stuff of our experience. Its business is to reveal, by various strategic means, the larger relations between the facts of human experience. In its highest forms, the relations revealed are those that endure so far as we are able to know, and that is far enough for our finite purposes. At least the relations revealed are unchanging in our little world of ever changing fact that seems to boil like quicksand. Our store of facts has increased enormously since the Greeks of fifth century Athens; but their human truths remain true. And how can this be, since they could not have considered more than a small portion of our facts? Because all our new facts fall naturally into old classifications.

However the separate classifications may be enlarged to hold the new facts that have sprung up, the relations between the classifications do not change, so far as men may know. If this were not true, there would be no place in the modern world for the Bible; Socrates would seem no longer wise; and Homer and Aeschylus and Shakspeare would not now be worthy the attention of intelligent men.

It is easy to see why so many people nowadays find the old classics dull. It is the facts, the raw material of literature, that really interests them; and, naturally, they find the facts outmoded. For instance, some cannot get past the childish gods of Homer, the strange customs of Homeric times, to find the sadness and the glory of the human truth that is still true about us now.

Many will remember how, during the days when Zola, the great French "realist," was flourishing. It was made to seem the wise thing to say that what we mortals needed was "the bitter truth" about life. We had, presumably, grown up at last, and we had put away childish things. No more fairy stories for us! We could stand the shock of things as they were. Let the mollycoddles "kid" themselves with pretty lies about human nature. There we stood, disillusioned, but undaunted. "Bring on your worst and serve it rare! There is hideous vice and crawling poverty and unmitigated meanness in the world." We were proud that we could see the ends of our noses.

It is good to be able to see the end of one's nose; but one gets cross-eyed looking at it. Nevertheless, it became the literary fashion to insist upon the superior virtues of myopia. It is still being done because it is extremely difficult to see all around the facts that hold our attention. Accordingly we have what is erroneously called "realism" in literature.

Zola used to say that "a novel is a slice of life seen through a temperament"; and such was his temperament that he usually, though not always, took his slice where the meat was tainted. This was hailed as a triumph for "the bitter truth." It was only a doubtful triumph for certain bitter facts; which was something different. It is not yet proven that the truth is bitter, though certainly there is a chastening and ennobling sadness about it always.

There are no facts to which men can afford to close their eyes. There are no facts so important as to deserve the exclusive attention of men. Realism, to deserve the name, must be concerned with the largest possible view of the facts under consideration; and whenever that view is achieved by a writer, some phase of beauty is certain to result, however ugly the facts themselves may seem.

The resultant beauty will not necessarily be concerned with morals. The saying that art is unmoral is easy to defend. But always genuine art is ethical; that is to say, it is somehow concerned with the abiding, as opposed to the accidental and transient. It is the facts that may be accidental and transient. It is the truth about their relations that abides; and the harmonies to be felt in those unchanging relations are what we love as beauty.

Concentrated Beauty
REVIEW OF *EDEN*, BY MURRAY SHEEHAN (NEW YORK: DUTTON, 1928)

Anyone who has thought much upon the subject must have suspected, at least, that truth (if the word is to have any meaning of its own), can be expressed only through poetic devices. You have only to wander about through the dictionary awhile to discover that language has been developed on a factual basis for urgent utilitarian ends. Now and then you will come across words that seem strangely charged with over-meaning to be felt but hardly to be stated; and in every case, you may be sure, such meanings have been generated by the poetic process without reference to etymology.

Expose an unimaginative literalist to such a word, and it will do nothing to him. For him, its meaning will in no way rise above or spread beyond the solid factual structure—the mere flesh and bones of the term. The over-meaning, that might well be called the soul of the word, will be as though it were not, though it may have been created out of the common joys or sorrows of innumerable men and women.

It is this difference between fact and truth that renders all the higher aspirations of men so pitifully vulnerable to ridicule. Try to state any vital truth in terms of fact alone and see how funny it will seem! It is probable that such an attempt is involved in all the strife between the scientist and religionist; and perhaps the tragic joker in such strife lurks not so much in the antagonism of the scientist as in the mistaken eagerness of the dogmatic religionist to identify with some hard structure of alleged fact the truth that he feels and loves. In other words, is not his truth poetic, if it be truth at all, and does he not concede too much when he strives to meet the scientist on his own ground of physical sense? Certainly no poet worth his salt will make such a concession, however much he may admire science in its own realm.

The Garden of Eden story offers an excellent example of profound human truth expressed in highly charged symbolisms, and of the manner in which such symbolisms may be made to appear ridiculous by the literalist, whether friendly or hostile. We have that story here in *Eden*. But it is no literalist, no seeker after the easy guffaws of our sense-bound sophisticates, who has retold the ancient story. Murray Sheehan is a poet, though it does not appear that he has written any verse, and out of the various versions of the Edenic legend he has woven a rich pattern of meaning that must have been humanly true long before the legend began to take form and shall be true, no doubt, as long as there are men and women and the sad longing to be happy.

To attempt to review Sheehan's book in the usual sense of the word would be to fall into the fatal trap of the literalist. For here is the tale of Lilith's passionate love for Adam before Eve was made, and of the far reaching results of her revenge upon her rival. Surely it is all very silly when you come to tell it in a few forthright words. But just as surely, anyone who has ever been young, and remembers, will recognize at once in Sheehan's story the old land of Eden. To few men—and they the luckless ones—will Lilith be a stranger, and Eve's will be a face well known and dear. Also, there will be something more than amusement in the plucking and the eating of the apple, the pursuing thunder and the flashing of the angelic sword, the weary journey eastward into a land where brambles grow and the stubborn soil yields only under sweat, and death seems waiting at the end of every trail. Cain, who was born in Paradise and shares with all wild and unspoiled creatures the precious secret of the way back, will come to mean something rather more exalted than murder; and Abel will be dismally familiar.

Few books have so much concentrated beauty in them as one finds here. Only once, and that for but a few pages, does it seem that the magical tale is about to be cheapened in keeping with the prevalent mania for being funny at any cost. It is after Adam and Eve have been driven from the Garden, and the harsh facts of the hard new life have blinded them and the family rows begin. This has vital meaning, too; but many will feel that Sheehan allowed himself to be influenced too much at this one point by the cynical attitude toward marriage now fashionable. Even now that the world has become so excessively modern and wise, there are many who still know a short way back from the sordid world that stretches east from Eden.

A Neglected Principle (1928)

In writing a friendly puff for Vere Hutchinson's recently published volume of short stories, entitled *The Other Gate* (Knopf), Sheila Kaye-Smith raises the question as to the relative literary power of the sexes. Very sensibly, she concludes that men and women are different and that to compare them is as foolish as to compare "a soprano and a baritone." It might be reasonable to object that the difference is far more profound than the chosen analogy indicates, but the point need not be labored.

"It is true," continues the laudatory preface, "that men and women do not respond to inspiration in quite the same way. A woman is by nature both more spiritual and more concrete than a man. Hence we find that poetry, which is almost entirely an emotional self-expression, has throughout the ages been chiefly in the hands of men, and that men have given it the most illustrious names."

It seems that there may be something wrong about this statement. The very inadequate conception of poetry here betrayed is held almost universally in these days, when the feminine influence is overwhelmingly evident in literature. " . . . Poetry, which is almost entirely an emotional self-expression!" Surely this is a distinctly feminine conception of poetry applying in no way to the great poetry that "has throughout the ages been chiefly in the hands of men." Is it possible to regard any of the greatest masterpieces of poetry as "almost entirely emotional self-expression?" What of the *Iliad* and *Odyssey*, the *Agamemnon* and *Prometheus* of Aeschylus, the *Oedipus* of Sophocles, the *Trojan Women* of Euripides, the *Aeneid* of

Vergil, Goethe's *Faust*, Shakspeare's plays? The list may be extended, to the same effect, by anyone who has any acquaintance whatever with world literature.

"But when we come to the novel," the argument continues, "—a comparatively recent form of literature, occupying itself chiefly with the facts of life and theories concerning them—we find women playing as big a part in its development as men, and giving to its roll of honor, from the first, names which, if not more illustrious, are at least equal in glory."

That is, no doubt, a true statement, as far as it goes; but might not something very pertinent be said about the type of novel that has become most fashionable in an age of feminized literature—an age in which such a conception of poetry may be held as that which Sheila Kaye-Smith betrays? Can it be said that this type is notable for its architectural quality? Is it conspicuously concerned with the creation of self-completing wholes? Does it reveal demiurgic power, or is it characterized rather by a painstaking accumulation of details—a sort of emotionally heightened gossip on a large scale? And if there be any meaning in these questions, does it not apply to as many fashionable men writers of the day as women writers? And, if this also be true, may it not be explained by the fact that the book-reading public today is largely feminine? And if the great poetry of the world has been distinctly a masculine product, was it not so because it was characterized by that creative, integrating vision that is generally lacking in the typical modern novel—and in typical modern poetry?

As an example of the demiurgic type of novel, *The Tree of the Folkungs* by Verner von Heidenstam may be named. This writer is aware that there are notable exceptions to the general idea suggested in the foregoing, but the point raised by Sheila Kaye-Smith in concerned, not with exceptions, but with a generality. In dealing with that generality she has overlooked a fundamental principle in the criticism of any art. This is not strange, for that principle is now very commonly overlooked by critics. It is the principle involved in the theory of emergent evolution, and may be stated thus: As a result of the creative combination of fragments into a self-completing organism, whether in the physical or mental realm, new values of a higher sort emerge—values that were not to be found in the previously unrelated fragments.

Art of any sort is concerned with the creation of such organisms with newly emergent values. All art is poetic in the original Greek sense of the word, the only sense that justifies poetry at all. Collection is not creation, nor is the greatest art of a personal nature.

A Great Personality

REVIEW OF *AMERICA, THE DREAM*, BY KATHERINE LEE BATES (NEW YORK: CROWELL, 1930)

There are two distinct ways in which men and women may achieve greatness, and there are those who suspect that the less conspicuous way may be the better, as well as the rarer. The more common way, perhaps, is to produce work that may survive the doer; and such is the mysterious character of the human mind that often the thing done is superior to the doer as he is known to men. Many works of genius have been of this sort. The other way is to develop a personality that is in itself its own masterpiece.

The greatness of Katharine Lee Bates, who died just a year ago at the age of 70, was chiefly of the latter kind; for though she published a score or more of books over a period of nearly 40 years, nothing that she wrote, fine as much of it is, suffices to give an adequate conception of the real masterpiece that was her own strong and wise and gentle spirit. There was New England granite in the integrity of her character, but her intuitive understanding and her deep human sympathies were as great as her strength.

One who remembers her with reverence for the personality that she was, might feel at first some disappointment in glancing through this collection of her patriotic poems. Lesser characters in the life sense have certainly produced greater poetry in the literary sense than is to be found here. But upon closer examination very much that was fine and rare in the life is to be felt in the poems.

Nearly everyone is acquainted with Miss Bates' *America the Beautiful*, which seems definitely to have become one of our national hymns; but relatively few can be aware of the depth of the author's love for America out of which the famous song grew. Here the whole story of that love is told in more than a hundred lyrics and ballads, covering our whole history. The volume is divided into sections, corresponding to the various stages of our national development, beginning with "the Discoverers" and carrying the story on through the periods of colonization, exploration, the Revolutionary War, the Civil War and the World War.

It is a book worth owning.

A Poet

REVIEW OF *LONESOME WATER*, BY ROY HELTON (NEW YORK: HARPER, 1930)

Since the so-called "Renaissance of Poetry" began along about 1912 with the free verse movement, it is practically certain that there have been far more professing poets in the world than ever before during any single generation. The number of those who have managed in one way or another to get their verse printed has been very great and they can not have constituted more than a very small minority of verse addicts. Nevertheless, anyone who has really experienced the poetic mystery intensely and often, not as literature, but as a state of expanded and uplifted consciousness, must have noted that in our time, as doubtless in former times, poetry very seldom happens. So seldom does it happen, that hundreds of books written in verse, even though some of them are notably well written, may be read eagerly with only an occasional moment of the genuine psychic expansion and uplift. On the contrary, such moments are frequent and intense in the best work of a very few of our lyric poets—Edna Millay being a notable example. It has happened that certain collections of verse have been praised in the most extravagant terms for a season, although not one such moment was to be experienced in reading them. As a matter of fact, the man in the street is almost right in his judgment of "poetry" in the bulk. In the main, it is largely a matter of vain pretense and self-fooling, the saying of something in an awkward insincere way that was not worth saying.

So confused has the whole question of poetry become as the result of its democratization in the worst possible sense, that to say of a book of verse simply that it contains much genuine poetry is to give to most people no impression whatever of one's meaning. Such a statement should constitute the highest praise, without any attempt being made to rate the writer as "greater" or "greatest," or even "great." Nearly all of the unquestionably genuine poetry of our day is minor in character, for that matter, the mood being personal and concerned with broken fragments of experience, not with the building of objective wholes vital with emergent meaning of a general character.

The purpose of the foregoing remarks is to prepare the reader, who may have come to regard the poetical game of the day as rather piffling on the whole, to read an extraordinary meaning into a simple statement about one Roy Helton, whose volume of verse, *Lonesome Water*, has just appeared. And this is the statement: Roy Helton is a poet.

The collection is composed almost wholly of Kentucky mountain ballads and lyrics of life in the hills. It is not primarily the nature of the material treated nor the convincing use of mountain dialect that makes this a notable book. Whatever might deeply interest a man like Helton would be certain to result in poetry; but his evidently intimate knowledge of the hill people has given him the opportunity to deal with fundamental human nature, and with the insight and verbal magic at his command he has produced some strangely impressive poems for which many a lover of poetry will be deeply grateful.

After all, talk about poetry really doesn't get anywhere. The important thing is to experience it—and here in *Lonesome Water* is an opportunity.

A Great Indian Poet (1931)

This writer has just returned to the modern world after spending a month in a contemporary antiquity that, in certain cultural respects, may be described as pre-Homeric. In company with his two daughters he has been living with his friends, the Oglala Sioux, in lonely country empty of white men where there was little to remind one of our civilization save the usual injustice and the resultant poverty of a conquered people who deserve a better fate.[3]

The writer had only casual contacts with the younger generation, who, having little of their own racial culture and less of ours, seem lost somewhere in a shadowy borderland that lies between the white man and the red and that has been crossed far less often by people of our race than is generally supposed. The writer's host and intimate associates were the old pahuskas, that is to say, the long-haired old-timers who have retained their "pagan" culture with a passionate devotion; men who were in at the death when Fetterman and his 80 troopers died that blizzard day on Piney Creek now more than 60 years ago; men who, as boys of 12 and 14 and 16, slaughtered Reno's panic-stricken cavalrymen "like fat cows" in the valley of the Little Big Horn, and helped to rub out Custer in the darkness of the hoof-dust and the smoke upon the hill; men who went through the tragic affair at Wounded Knee when their fleeing women and children were murdered as they fled and where a great dream died in the bloody snow.

Well, we killed a bull and had a feast, cooking in the ancient way, and there were enough of us so that when the feast was finished little remained but the hide and the horns and hoofs. (To be quite accurate, later on we ate the hoofs.) And the old men and women danced in full dress and wrinkled old-timers made "kill-talks," remembering their youth before they had become prisoners of war, recounting deeds of prowess in quite the true Homeric manner while the rawhide drums boomed at high points in the story and the old women sent forth the tremolo of admiration.

And it happened, so powerful was the spell of it all, that we three danced, too, mere white folks that we were, and we did it in no spirit of derision, but with a happy humility, as was fitting. And that night we danced the rabbit dance under the stars to the booming of the big drum while the young drummers sang and the old and the young, the dark and the white, the men and the boys and the women and the girls, seemed of one age and of one color and of no sex at all. The pure lyric joy of it is very good to remember.

But it wasn't the dancing or the Gargantuan feasting that mattered most in the end. It wasn't even the eating of raw liver hot from the bull—an act of communion with the old warriors and hunters far more satisfactory as a symbolism, be it confessed, than as a gustatory experience! The best of it all came out in the long days of constant talk with the old men, and especially with our host, Hehaka Sapa (Black Elk), who is the second cousin of the great chief Crazy Horse. Black Elk is a great "medicine man," that is to say, a priest and a seer of visions. At the age of 13 he did a man's share of the bloody work on the Little Big Horn, and he fought at Wounded Knee and at the Mission Fight and at White Clay Creek in the Badlands during the Messiah trouble of 1890. But war, to him, was only an unavoidable necessity. He has lived for spiritual values and his visions, as set forth in careful detail for this writer, rank easily in beauty and profundity of significance with the supreme things in the rich literature of the Aryan peoples. His great vision, which came to him first at the age of 9, during a 12-day period of apparent unconsciousness, is in itself a very great work of art, both as to form and to content. Unfortunately, for us white people, literature, in our sense, never developed among Black Elk's people. His culture never passed the evolutionary stage of the dance ritual and accordingly the great vision can be adequately expressed only in the dance ceremony, with its accompanying song. One portion of the vision alone—the horse dance, which is poetry of a sublime order—would require some five or six hours to produce. No white man has ever seen it performed, and no white man until now has ever heard it described in its astonishing beauty; but that one white man, who has spent his life in awe of the great ones of our literature, felt that he had been sitting at the feet of a poet fit to dine with the finest spirits that have sung in his discordant world and are now among the tallest of the dead. Black Elk is truly a great poet; and if ever our world shall be privileged to see and understand his masterpiece, the horse dance—as this writer hopes it may—there will be few to question the indubitable truth of this statement.

WHAT IS POETRY? (1933)

One who has served as judge in many so-called "poetry contests" has wondered often if some much-needed change in the prevailing conception of poetry might not render it impossible to conceive of competition in such a field of experience. The following remarks may serve to indicate the direction of the needed change:

Verse can be defined in terms of literature. Poetry cannot. Although commonly conceived as a literary form, it can be explained, rather than strictly defined, only in terms of psychology.

Essentially, poetry is not the opposite of prose, but of science. The difference is between two different modes of being aware. It is the function of science to relate and systematize the phenomena of the physical senses. It is the function of poetry to present those larger relations of human experience commonly described as spiritual, and by virtue of those revealed relations to create patterns of meaning not to be found in any possible arrangement of sense data.

The question of poetry is concerned with states of being aware. By way of making the matter clear, it may be pointed out that the awareness of a bug can hardly be so inclusive as that of a horse, nor can the awareness of a horse include as much of the world as does the consciousness of a man. We commonly assume, without thought, that every man and woman is equally conscious of an identical world in the same way. But on taking thought, we know this conventional assumption to be false. There is indeed a conventional world commonly shared by conventional mentalities, but even this must differ in detail far more than is generally assumed.

Assuming that the foregoing statements are understood, we are in position to consider that mode of understanding and expression which is called poetry. For the problem involved is concerned with the fact that human consciousness is expansive and not limited to the awareness of mere physical relationships. If it were so limited, there would be no difference between human and brute.

Poetry is both a mode of understanding and a means of communicating the understandings of a more inclusive state of awareness to a less inclusive state. It is a means of expressing through the mediumship of language what language was not designed to express; for language was developed under the pressure of necessity for utilitarian purposes.

Accordingly, since language is in its nature utilitarian, poetry employs various devices by way of increasing the expressiveness of words. For instance, it uses symbols, suggests far more than it tells, and employs meter, rhythm, rhyme and varying internal vowel and consonant schemes which serve somewhat in the nature of hypnotic agencies, aiding in the task of creating in the consciousness of the hearer by suggestion a vivid sense of that which could not be told as science.

As for what happens to one who is suddenly made aware through poetry of illuminating relations other than those of ordinary brute sense living, we may cite the experience of a man walking in a dark night and carrying a lantern. He proceeds well enough for all immediately practical purposes and for his individual needs of the moment, for the lantern illuminates a small circle about him, so that he is aware of his immediate lesser relationships. But suddenly, as he proceeds, a great flash of lightning renders dim his little lantern glow, and in a moment of larger illumination, he becomes aware of a vast landscape all about him in all its relationships; a landscape of which he may not previously have been aware but of which nevertheless his little moving circle of dim light was an integral part. Surely with that revelation he will be a more understanding traveler.

The illustration is necessarily crude; as analogies are likely to be; but it serves well to indicate the nature of the genuine poetic experience.

In the literature of poetry, the poetic illumination may occur briefly in a single epithet or in a line or a passage; or it may emerge from the whole structure of the poem. The latter is true of all great world poetry.

Two Adult Lyric Poets
REVIEW OF *POEMS: 1911–1936*, BY JOHN HALL WHEELOCK (NEW YORK: SCRIBNER'S, 1936), AND *HILL GARDEN*, BY MARGARET WIDDEMER (NEW YORK: FARRAR, 1936)

It is highly improbably that better lyric poetry will be published this season than is to be found in the two volumes here noted—one by a man, one by a woman, and both not only unquestionably authentic poets, but mature.

It has been remarked with good reason that the supreme feat of the poet must be undergone near the age of 30 when the romantic period normally ends. By that time the extravagantly promising ecstasy of vernal blossoming is definitely on the wane and the pain of fruiting begins. It is a time of progressive disillusionment, and for most, whether professing poets or not, the "shades of the prison house begin to close." That, perhaps, is what maturity means to the vast majority.

Maturity kills most poets; and fortunately so, since it is precisely the adult vision that can make verse worth the paper that it blackens. For who cannot see alluring visions when the young blood riots? The test is in seeing the enduring vision when early dreams have dimmed and facts are brutal tyrants and duty is a galling harness. Some, it is lamentably true, continue poetizing without vision long beyond the killing test—a pathetic and profitless industry.

Both John Hall Wheelock and Margaret Widdemer have lived and continued to sing far beyond the crucial period, and each has seen the only vision that can justify a continued interest in the writing of poetry after the death of youth. Not only have they survived the biological crisis, but they have come through the more than 20 years of cultural madness that began in America about the year 1912 and resulted in the incredible insanities of the "new poetry." There is nothing in their verse to indicate exposure to that madness. The point that greatly matters here is this: that John Hall Wheelock, poet, is, first of all, truly a grown-up man; that Margaret Widdemer, poet, is first of all truly a grown-up woman; that both have been spiritually enriched with sacrifice and pain, and therefore have, as by divine gift, a license to sing to the rest of us who go about our tasks too often songless and certainly a little lonely.

These two voices—a man's and a woman's—sing beautifully in unison, for in the final appraisal they are singing the same song. Each has grown to the point where the personal view, the hurts and joys of the self, give way to the vast impersonal vision. Wheelock expresses this most powerfully in his "Unisons," the next to the last poem in the volume; Margaret Widdemer sings it exquisitely in "Curtains," the last of her collection; and perhaps the difference in expression is not unlike that between a baritone and a soprano voice.

If one were called upon to compare the two volumes, it would be necessary to say that Wheelock's is by far the greater from the viewpoint of literary achievement, for it contains the best of his work over a period of a quarter of a century, and Wheelock is indubitably one of the finest poets our generation has produced. Margaret Widdemer's volume is the product of the last four years.

But, after all, poetry, which happens much more rarely than most readers suppose, is poetry, and in its essence there is only equality.

SIXTEEN

What Is Literature Good For?

Unparalleled success by science in the material realm left early-twentieth-century society with the expectation that science could meet all needs. Not so, as far as Neihardt was concerned. Poetic values are necessary to human existence, Neihardt argued, and in the following essays he explains why. He suggested that the great deeds of his contemporaries were active expressions of the creative dream in humanity; in 1912 he linked the energy driving technological progress to an emerging poetic sensibility, in spite of the fact that "we have been so busy fitting up a vast continent with strictly modern improvements that we have not listened to the singing voices in our land."[4]

For those who cannot actively achieve, their dreams can be sung. When putting dreams into words, ordinary language is inadequate; here the gifts of the poet come into play, giving shape to those longings of the spirit that are difficult to express, "the beautiful difference between our dreaming and our doing."[5] The record of these attempts to put the expressions of the spirit into words can be found in the literature of the ages. The person whose environment is limited (and that includes all of us) can turn to literature to transcend boundaries of space and time. Through literature, anyone can connect to the encompassing body of humanity in whose literature the "restless, dreaming human spirit" finds expression.

Neihardt challenged prevailing definitions of "practical" as "little more than hustling after money." He called for an awareness of the need—met by poetry—to help humans learn how to live fully once the means of life have been acquired. He charged education with this responsibility, to the "process of making a man rich in the only values that can not possibly be acquired by accident, or theft in any of its many disguises" nor lost by the same means.[6]

THE RENASCENCE OF POETRY IN AMERICA (1912)

There is a saying abroad to the effect that poetry is dead and buried. It has become a catch-phrase. You may hear it any day from almost anyone to whom you may broach the subject.

If you say "Ivory Soap" to the average American, he will immediately either say or think, "It floats." Likewise, if you say the word poetry the same man will either think or say, "There are no longer any poets worth reading."

This is the age and America is the country of the catch-phrase; and it is by no means a negligible fact; it has a deep psychological significance. For several generations most of us have been so busy making and spending money, so occupied with the utilitarian side of life, that we have, as a body, neglected the finer aspects of living. We think, as we eat, on the run. It is the time of predigested foods and ready-to-wear culture. The former can be had at 15 cents the package, and the latter is free in the form of catch-phrases. Conversation hardly exists. To converse in the fine old sense, one must have thought in leisure about many things and their relations. So when we wish to appear cultured, the majority of us merely get out our stock of embalmed sentiments and pass them around—like bon bons. For instance, when religion is under discussion, you are sure to hear from someone present that "religion is dying." This startling bit of information is given out blandly and without the least indication of alarm. And yet, not since the early centuries of Christianity, has the Christ idea been so strongly in evidence as now; not that the temporal masters are led by it, but that it is the yeast in a world-wide ferment.

The Christ idea dead! Poetry dead! These are absurdities. Neither can die, as each has to do with the unchanging spiritual hunger of Man. And, indeed, poetry is essentially more closely connected with religion than is supposed by one in ten thousand; for poetry is one of the arts—many think it to be the greatest of them—and the arts are the vehicles of expression for the divinity in man.

Hugo, in his magnificent, though sometimes erratic work, which treats of everything and is called *William Shakspere,* thunders against this periodical cry of the ubiquitous Philistine regarding the death of poetry.[7] Even in that time, when the gorgeous flower of romanticism was bursting forth from the aridity of a worn-out classicism, men said what they are saying today, and mourned over the vanished days of Corneille and Racine. Yet the manner in which the grizzled old bard unleashed his lightnings should have been proof enough, even to his purblind contemporaries, that the strain of the elder prophets had not perished from the earth.

Not only in Hugo's time, nor in our own twentieth century, has the cry gone up that the time of great poetry is past. As early as the sixth century B.C., when the rhapsodoi—"sons of Homer," singers of the stitched song—chanted the epics of the blind bard of Chios, men doubtless looked back longingly upon the golden past, shook their heads and said, "Homer was—and the great harp is silent forever." And yet, Vergil was on the way—and Dante and Milton and Tasso. And in the time when the literary gossip of Athens was all about the plays of Euripides, were there not many of those who spoke sadly of the younger days of Eschylus, saying that virility was dead and that poetry had become effeminized? Who could ever awaken again the thunders of the Orestean trilogy? No less a man than Aristophanes was of that number. And yet far away in an island of the Northern seas, not as yet discovered, the Avon flowed quietly by the spot where Stratford was to stand, where Shakspere was to be born in good time. And in the Augustan age of Rome, in those days when Vergil sat before the emperor of the world and chanted his latest lines from the growing Aeneid, was there not a cult that, while lounging in the baths, quoted Greek verses and sneered at the Mantuan as the petted and very much overestimated darling of the aristocracy?

"Shakspere," says a critic who lived shortly after the Elizabethan age, "had neither the tragic talent nor the comic talent. His tragedy is artificial, and his comedy is but instinctive." Shakspere was "a plagiarist," a "copyist," "a crow adorned with the plumes of others!" His *Hamlet* was but a rehash of the *Orestes* of Eschylus; his *Lady Macbeth* but a garbled version of *Clytemnestra,* his *Lear* but a poor adaptation of *Edipus!* So said certain scholarly critics and went back to the ancients.

When John Keats died in Rome, "not a dozen men in England knew that a great poet had passed away," says Rossetti. And yet, without Keats there could have been no Tennyson, no Swinburne, no Morris!

In all great ages men have looked longingly backward at "the good old times." The man on the mountain cannot see the mountain upon which he stands; the purple of some distant peak will attract him. It is a matter of perspective. Nevertheless there are unfailing means of ascertaining the altitude of a mountain upon which one stands; and just as surely it is possible to judge the greatness of a poet before he is dead. But there is this difference: The world at large will readily accept the stated altitude of a mountain; but the poet must, as a rule, bide his time until tradition has flung the purple mantle about him, when he will be gazed at to the detriment of those nearer singers whom tradition has not yet clothed.

We moderns, especially in America, have a way of priding ourselves upon what we term our "materialism"; and being, as we fancy, intensely materialistic and commonsensical, we think that great poetry cannot grow in the atmosphere of our time. Yet, never in the history of man has there been such a time for dreaming and for realizing dreams. Put yourself, if possible, in the mental state of a man of the middle ages, and take a good look at us. What do you see? Was ever monster of the dark ages more a creature of the creative imagination than the Twentieth Century Limited? We have dreamed with Icarus, but with more success. Having conquered the sea, we coveted the lordship of the air. We make day by pressing a button. We talk casually over leagues and leagues of wire. We hurl messages across the sea in the twinkling of an eye, very much as a small boy throws a stone over a frog pond. Ships parley with each other across a thousand miles of ocean wilderness. Some of us are seriously talking of calling up Mars for a friendly chat. We weigh the stars and determine the elements of the sun. Was the Colossus of Rhodes quite so audaciously romantic an undertaking as the Woolworth building in New York? Is an automobile less charged with mystery (because it is real) than the Chimera? Some of our biologists have dared to dream of the generation of life from inert matter and lately the news has gone forth that this seeming miracle has been accomplished. Chemists are dreaming of the possible transmutation of metals—alchemy become scientific. We discuss the invisible rays of the spectrum, and have devised a means for rendering opaque bodies transparent. Dreaming mariners have stood upon both poles of the earth. An international society exists for the avowed purpose of communicating with an alleged world of disembodied spirits. All over the world the unlettered toilers are dreaming of an ideal commonwealth, and are most decidedly working toward its realization.

Why, our age is packed with imagination, and more wonders are told than Marco Polo brought back to startle Venice! A prosy age? An age in which poetry cannot thrive? But it is precisely the kind of an age in which it can and does thrive! We have been so busy fitting up a vast continent with strictly modern improvements that we have not listened to the singing voices in our land. We have taken our poetry in the form of skyscrapers and aeroplanes and ocean liners and limited trains and automobiles and wireless telegraphs and the like. The trouble is not with the singers, but with those who have not yet listened.

All great literary ages have seemed to be materialistic ages—to the myopic eyes of contemporaries. What of the Periclean age of Greece, the Augustan age of Rome, the Elizabethan age of England? Always the great singers have come when the fever of great enterprises was in the air. And when before was there such a stirring in every conceivable branch of human endeavor as now?

Science has been likened to a river, art to an ocean. Science is progressive—it advances. Art does not progress—it rises and falls. Once again the wave is rising, and it is safe to say that we are now in a remarkable lyrical age. All over the land the fires have burst forth. We have at least a dozen singers who would have added glory to any age. There are those, doubtless, who will look upon this statement with suspicion; but the sacred fire burns. It has touched George Sterling out in California; Sara Teasdale down in St. Louis; Ridgeley Torrence in Ohio; Anna Hempstead Branch in Connecticut; Lizette Woodworth Reese in Baltimore; Cale Young Rice and Madison Cawein in Louisville; Edwin Arlington Robinson in New York; William Ellery Leonard in Wisconsin. Then there are Percy Mackaye, Ezra Pound, Josephine Preston Peabody. Our own city may boast of Richard Burton and the lamented Arthur Upson. Verily, poetry is not dead.

In the spring of 1910, the Poetry Society of America was organized for the purpose of encouraging our rising singers, and to "secure for the art of poetry a fuller public recognition as one of the important forces in higher civilization." This society has been eminently successful from the start, and is just now entering its third year of existence with a large membership, including important persons in all lines of human endeavor. And, what is probably more to the point in this time of money valuation, the lists of the publishers show an increasing percentage of books of verse. A magazine, given over entirely to the productions of modern American poets, will be launched in Chicago soon.[8] A hundred poetry lovers have subscribed $5,000 per year for five years toward the support of the venture.

This department will, from time to time, print articles dealing with the works and personalities of those who are reviving in America the fine old traditions of English poetry.

EDUCATION AND LITERATURE (1926)

What is education? It must be, fundamentally, a spiritual process. In its proper function it is concerned less with the problem of acquiring the means of life than with the far more difficult one of knowing what to do with life after one is in possession of the means to live. We have heard much of practical education; and there is no fault to find with the expression; for "practical" means that which will work, and surely only that which will work may be regarded as good. But there has been something radically wrong with our understanding of the word "practical." Owing to the tremendous economic pressure of our time, we have been forced to interpret the word as meaning that which contributes directly to material success; and for a great many people practical education has come to signify that mental training which is calculated to give the maximum of income in the minimum of time.

Obviously, if that conception be a true one, a human being is little more than a machine designed for the purpose of diverting to his own uses as great a portion of the world's stream of wealth as may be possible under the circumstances. Thus, the emphasis of life is placed upon a purely material scale of values—which is the scale of the brute. That conception of education results in the classification of men and women by what they possess rather than by what they are; and it is a matter of common knowledge that, in the anarchic scramble for possession of material things, it is not infrequently the admittedly lower type of man that arouses the envy of the neighborhood.

A man can be no other than that which he truly is, as distinguished from what he has. And it is with what a man is—that is to say, with personality—that education must be chiefly concerned. It is the process of making a man rich in the only values that can not possibly be acquired by accident, or theft in any of its many disguises, and that can not be lost by such means. And in what do these values consist? In those impersonal spiritual and mental attitudes that have resulted from man's age-long struggle. And in this sense, it is the prime function of education to make men social beings; to make them, insofar as may be possible, citizens of all time and of all countries; to give them the widest possible comprehension of a man's relation to other men and to his physical environment; to substitute sympathy for prejudice in the list of human motives. In other words, the consciousness of the individual must be extended to include the race consciousness. It must be made possible for the one to live vicariously the life of the many from the beginning.

It will be said by some that this is a large order, indeed; but it must be remembered that education is not an end, but rather an endless process, a manner of becoming, a spiritual direction. The fundamental importance of World Literature in this connection ought to be obvious. Institutions of learning are devices for facilitating the educational process; but insofar as they neglect world literature, they fall short of their purpose; for what is world literature but a record of the continuous consciousness of the race? And what is Science but a running commentary on that tremendous text?

It may be remarked by some that this is old fashioned humanism, impractical in the modern world. It is not humanism that is impractical, but rather the lack of it; for what is it that all men seek if it be not happiness? And what is happiness but the spiritual result of harmonious adjustment to the world of men and things? And can one logically hope to achieve that state solely through a material process? A thousand seers have agreed that happiness does not come from without; that it is not something to be pursued and captured; that possession of things can not produce it; that the desire to possess is like a flame growing upon the fuel that feeds it, or like one's own shadow that one pursues in vain. A certain amount of material goods is necessary to existence; but the needed amount is not great, and what could be less wise than to spend one's life in acquiring the means of life, and neglecting to live?

It is especially fitting that this view of education should be emphasized at this time when the word "democracy" is in every mouth. Though democracy is fundamentally an economic concept, concerned with the nice adjustment of individual rights and duties that all may contribute to, and share, the means of life; yet its ultimate purpose should transcend the grosser world and emphasize the equality of opportunity in the spiritual realm as well. The so called "practical" education is too much concerned with the economic world, too little with the more important business of the soul. The education of the future should not make us less efficient in the economic realm; but it should certainly make it possible for all to share according to their abilities that priceless racial inheritance, preserved for us in the great literature of the world, which is the very essence of genuine education.

There is Nothing to Escape

A recent literary note reads as follows: "One of the biggest men in Wall Street, we are told, keeps the salesman of a bookstore near his office hunting distractedly for a new mystery novel daily. The financier finds no other such relaxation and complete escape from business, he avers, as that offered by his evening detective stories. The demand for novels of mystery and its solution, whatever elements may be its cause, has grown so of recent years that it almost deserves a separate literary category."

The implied conception of literature as a means of escape from life is very common in our time, as a cursory examination of the stream of books will prove. It is so common that even many critics have come to regard all the arts as devices for living briefly in an unreal world of the imagination. The assumption must be that life itself is rather a dull business to be borne somehow. Upon what other assumption could that view of the arts be based? For if life be not a bad business, why the wish to escape it?

Since we can not afford to grant that human life is a bad job at best—and in the larger view there is no justification for granting it—we must conclude that the error involved is concerned with the conception of life out of which such a conception of literature must grow. If men want to escape what they are persuaded to regard as "real life," then there is something radically wrong with their notion as to what "real life" is, and there will be something radically wrong with their literature, too.

By the very fact of being human, "men can not live by bread alone." They are human by virtue of other values that are not to be expressed in terms of price; and when, as now, most people are persuaded or forced to believe that the getting of material things is a man's best reason for existence, frequent escapes from life will seem necessary, and literature will be conceived as a means of escape.

But genuine literature is not and can not be a means of escape from life. Rather it must be, in some degree, a larger revelation of human life, to the end that life may not seem a bad business. This does not mean that literature will preach the sentimental sunshine doctrine. That, itself, is merely another attempt at escape. Genuine literature will reveal life with its larger compensations. A great work of literature should be as a lofty hill from which you may get a just view of the whole landscape in which you move your little while. And from that hill of vision you may know that there is nothing to escape in this world but one's own shortsighted view of things.

What Is Poetry Good For? (1926)

In this practical time men justly demand that nothing shall survive without some utilitarian reason for existence. If it could be shown that poetry performs no important function, the writing of it might well be forbidden and poets set to useful tasks. But poetry does not suffer under such a test.

Perhaps everyone will agree in defining language as a means for communicating states of mind. If all states of mind were capable of communication by direct statement, then the study of language would be no more than the study of words arranged according to the rules of grammar and syntax. But everyone has noted, or should have noted, that in the higher reaches of human expression certain effects are obtained that cannot be explained by the most industrious parsing and analysis. Something subtle and powerful escapes between the parts of speech. At such moments it becomes evident that the thing analyzed is a mere skeleton and that some mysterious spirit moves among those dry bones. At such moments it is apparent that one might as well hope to explain *Aeneid* by analyzing the food that Virgil ate, as to account, by means of verbal mechanics, for the miracle that has happened among those words.

And what is this miracle that grammar and syntax cannot explain? It is the universal language, and it operates alike in all countries and times. It is grounded in human nature, and the devices through which it works attain their highest power in what we call poetry.

It has been remarked that "we are all islands shouting lies to each other across seas of misunderstanding." Stripped of its obvious exaggeration, the saying contains an important truth. Language has always been an inadequate means of expression, as a little thought will prove to anyone. Thought outruns expression for the reason that language has developed out of fundamental human need, while the restless, dreaming human spirit has always groped for values unrelated to physical necessity. That is why human nature is human and not merely brutal.

So long as men communicate only such ideas as are more or less directly concerned with fundamental needs there can be no confusion. We can all meet on that common ground and we have a language well adapted to such expression. But man is master of the earth solely because he is gifted with the power to dream constructively, transcending his physical environment; and, accordingly, the dictionaries of the world record numerous attempts, only partially successful, to express in sound the high adventuring of the human spirit. It is well known that limitation may be a means to power; and out of the very inadequacy of language have grown the arts. Poetry (not verse) is the essence of all the arts.

Mission of Poetry

Poetry may be defined as a means of communicating what can not be said by direct statement. In its highest moments, in any art, it tells nothing; rather it induces the desired mood of understanding. Its appeal is to the stored up experience of the reader—experience that, in many cases, may have seemed to have been forgotten. Some of such experience must have been acquired directly by living. Most of it, in the matter of appreciating great poetry, could not be acquired so but must be the wider experience of other men in many times, absorbed through contact with literature and the other arts.

For the manner in which poetry works as a means of communication, we have a close analogy in the wireless telegraph. When, for instance, the faint electric thrill has traveled, say, from Ireland to Newfoundland, it is too weak to operate the receiving mechanism. For this reason, in the early days of the wireless, a device called a "coherer" was employed. It consisted of a glass tube filled with iron filings. Through this the faint electric thrill passed, and as it did so it caused the filings to cohere, thus completing a circuit between the receiving instrument and a powerful battery belonging to the receiving station. It was the receiving station's own battery that did the work.

In the manner of poetry, to apply the analogy, the written or spoken word is the coherer that conducts the poetic suggestion, and serves to hurl across the mind of the hearer or the reader the latent and often unsuspected power with which his own memory is charged. It is the stored up experience of the receiver that must complete the work of understanding; and thus, in all the arts precious messages are passed from mind to mind across "the seas of misunderstanding." But a receiving station must have a well charged battery!

You May Be Out Of Tune

And so it happens that when you think of a poet or artist of any sort whom time has proven great, and yet feel in no way moved, you are in exactly the position of one who has no receiving set with which to catch, we will say, the music of a Heifitz or a Paderewski or a Galli-Curci that may be living all about you in radio vibrations from the distant broadcasting station. Or it may be that you are in the position of one who possesses a receiving set capable of being tuned to only a few wave lengths, and who can not pick up the greater stations. You will not note the lack of what is hidden from you. But the fact remains that you are quite as dead to an important portion of your environment as any tree. We may be certain that every mere human being is quite unconscious of by far the vaster portion of his environment. This merely is to say that we have finite minds. But it is also true that relatively few people ever become conscious of the larger environment that is quite within the reach of their latent powers, if they only knew.

LIVING WATER

REVIEW OF *SELECTED LYRICS OF AMELIA JOSEPHINE BURR* (NEW YORK: DORAN, 1927)

During the past 15 years there has been a great deal of acrimonious argument concerning poetic theory and poetic form. For a much longer time there has been a great deal of acrimonious argument concerning religious theory and form. To some it seems fairly clear that all such contentiousness is based upon some misunderstanding of the function of form.

Just as, in its essence, religion is an intimate personal experience of larger relations than those revealed by the senses, an experience that can be shared with other men only through some medium of form, so is poetry, in its nonliterary and truer meaning, an intimate personal experience of larger relations to be shared through the mediumship of literary devices.

In each case it is the vision that matters, and the vision is not of the senses. But since the structure of our common world is built of such stuff as the senses may know, it is not strange that we should so often set the visible form above that for which the form is only a medium.

Famishing men dip up the living waters with cups and cans and goblets of varying designs and costliness; and most of them forget to drink while they run about wrangling bitterly over the relative merits of their utensils. There is no good reason why a thirsty man should not drink from a finely jeweled goblet; there may be good reasons why he should, if he so desires and can, for esthetics may be more than a dilettante whim. There is no reason why another should not drink from a gourd. And those who, having no cup at all, yet find the living spring with their lips are surely not to be condemned.

The important question to be asked of those who hawk their brand-new cups about the literary world is this: Do they, by chance, hold any living water? Some undoubtedly do. But the important question has been overlooked pretty generally, else there would have been less acrimony.

Meanwhile there have been those who knew, in spite of all the confusing clamor, that the business of a poet, if he may be said to have any, is to see at least a little more than naked eyes have seen and to say what he has seen so that others may see, too. And that is to bear the living water.

These oblique remarks would serve to introduce the work of any one of at least a dozen honest singers of our day, both men and women. Amelia Josephine Burr is such a singer, as she has been proving for years and as her *Selected Lyrics* show. There is no indication that she has ever mistaken form for substance, and she strives for no "original" effects. Having seen, she sings quite simply in the measures that she knows and she has mastered them that they may serve her purpose well. Over and over in the reading of her lyrics one feels the sudden breathlessness, the quick half-hurt of beauty seen where common things had been.

LITERATURE AS ENVIRONMENT (1927)
We hear a great deal about heredity and environment in these days, and there seems to be no reason to doubt that what a man becomes is the result of his inheritance acted upon by the environment in which he develops. Formerly the greater emphasis was placed on heredity, but there is now a growing tendency to emphasize the power of environment in shaping human beings. With a certain school of psychologists, this tendency has

gone so far as to make the mind of man seem no more than the result of muscular reaction to stimuli. No doubt this tendency will lead thinkers far on the other side of the truth, as generally happens when there is a new persuasion to be defended; but it is not wholly a bad tendency, since it makes society responsible for the welfare of its members.

Whatever the truth may be as to the exact relative importance of heredity and environment, this much may be taken as true; that, granting the inherited potentialities of an individual, environment is everything thereafter.

But what do we mean by environment?

Environment is that which surrounds a man. From his viewpoint, he may be regarded as the center of his environment; but what is the circumference of it? How far does it extend?

It is probable that most people think of environment only in the physical sense. A child born in dire poverty is discussed as having a certain environment characteristic of want; but the literature of biography disproves this over and over. A thousand children of all sorts are born in a county where no one seriously considers anything but the prices of land and agricultural commodities; but among the thousand children, two or three may show very early in their lives that they are being acted upon by some environment greater than that of which the rest of the population is conscious. One of these youngsters, for instance, may by accident acquire a cheap copy of some great book, and such may be his hereditary traits that the book may become dear to him; so dear that he will manage somehow to get more and more joy of the same sort. And since the passion to understand develops by geometrical progression, the fixed and duller passions of the community will have little power to check the development of the youngster. He will not be the product of his county. And yet it will remain true that a man develops by virtue of his potentialities acted upon by his environment.

Then what, in reality, is that boy's environment?

There is environment in space and there is environment in time, and the latter is beyond computation the more important. It is possible to spend a lifetime in traveling all over the globe, as many illiterates have done, and never get out of the smaller environment. It is possible to dwell a lifetime in one place, yet live almost wholly in the larger environment. There is no escape from the self by changing one's geographical position. The only escape is through development of self; and the larger development of the self is the result of contact with that environment which is in time and which consists of the best that men have "thought and felt and done." The enduring literature of the world is the medium through which contact with this larger environment is made possible.

And so we come to a very thrilling fact, that great numbers of people in our time are right now able to connect with the largest environment if they care to do so. It surrounds them like an atmosphere that all but a relative few have never breathed. Wealth is by no means an essential, and not very much leisure is demanded. A little well-guided reading every day will accomplish wonders in a few years, as no doubt many of our readers could testify from experience; but relatively the number of those must be small.

It is an obsession with us nowadays to be what we call "practical." By that term we mean, as a rule, little more than hustling after money. This is not strange, for need drives where greed does not, and the economic pressure is very great in a civilization that is so largely devoted to the artificial stimulation of consumption that production of commodities may be profitable.

Also the astonishing exploits of science tend to encourage us in focusing our attention on the purely physical, the immediate thing. This, too, has its justification; for, as we have learned, there is a great deal we need to know about the purely physical, the immediate thing.

But we should not forget that we are human, and not mere brutes, only because we are able to store up human experience for the use of our posterity. We now are both ancestors and posterity. And, as posterity, is it practical for us to overlook our great inheritance—the stored-up experience of those who were before us, as recorded in the literature that has survived so many changes in the moods of men?

Three thousand years is not long. It only seems so. In fact, all the great ones, whose lives and works have been saved for us, are not so much as a minute away from us right now. They are "nearer to us than breathing, closer than hands and feet."⁹ In the realm of the greatest there is only now; and most of us may be citizens of that richest realm if we only wish to be.

Notes

INTRODUCTION

1. Neihardt, "Folk Lore of the Antilles," review of *As Old as the Moon*, by Florence Jackson Stoddard, *New York Times Book Review*, 1 January 1910, 4 (hereafter cited as *Times*).

2. Neihardt, *Black Elk Speaks: Being the Life Story of a Holy Man of the Oglala Sioux* (1932; reprint, with a new preface, illustrations, and appendixes, and with an introduction by Vine Deloria Jr., Lincoln: University of Nebraska Press, 1961, 1979).

The five Songs in Neihardt's epic were originally published individually. *The Song of Hugh Glass* (New York: Macmillan, 1915), *The Song of Three Friends* (New York: Macmillan, 1919), and *The Song of Jed Smith* (New York: Macmillan, 1941) have been reprinted in *A Cycle of the West* (1949; Lincoln: University of Nebraska Press, 1963, 1991) and *The Mountain Men* (Lincoln: University of Nebraska Press, 1971). *The Song of the Indian Wars* (New York: Macmillan, 1925) and *The Song of the Messiah* (New York: Macmillan, 1935) have been reprinted in *A Cycle of the West* (1949; Lincoln: University of Nebraska Press, 1963, 1991) and *The Twilight of the Sioux* (Lincoln: University of Nebraska Press, 1971).

3. Except where noted, biographical information on Neihardt's critical venture comes from Lucile Aly, *John G. Neihardt: A Critical Biography* (Amsterdam: Rodopi, 1977).

4. Neihardt, "The Political Essays of John Jay Chapman," review of *Causes and Consequences* and *Practical Agitation*, by John Jay Chapman, *Minneapolis Journal*, 12 September 1912, ws7 (hereafter cited as *Journal*).

5. Hilda Neihardt, "John Neihardt, Essayist" (paper presented at the Nebraska Literature Festival, Omaha, Nebr., 26 September 1994), 2.

6. Neihardt to Sterling, 16 September 1921, Sterling Collection, GS 340, Huntington Library (hereafter cited as Sterling Collection). Items from the Sterling

Collection are reproduced by permission of The Huntington Library, San Marino, Calif.

7. Neihardt to Aly, Manuscript notes, n.d., Aly Collection, file J2.7, John G. Neihardt Center, Bancroft, Nebr. (hereafter cited as Aly Collection).

8. Neihardt to Sterling, 6 July 1918, Sterling Collection, GS 321.

9. Neihardt to Jordan, 10 November 1918, Jordan Collection, Hoover Institution Archives, Stanford University.

10. Aly, *Neihardt*, 89.

11. Neihardt, "What Did Paul Mean?" *Journal*, 26 September 1918, 11; Neihardt, *The Song of Jed Smith*, 56.

12. Neihardt, "An Iconoclast," review of *Prejudices—Second Series*, by H. L. Mencken, *Journal*, 20 December 1920, Ed. 8; Neihardt, "Provincialism," review of *The American Credo*, by H. L. Mencken and George Jean Nathan, *Journal*, 21 June 1920, 4; Neihardt, "A Bird's-Eye View," review of *Living Philosophies*, *St. Louis Post-Dispatch*, 6 July 1931, n.p. (hereafter cited as *Post-Dispatch*); Neihardt, "Rich Purple Wraths," review of *Menckeniana*, *Post-Dispatch*, 19 January 1928, 17.

13. Neihardt, "An Iconoclast," Ed. 8.

14. Neihardt, "Going to the Dogs?" review of *The Revolt against Civilization*, by Lothrop Stoddard, *Journal*, 5 November 1922, Ed. 8.

15. Neihardt, *Poetic Values: Their Reality and Our Need of Them* (New York: Macmillan, 1925).

16. Neihardt, Manuscript notes to p. 51, Aly Collection.

17. Aly, *Neihardt*, 157.

18. Neihardt, "Erskine Scores Again," review of *Galahad*, by John Erskine, *Post-Dispatch*, 30 October 1926, 13; Neihardt, "Jazzing into the Garbage Can," review of *The Garbage Man*, by John Dos Passos, *Post-Dispatch*, 30 October 1926, 13; Neihardt, "Einstein and the Average Man," review of *Relativity*, by Sir Oliver Lodge, *Post-Dispatch*, 30 October 1926, 13; Neihardt, "Who Is My Mortal Enemy?" review of *My Mortal Enemy*, by Willa Cather, *Post-Dispatch*, 30 October 1926, 13.

19. Neihardt, "More Famous Writers Comment on Our Literature," *Post-Dispatch*, 22 December 1926, n.p.

20. Neihardt, Manuscript notes to p. 53, Aly Collection.

21. Neihardt, *Post-Dispatch*, 4 April 1929, 19.

22. "The Journalistic Smart Alec," *St. Louis Star*, 8 April 1929, 14.

23. Neihardt, Notes to essays, 4 July 1971. Florence Lueninghoener worked with Neihardt to begin gathering essays for publication, a task uncompleted at the time of his death in 1973. Mrs. Lueninghoener gave me copies of the essays that they had collected along with notes made at the time.

24. Neihardt, Review of *Hindu Fables for Little Children*, by Dhan Ghopal Mukerji, *Post-Dispatch*, 30 April 1929, 25; Neihardt, *Poetic Values*, 19–22.

25. Neihardt, "Valuable and Enthralling."

26. Neihardt, "A Great Indian Poet," 3C.

27. Neihardt to House, 17 December 1930, John G. Neihardt Papers, c. 1858–1974, Western Historical Manuscripts Collection, University of Missouri–Columbia (hereafter cited as Missouri Collection).

28. Neihardt to McAdams, n.d., Missouri Collection.

29. Neihardt to Pulitzer, n.d., Missouri Collection; Neihardt, "History of New Type," review of *Over Here*, by Mark Sullivan, *Post-Dispatch*, 3 December 1933, n.p.; Neihardt, Review of *After Such Pleasures*, by Dorothy Parker, *Post-Dispatch*, 10 December 1933, n.p.

30. Neihardt, Manuscript notes to p. 53, Aly Collection.

31. Neihardt, "Crazy Horse, Who Led the Sioux at Custer's Last Fight," review of *Crazy Horse*, by Mari Sandoz, *Times*, 20 December 1942, VI-4.

32. Neihardt, "Art and Democracy," *Journal*, 16 May 1916, 15.

33. Neihardt, "Remarks on a Much-Used Word," *Post-Dispatch*, 22 October 1928, 15.

34. Neihardt to N. Chatterji, n.d., Missouri Collection.

35. Neihardt's personal library of more than five thousand volumes was donated to the University of Missouri at the time of his death.

36. Neihardt, "The New Reading Public," *Kansas City Journal-Post*, 7 March 1926, 7D (hereafter cited as *Journal-Post*).

37. Neihardt, "Contemporary Literature Is News," 12.

38. Neihardt, "Too Clever," review of *One Crystal and a Mother*, by Ellen DuPois Taylor, *Post-Dispatch*, 17 February 1927, 19.

39. Neihardt, "Why Scream?" 23.

40. "Modern American Poetry," review of *The New Era in American Poetry*, by Louis Untermeyer, *Journal*, 1 July 1919, 15.

41. Neihardt, "Provincialism," 4.

42. Van Wyck Brooks, "On Creating a Usable Past," in *Critics of Culture: Literature and Society in the Early Twentieth Century*, edited by Alan Trachtenberg (New York: Wiley, 1976), 165–71.

43. Neihardt, "Self-Determination for Words," review of *Transition Stories*, edited by Eugene Jolas, *Post-Dispatch*, 21 January 1929, 15.

44. Neihardt, "John Morley and His Recollections," review of *Recollections*, by John Morley, *Journal*, 20 December 1917, 16.

45. Neihardt to Woodberry, 4 August 1917, Woodberry Collection, bMS Am 1587 (174), by permission of the Houghton Library, Harvard University (hereafter cited as Woodberry Collection).

46. George E. Woodberry, *America in Literature* (New York: Harcourt, 1903).

47. George E. Woodberry, *The Appreciation of Literature* (New York: Harcourt, 1907), 5, 8–9, 196.

48. Irving Babbitt, *Masters of French Criticism* (Boston: Houghton, 1912); Neihardt, "A New Fad?" 3B.

49. Neihardt to Aly, 14 October 1962, Aly Collection.

50. Sir Arthur Quiller-Couch, *Studies in Literature* (New York: Putnam's, 1918), 77, 235–36; Neihardt, "Critic and Regular Fellow," review of *Studies in Literature*, by Sir Arthur Quiller-Couch, *Journal*, 11 April 1919, 42.

51. Stuart P. Sherman, "R. L. S. Encounters the Modern Writers," in *Critical Woodcuts: Essays on Writers and Writing* (New York: Scribner's, 1926), 160.

52. Sherman, *Critical Woodcuts*; Neihardt, Review of *Perhaps Women*, by Sherwood Anderson, *Post-Dispatch*, 15 August 1931, n.p.; Neihardt, Review of *The Woman Who Rode Away*, by D. H. Lawrence, *Post-Dispatch*, 21 June 1928, 27; Neihardt, "Who Is My Mortal Enemy?" 13.

53. Neihardt, "Natural Aristocracy," review of *Aristocracy and Justice*, by Paul Elmer More, *Journal*, 7 December 1915, 17.

54. Neihardt, "The Vertical Cleavage," *Post-Dispatch*, 17 February 1931, n.p.

55. Neihardt, "Good for What?" review of *The Genteel Tradition at Bay*, by George Santayana, *Post-Dispatch*, 27 July 1931, n.p.

56. Review of *Humanism, a New Religion*, by Charles Frances Potter, *Post-Dispatch*, 28 April 1930, 3C.

57. Neihardt, *Poetic Values*, 135.

58. Neihardt, "Satire and Sublimity," review of *News of the Devil*, by Humbert Wolfe, *Post-Dispatch*, 16 February 1927, 17.

59. Neihardt, "The Man in the Ranks," review of *Yank the Crusader*, by Earl Van Zandt, *Journal*, 1 October 1920, 25.

60. See, for example, Richard Stokes to Joseph Pulitzer, 3 February 1933, Missouri Collection, and Julia Patton to Neihardt, 25 March 1919, Aly Collection.

61. Neihardt to Parker, 18 November 1933, Missouri Collection.

62. Neihardt, "Contemporary Literature Is News," 17.

63. Neihardt, "Traditionalists," in *The Young Idea: An Anthology of Opinion Concerning the Spirit and Aims of Contemporary Literature*, edited by Lloyd R. Morris (New York: Duffield, 1917), 188–89; Neihardt, "A Noble Book," review of *Seven Days' Darkness*, by Gunnar Gunnarsson, *Post-Dispatch*, 26 November 1930, n.p.

64. Neihardt, "Growing Debt," 25.

65. Neihardt, "The Bitterness of Truth," 15.

66. Neihardt, "Contemporary Literature Is News," 12.

67. Neihardt, "Men and Insects," review of *Emergent Evolution and the Development of Societies*, by William Morton Wheeler, *Post-Dispatch*, 8 March 1928, 19.

68. Neihardt, "Laughing Women," *Post-Dispatch*, 9 September 1934, n.p.

69. Neihardt, "Not Indifferent to Literature," *Post-Dispatch*, 28 March 1927, 14.

70. Neihardt, "Traditionalists," 190–91.

71. Neihardt, "The White Radiance," 13.

72. Neihardt, "Literature of the Trail," review of *The Wilderness Trail*, by Charles A. Hanna, *Times*, 12 March 1911, 142.

73. Neihardt, "Edwin Arlington Robinson," *Journal*, 3 November 1912, ws5.

74. Neihardt, *The Song of Three Friends*, viii.

75. Neihardt, Review of *Dawn over Samarkand*, by Joshua Kunitz, *Post-Dispatch*, 26 May 1935, n.p.

76. Neihardt, "We Forget Them," 17.

77. Julius T. House, *John G. Neihardt: Man and Poet* (Wayne NE: Jones, 1920), 18–19.

78. Neihardt, Manuscript notes to p. 67, Aly Collection.

79. Neihardt, "Traditionalists," 191.

80. Neihardt, "The Free Verse Movement," *Journal-Post*, 11 April 1926, 6D.

81. Neihardt, "A Neglected Principle," *Post-Dispatch*, 13 December 1928, 21.

82. Neihardt, "Misleading Labels," *Journal-Post*, 14 March 1926, 6D.

83. Neihardt to House, 4 April 1930, Missouri Collection.

84. Neihardt, "Cabell's Latest," review of *Something About Eve*, by James Branch Cabell, *Post-Dispatch*, 17 September 1927, 5.

85. Neihardt, *Poetic Values*, 8, 99.

86. Neihardt, "April Theology," in *Lyric and Dramatic Poems* (1926; reprint, Lincoln: University of Nebraska Press, 1965, 117–18.

87. Neihardt, *Poetic Values*, 104–5.

88. Neihardt, *Poetic Values*, 115–16.

89. Neihardt, *Poetic Values*, 113–14.

90. Neihardt, *Poetic Values*, 42.

91. Neihardt, *Poetic Values*, 132.

92. Neihardt, "Why Not Both?" 23.

93. Neihardt, "The Mathematical Mind," review of *Mole Philosophy*, by Cassius J. Keyser, *Post-Dispatch*, 13 May 1927, 31.

94. Neihardt, *Poetic Values*, 73–74.

95. Neihardt, *Poetic Values*, 104.

Part 1. Tradition

1. Neihardt, "Radicals and Conservatives," *Journal*, 7 April 1914, 10.

2. Probably *Notorious Literary Attacks*, edited by Albert Mordell (New York: Boni, 1926).

3. Percy Bysshe Shelley, *Adonais*, lines 462–63.

4. Neihardt to Sterling, 16 June 1918, Sterling Collection, GS 320.

5. Robert Lewis Stevenson, "Happy Thought," in *A Child's Garden of Verses* (London: Longmans, 1885).

6. Neihardt is referring to Oswald Spengler's 1928 book *The Decline of the West* (New York: Knopf).

7. George E. Woodberry, *Great Writers: Cervantes, Scott, Milton, Virgil, Montaigne, Shakespeare* (New York: Macmillan, 1912), 144–45.

8. Alfred, Lord Tennyson, *Idylls of the King*, line 408.

9. Neihardt, *The River and I* (1910; reprint, Lincoln: University of Nebraska Press, 1968).

10. Neihardt, "Literature of the Trail," 142.

11. Jane Harrison, *Ancient Art and Ritual* (New York: Holt, 1913), 159–60, quoted in Aly, *Neihardt*, 72.

12. Woodberry, *America in Literature*, 151, 253.

13. Neihardt, Review of *Dawn over Samarkand*.

14. Neihardt, "We Forget Them," 17.

15. John Bradbury, *Travels in the Interior of America. . . .* (London: Sherwood, 1817); Washington Irving, *Astoria, or Anecdotes of an Enterprise beyond the Rocky Mountains* (Philadelphia: Carey, 1836).

PART 2. TROUBLED PLANET

1. Neihardt, "Burning Conviction."

2. *The World Tomorrow* was a Christian socialist monthly magazine from 1921 to 1934.

3. Charles A. Beard, *The Open Door at Home* (New York: Macmillan, 1934).

4. Neihardt, *Omaha World-Herald*, 14 February 1937, quoted in Aly, *Neihardt*, 201.

5. Neihardt to Aly, 2 November 1957, Aly Collection.

6. Neihardt, "Stable for What?" review of *Permanently Curing Depressions*, by H. M. Reymond, *Post-Dispatch*, 2 April 1933, n.p.

7. Books written by Pitkin include *The Twilight of the American Mind* (New York: Simon, 1928); *New Careers for Youth* (New York: Simon, 1934); *The Psychology of Achievement* (New York: Simon, 1930); *Chance of a Lifetime: Marching Orders for the Lost Generation* (New York: Simon, 1934); *Life Begins at Forty* (New York: Whittlesey House, 1932); *Capitalism Carries On* (New York: Whittlesey House, 1935); *The Psychology of Happiness* (New York: Simon, 1929); and *A Short Introduction to the History of Human Stupidity* (New York: Simon, 1932).

8. Neihardt, "Light on Our Grayness," review of *Drink: Coercion or Control?* by Rheta Childe Dorr, *Post-Dispatch*, 5 December 1929, 3B.

9. Neihardt, "How Shall We Be Saved?" 5D.

10. Ethel Harriman, *Romantic, I Call It* (New York: Boni, 1926).

11. Alfred Korzybski, *Manhood of Humanity* (New York: Dutton, 1921).

12. Panait Istrati, *Kyra Kyralina* (Jerusalem: n.p., 1926).

13. Neihardt credited P. D. Ouspensky with elaborating idealistic theory and challenging the validity of Western thought patterns in *Tertium Organum* (Rochester NY: Manas, 1920).

14. James Harvey Robinson, *Mind in the Making* (New York: Harper, 1921); John Herman Randall, *The Making of the Modern Mind* (Boston: Houghton, 1926); Lewis Browne, *This Believing World* (New York: Macmillan, 1926).

15. Jackson's *A Century of Dishonor* (New York: Harper, 1881) chronicles one hundred years of violated treaties and broken promises on the part of the United States in its dealings with tribal governments.

16. Neihardt refers to Black Elk, whose conversations with the poet are recorded in *Black Elk Speaks*.

PART 3. TRENDS IN CONTEMPORARY LITERATURE

1. Frank Harris, *The Man Shakespeare and His Tragic Life Story* (New York: Kennerley, 1909).

2. Van Wyck Brooks, *The Ordeal of Mark Twain* (London: Heinemann, 1922).

3. Erich Maria Remarque, *All Quiet on the Western Front* (Boston: Little, 1929). See Neihardt's review, "The Heart of a Hun," in chapter 10.

4. Irving Babbitt, *Masters of French Criticism* (Boston: Houghton, 1912).

5. Fred L. Pattee, *History of American Literature Since 1870* (New York: Century, 1915).

6. Neihardt, "Great Skill for What?"

7. Neihardt, "The Personal Note Wears Out," 5D.

8. Neihardt to Teasdale, 18 July 1912, Missouri Collection.

9. Neihardt, "The Personal Note Wears Out," 5D.

10. Havelock Ellis, *The New Spirit* (London: Scott, [1891]).

11. Gopher Prairie is the fictional Minnesota town in Sinclair Lewis's *Main Street* (New York: Harcourt, 1920).

12. Bryan, the unsuccessful Democratic Party candidate for U.S. President in 1896, 1900, and 1908, in his speech before the Democratic National Convention in Chicago (9 July 1896) called for a bimetal standard, rather than an exclusively gold standard, to back the U.S. paper currency, asserting: "You shall not press down upon the brow of labor this cross of thorns, you shall not crucify mankind upon a cross of gold."

13. Padraic Colum, *Balloon* (New York: Macmillan, 1929).

14. Walter Lippmann, *A Preface to Morals* (New York: Macmillan, 1929).

15. A. S. Eddington, *The Nature of the Physical World* (Cambridge, England: Cambridge University Press, 1928).

PART 4. OF MAKING MANY BOOKS

1. Neihardt, "Contemporary Literature Is News," 17.

2. F. Scott Fitzgerald, *This Side of Paradise* (New York: Burt, 1920).

3. Grace Hebard and A. E. Brinninstool, *The Bozeman Trail: Historical Accounts of the Blazing of the Overland Routes into the Northwest, and the Fights with Red Cloud's Warriors* (Cleveland: Clark, 1922); Grace Hebard, *Washakie: An Account of Indian Resistance of the Covered Wagon and Union Pacific Railroad Invasions of Their Territory* (Cleveland: Clark, 1930).

4. Neihardt entered a public discussion as to why Hardy had been overlooked as a candidate for the Nobel Prize in a column for the *Journal-Post* subtitled "Perhaps Committee Has Not Overlooked This Author, as Many Believe, but Has Merely Exercised a Sense of Humor" (18 April 1926). Bunin was the 1933 recipient of the award.

5. Upton Sinclair, *Profits of Religion* (Pasadena CA: The Author, 1918), *The Brass Check* (Pasadena CA: The Author, 1920), and *The Goose Step* (Pasadena CA: The Author, 1923).

6. Neihardt considered his friend George Sterling, author of *Lillith* (1919), to be one of the greatest contemporary poets.

7. H. G. Wells, *Outline of History* (London: Newnes, 1919–20).

8. Neihardt, Review of *I Thought of Daisy*, by Edmund Wilson, *Post-Dispatch*, 2 December 1929, 3B.

9. Neihardt, "Modern American Poetry," 15.

10. Robert Frost, *North of Boston* (London: Nutt, 1914), and *A Boy's Will* (London: Nutt, 1913).

11. Harriet Monroe, ed., *Poetry* (Chicago: Modern Poetry Association). Initially, Neihardt had enthusiastic praise for the magazine, but soon quarreled with editor Monroe over the direction taken by the magazine—for example, in the support of poets like Pound, who figured prominently in early issues of the publication.

12. Bruce Barton, *The Man Nobody Knows: A Discovery of the Real Jesus* (Indianapolis: Bobbs, 1925).

13. Knut Hamsun, *Hunger*, translated by George Egerton (New York: Knopf, 1920), and *Growth of the Soil*, translated by W. W. Worster (New York: Knopf, 1921).

14. Verner von Heidenstam, *The Charles Men*, translated by Charles Wharton Stock (New York: American-Scandinavian Foundation, 1920), and *The Tree of the Folkungs*, translated by Arthur J. Chater (New York: Knopf, 1925).

15. Paul Radin, ed., *Crashing Thunder: The Autobiography of an American Indian* (New York: Appleton, 1926).

16. Neihardt, "The American Indian," review of *Crashing Thunder,* edited by Paul Radin, *Post-Dispatch,* 24 December 1926, 11.

17. James Mooney, *The Ghost Dance Religion and the Sioux Outbreak of 1890* (Washington: Government Printing Office, 1896).

PART 5. THIS MYSTERIOUS UNIVERSE

1. Neihardt to House, n.d., Missouri Collection.

2. Neihardt, *Poetic Values,* 36.

3. Neihardt, "Einstein and the Average Man," 13.

4. Neihardt, "A Burning Issue."

5. Cassius J. Keyser, *Thinking about Thinking* (New York: Dutton, 1926).

6. George Eliot, *The Legend of Jubal and Other Poems* (London: Blackwood, 1874).

7. A. S. Eddington, *Science and the Unseen World* (New York: Macmillan, 1929).

8. Henshaw Ward, *Thobbing: A Seat at the Circus of the Intellect* (Indianapolis: Bobbs, 1926).

9. The description was written by Neihardt of the terrain over which Hugh Glass crawled, recorded in *The Song of Hugh Glass.* Aly records the discovery in 1923 by Neihardt and a group of friends of the uncanny likeness of the description to the actual landscape (*Neihardt,* 83–84).

10. Neihardt, "A Valuable Interpretation," 21.

11. Neihardt to Aly, 16 February 1958, Aly Collection.

12. Rudyard Kipling, "The Ballad of East and West," 1889: "Oh, East is East, and West is West, and never the twain shall meet, / Till Earth and Sky stand presently at God's great Judgment Seat."

13. Probably *The Story of Philosophy: The Lives and Opinions of the Greater Philosophers,* by Will Durant (New York: Simon, 1926).

14. John B. Watson. See "Mob Flattery," review of *The Ways of Behaviorism,* in chapter 11.

15. Joyce Kilmer, *Trees* (New York: Doran, 1914).

16. Job 3: 13–14: "For now should I have lain still and been quiet, I should have slept: then had I been at rest, / With kings and counsellors of the earth, which built desolate places for themselves."

PART 6. POETIC VALUES

1. *Journals of Ralph Waldo Emerson,* edited by Edward Waldo Emerson and Waldo Emerson Forbes (Boston: Houghton; Cambridge: Riverside, 1909–14).

2. Stevenson, "Happy Thought."

3. Conversations that took place over a three-week period between Neihardt and Black Elk resulted in the book *Black Elk Speaks*.

4. Neihardt, "The Renascence of Poetry in America," WS7.

5. Neihardt, "The Beautiful Difference," *Post-Dispatch,* 23 June 1927, 23.

6. Neihardt, "Education and Literature," 4D.

7. Victor Hugo, *William Shakespeare* (London: Hurst, 1864).

8. Monroe, *Poetry.*

9. Alfred, Lord Tennyson, "The Higher Pantheism," in *Works* (London: Macmillan, 1891).

Sources

PART I. TRADITION

I. AS FROM A HEIGHT OF TIME

"The White Radiance." *Post-Dispatch*, 30 October 1926, 13.

"Literature and the Unlettered." *Post-Dispatch*, 4 December 1926, 6.

2. ANCIENT SEERS

"Galvanic Shocks in Essay Form." Review of *Learning and Other Essays*, by John Jay Chapman. *Times*, 25 June 1911, 402.

"Excellent Aeschylus Translation." Review of *Aeschylus with an English Translation*, by Herbert Weir Smyth. *Journal-Post*, 16 May 1926, 4D.

"An Admirable Translation." Review of *The Aeneid of Virgil*, translated by Harlan Hoge Ballard. *Post-Dispatch*, 11 August 1930, 3C.

"Greatness." Review of *Socrates*, by A. E. Taylor. *Post-Dispatch*, 19 March 1933, 2B.

"Cheers for Humanity." Review of *The Platonic Legend*, by Warner Fite. *Post-Dispatch*, 9 December 1934, 2B.

3. EPIC LANDSCAPE

"The Stuff of Our Unwritten Epic." Review of *Economic Beginnings of the Far West*, by Katherine Coman. *Journal*, 24 November 1912, WS5.

"Valuable and Enthralling." Review of *Indian Heroes and Great Chieftains*, by Charles A. Eastman. *Journal*, 17 February 1920, 17.

"We Forget Them." Review of *John Colter*, by Stallo Vinton. *Post-Dispatch*, 19 January 1927, 17.

"A Magnificent Story." Review of *The Santa Fe Trail*, by R. L. Duffus. *Post-Dispatch*, 10 September 1930, 3C.

"A Book with Light in It." Review of *Ancient Life in the American Southwest*, by Edgar L. Hewett. *Post-Dispatch*, 1 December 1930, 3B.

Review of *The Pony Express Goes Through*, by Howard R. Driggs. *Post-Dispatch*, 18
August 1935, 2H.

PART 2. TROUBLED PLANET

4. TREMENDOUS MOOD OF WAR

"War and Society." Review of *Social Progress and the Darwinian Theory*, by
George Nasmyth. *Journal*, 28 February 1917, 6.

"Excellent Intentions." Review of *The Fight for Peace*, by Devere Allen.
Post-Dispatch, 24 November 1930, 3B.

"Hitler's Book." Review of *My Battle*, by Adolph Hitler, abridged and
translated by E. T. S. Dugdale. *Post-Dispatch*, 12 November 1933, 2H.

"Burning Conviction." Review of *"Halt!" Cry the Dead*, edited by Frederick
A. Barber. *Post-Dispatch*, 2 June 1935, 2H.

5. BREADLINES AND BURSTING GRANARIES

"Dissertation on Fear." Review of *Casting Out Fear*, by Flora Bigelow Guest.
Journal, 4 April 1919, 7.

"Perpetual Motion." Review of *Our Biggest Customer*, by George Harrison Phelps.
Post-Dispatch, 8 July 1929, 21.

Review of *Criminals and Politicians*, by Denis Tilden Lynch. *Post-Dispatch*, 18
December 1932, 2B.

"For Those Who Care." Review of *Human Aspects of Unemployment and Relief*, by
James M. Williams. *Post-Dispatch*, 29 January 1933, 2B.

"Do They Know Enough?" Review of *Finding a Job*, by Roger W. Babson. *Post-
Dispatch*, 19 November 1933, 2H.

"Beware of Substitutes!" Review of *Let's Get What We Want*, by Walter B. Pitkin.
Post-Dispatch, 16 June 1935, 21.

6. SOCIAL TURMOIL

"A Plea for Education." Review of *College Sons and College Fathers*, by Henry Seidel
Canby. *Journal*, 7 December 1915, 17.

"Civilization and Mrs. Shimmyall." *Journal-Post*, 17 October 1926, 5D.

"How Shall We Be Saved?" Review of *The Escape from the Primitive*, by Horace
Carncross, and *Thinking about Thinking*, by Cassius J. Keyser. *Journal-Post*, 17
October 1926, 5D.

"Straws in the Wind." Review of *This Ugly Civilization*, by Ralph Borsodi, and
Our Business, Civilization, by James Truslow Adams. *Post-Dispatch*, 23 October
1929, 21.

Review of *Massacre*, by Robert Gessner. *Post-Dispatch*, 19 February 1931, 3B.

"Merejkowski's Thesis." Review of *The Secret of the West*, by Dimitri Merejkowski, translated by John Cournos. *Post-Dispatch*, 3 July 1931, 7A.

PART 3. TRENDS IN CONTEMPORARY LITERATURE

7. GENUINE CRITICISM

"The Socratic Spirit." Review of *On Contemporary Literature*, by Stuart P. Sherman. *Journal*, 19 March 1918, 4.

"Provincialism." Review of *The American Credo*, by George Jean Nathan and H. L. Mencken. *Journal*, 21 June 1920, 4.

"Contemporary Literature Is News." *Post-Dispatch*, 6 December 1926, 12.

"Luminous Sanity." Review of *Essays on Literature*, by A. Clutton-Brock. *Post-Dispatch*, 23 March 1927, 19.

8. VANDALS IN THE TEMPLE

"Modern American Poetry." Review of *The New Era in American Poetry*, by Louis Untermeyer. *Journal*, 1 July 1919, 15.

"Roses and Dead Cows." *Post-Dispatch*, 28 June 1927, 21.

"Revaluing the Classics." Review of *Literary Blasphemies*, by Ernest Boyd. *Post-Dispatch*, 16 November 1927, 19.

"Why Scream?" Review of *All Else Is Folly*, by Peregrine Acland. *Post-Dispatch*, 16 September 1929, 23.

"Growing Debt." Review of *Life and Letters of Stuart Sherman*, by Jacob Zeitlin and Homer Woodbridge. *Post-Dispatch*, 7 October 1929, 25.

"An Honest Book." Review of *Our Singing Strength*, by Alfred Kreymborg. *Post-Dispatch*, 20 November 1929, 3B.

"A New Fad?" *Post-Dispatch*, 7 March 1930, 3B.

"An Athletic Mind in Action." Review of *The New American Literature*, by Fred L. Pattee. *Post-Dispatch*, 4 November 1930, 3B.

9. ONLY SYMPTOMATIC

"The New Reading Public." *Journal-Post*, 7 March 1926, 7D.

"The Personal Note Wears Out." Review of *Dark of the Moon*, by Sara Teasdale. *Journal-Post*, 3 October 1926, 5D.

"The Truth About Small Towns." Review of *Home Town Sketches*, by Emile Paillou. *Post-Dispatch*, 26 January 1927, 17.

"Genuine Realism." Review of *God Got One Vote*, by Frederick Hazlitt Brennan. *Post-Dispatch*, 22 August 1927, 21.

"The Literary Bull Market." *Post-Dispatch*, 26 June 1928, 23.

"The Wisdom of Machines." *Post-Dispatch*, 21 June 1929, 31.

"An Exchange of Roles." *Post-Dispatch*, 10 August 1929, 5.

"Realism." Review of *As the Earth Turns*, by Gladys Hasty Carrol. *Post-Dispatch*. 18 June 1933, 2F.

"Great Skill for What?" Review of *Only the Fear*, by Lenore G. Marshall. *Post-Dispatch*, 7 July 1935, n.p.

PART 4. OF MAKING MANY BOOKS

10. THE GLOW OF THE MOMENT

"Fitzgerald Again." Review of *Flappers and Philosophers*, by F. Scott Fitzgerald. *Journal*, 21 October 1920, 3.

"An Excellent Biography." Review of *George Eliot and Her Times*, by Elizabeth Haldane. *Post-Dispatch*, 30 June 1927, 2S.

"An Old-Timer Remembers." Review of *A Two-Gun Cyclone*, by B. E. (Cyclone) Denton. *Post-Dispatch*, 31 August 1927, 21.

"Hurrah for Dorothy." Review of *Sunset Gun*, by Dorothy Parker. *Post-Dispatch*, 30 May 1928, 1S.

"A Book by a Seer." Review of *Jesus, the Son of Man*, by Kahlil Gibran. *Post-Dispatch*, 16 January 1929, 1S.

"The Heart of a Hun." Review of *All Quiet on the Western Front*, by Erich Maria Remarque, translated by A. W. Wheem. *Post-Dispatch*, 27 June 1929, 2S.

"An Oklahoma Epic." Review of *The Range Cattle Industry*, by Edward Everett Dale. *Post-Dispatch*, 31 October 1930, 3B.

Review of *Sacajawea*, by Grace Raymond Hebard. *Post-Dispatch*, 21 May 1933, 2H.

"Windstorms of the Spirit." Review of *An Upton Sinclair Anthology*, compiled by I. O. Evans. *Post-Dispatch*, 5 August 1934, 2E.

"Wells at 67." Review of *Experiment in Autobiography*, by H. G. Wells. *Post-Dispatch*, 11 November 1934, 2H.

11. IMPECCABLY UNREMARKABLE

"A New England Poet." Review of *Mountain Interval*, by Robert Frost. *Journal*, 23 March 1917, 8.

"Book of Great Significance." Review of *Is Five*, by E. E. Cummings. *Journal-Post*, 25 July 1926, 4D.

Review of *The Collected Poems of Ezra Pound*. *Post-Dispatch*, 11 January 1927, 1S.

Review of *Wild Honey*, by Frederick Niven. *Post-Dispatch*, 31 January 1927, 1S.

"Cervantes Read Backwards." Review of *The Life of Don Quixote and Sancho*, translated by Homer P. Earle. *Post-Dispatch*, 6 October 1927, 27.

"Knowledge and Opinion." Review of *The Outline of Man's Knowledge*, by Clement Wood. *Post-Dispatch*, 11 November 1927, 27.

"The Benefit of the Doubt." Review of *The Story of the American Indian*, by Paul Radin. *Post-Dispatch*, 16 January 1928, 1S.

"Mob Flattery." Review of *The Ways of Behaviorism*, by John B. Watson. *Post-Dispatch*, 14 May 1928, 21.

Review of *Green Hills of Africa*, by Ernest Hemingway. *Post-Dispatch*, 1 December 1935, 2E.

PART 5. THIS MYSTERIOUS UNIVERSE

12. ET TU, SCIENTIA?

"Socratic Questioning." Review of *The Breath of Life*, by John Burroughs. *Journal*, 7 March 1916, 15.

"Einstein and the Average Man." Review of *Relativity*, by Sir Oliver Lodge. *Post-Dispatch*, 30 October 1926, 13.

"The Mathematical Mind." Review of *Mole Philosophy and Other Essays*, by Cassius J. Keyser. *Post-Dispatch*, 13 May 1927, 31.

"Swapping Illusions." Review of *The Future of an Illusion*, by Sigmund Freud. *Post-Dispatch*, 9 November 1928, 29.

"Dare We Giggle Now?" Review of *Our Changing Human Nature*, by Samuel D. Schmalhausen. *Post-Dispatch*, 30 October 1929, 17.

"Light on the Peaks." Review of *The Revolt against Dualism*, by Arthur O. Lovejoy. *Post-Dispatch*, 12 June 1930, 3C.

"A Burning Issue." Review of *The Supreme Law*, by Maurice Maeterlinck. *Post-Dispatch*, 4 August 1935, 2E.

13. EXPLORING THE UNKNOWN

"Scientific Pessimism." Review of *Eos, or The Wider Aspects of Cosmogony*, by J. H. Jeans. *Post-Dispatch*, 19 July 1929, 29.

"Seed and the Soil." Review of *What's Life All About?* by Bertha Conde. *Post-Dispatch*, 25 June 1930, 3C.

"Something to Think About." Review of *The Story of Psychic Science*, by Hereward Carrington. *Post-Dispatch*, 27 April 1931, 3C.

"The Practicality of Prayer." Review of *Can Prayer Be Answered?* by Mary Austin. *Post-Dispatch*, 19 August 1934, 2F.

"Daring Academic Departure." Review of *Extra Sensory Perception*, by J. B. Rhine. *Post-Dispatch*, 3 November 1935, 2E.

14. THE FLESH AND THE SPIRIT

"O'Neill's New Play." Review of *Marco Millions*, by Eugene O'Neill. *Post-Dispatch*, 23 April 1927, 5.

"A Valuable Interpretation." Review of *The Story of Oriental Philosophy*, by L. Adams Beck (E. Barrington). *Post-Dispatch*, 28 August 1928, 21.

"Why Not Both?" Review of *Mysticism and Logic*, by Bertrand Russell. *Post-Dispatch*, 23 September 1929, 23.

"Humane Philosophy." Review of *Matter, Life, and Value*, by C. E. M. Joad. *Post-Dispatch*, 6 January 1930, 3B.

"The Message of the Dust." Review of *Deserts on the March*, by Paul B. Sears. *Post-Dispatch*, 5 April 1936, 4I.

PART 6: POETIC VALUES

15. HILL OF VISION

"Building of a Masterpiece." Review of *The Heart of Emerson's Journals*, edited by Bliss Perry. *Journal-Post*, 26 September 1926, 5D.

"Literature." *Post-Dispatch*, 16 March 1927, 21.

"A Lesson from Oriental Song." Review of *Lotus and Chrysanthemum*, edited by Joseph Lewis French. *Post-Dispatch*, 6 June 1927, 21.

"The Bitterness of Truth." *Post-Dispatch*, 11 January 1928, 15.

"Concentrated Beauty." Review of *Eden*, by Murray Sheehan. *Post-Dispatch*, 31 January 1928, 15.

"A Neglected Principle." *Post-Dispatch*, 13 December 1928, 21.

"A Great Personality." Review of *America, the Dream*, by Katherine Lee Bates. *Post-Dispatch*, 1 April 1930, 3B.

"A Poet." Review of *Lonesome Water*, by Roy Helton. *Post-Dispatch*, 24 October 1930, 3B.

"A Great Indian Poet." *Post-Dispatch*, 10 June 1931, 3C.

"What Is Poetry?" *Post-Dispatch*, 4 June 1933, 2H.

"Two Adult Lyric Poets." Review of *Poems: 1911–1936*, by John Hall Wheelock, and *Hill Garden*, by Margaret Widdemer. *Post-Dispatch*, 4 October 1936, 4J.

16. WHAT IS LITERATURE GOOD FOR?

"The Renascence of Poetry in America." *Journal*, 15 September 1912, ws7.

"Education and Literature." *Journal-Post*. 2 May 1926, 6D.

"What Is Poetry Good For?" *Journal-Post*, 9 May 1926, 4D.

"Living Water." Review of *Selected Lyrics of Amelia Josephine Burr*. *Post-Dispatch*, 28 March 1927, 15.

"Literature as Environment." *Post-Dispatch*, 15 August 1927, 21.

Index

www.ingramcontent.com/pod-product-compliance
Lightning Source LLC
Chambersburg PA
CBHW030633110726
47901CB00002B/425